The Nevada Constitution:
Origin and Growth

Fifth Edition

Nevada's most recent governors at the inauguration of Governor Robert List in January 1979. From left to right: Grant Sawyer (1959–1966); Paul Laxalt (1967–1970); Mike O'Callaghan (1971–1978); and Governor List. The construction equipment in the background was being used during restoration of the state capitol. (Courtesy of Governor List.)

THE NEVADA CONSTITUTION:

Origin and Growth

Fifth Edition

Eleanore Bushnell
with
Don W. Driggs

UNIVERSITY OF NEVADA PRESS
RENO, NEVADA
1980

NEVADA STUDIES IN HISTORY AND POLITICAL SCIENCE NO. 8

Series Editor

WILBUR S. SHEPPERSON

Editorial Committee

DON W. DRIGGS   ANDREW C. TUTTLE
JEROME E. EDWARDS   THOMAS C. WRIGHT

Library of Congress Cataloging in Publication Data
Bushnell, Eleanore.
   The Nevada constitution.
   (Nevada studies in history and political science; no. 8)
   "Constitution of Nevada (as amended to June 1980)":   p.
   Bibliography: p.
   Includes index.
   1.   Nevada—Constitutional law.   I. Driggs, Don W., joint author.   II. Nevada.
Constitution. III. Title.   IV. Series.
KFN1002.Z9B8   1980   342.793'02   80-23682
ISBN O-87417-060-5

University of Nevada Press, Reno, Nevada   89557 USA

Dedicated to Eric C. Bellquist

CONTENTS

TABLES

Preface to the Fifth Edition

NEVADA IN THE EARLY 1980s is experiencing a number of political, social, and economic problems. Some of them, such as taxes, inflation, and quality of the environment, afflict, in varying degrees, all the states; some of them, such as gambling control, nuclear waste, and placement of the MX missile system, are peculiar to this state or to only a few others. In the fifteen years separating the first and fifth editions of this book, the greatest changes that took place in Nevada arose from the state's rapid increase in population. The increase, occurring almost entirely in the urban areas of Reno and Las Vegas, is caused mainly by gambling, revenues from which continue to climb despite threats of recession or the ravages of inflation.

Population increase brings attendant pressures on schools, water supply, sewage capacity, roads, and on the entire complex of services strained by unremitting growth. Those of Nevada's leaders who would like to focus attention on the consequences of growth often face public indifference until people are confronted with smog, an inadequate supply of water, rising crime rates, and streets glutted with cars doing their share to increase pollution. Then cries for action are heard from certain groups, while other groups accept things as they are and prefer them to continue unimpeded. Politicians have difficulty in meeting or balancing the demands of these forces. The desire to serve the best interests of the public and also to be reelected exerts great pressure on officeholders. Even so, the 1980s require thorough, rational, and cautious policy formation and execution. Fragmented, piecemeal reactions to each new crisis offer a poor substitute for developing long-range policies.

Immediate problems of the early 1980s include the "Sagebrush Rebellion," an effort by Nevada (and certain other states) to assert title to federal land within the state's borders; reapportionment based on the 1980 census figures, and likely to modify the previous distribution of political power in the state; management of the state's major revenue producer, gambling, to insure honesty and continued state control; development of geothermal energy, a source with which Nevada is well endowed.

Additionally, two major and threatening difficulties confront the state, both characteristic of troubled intergovernment relations in a federal union. The first concerns the MX missile and whether Nevada should or must allow this giant racetrack system to be constructed here. The second centers on disposal of the lethal by-products of nuclear energy, with the health and safety imponderables contingent upon its storage; Nevada, and other states used as dumping grounds, experience political and social uneasiness in the absence of adequate control over a national, inadequately-resolved refuse problem. The ability of the state's government to analyze and deal with these and other problems will be the measure of its effectiveness and the source of citizen satisfaction or displeasure.

Chapters 1, 2, and 3 remain essentially as they appeared in the earlier editions. The other chapters have been expanded, reshaped, and brought up to date to make the book as nearly current as any work on so volatile a subject as the political process can hope to be.

Don W. Driggs, my colleague in the political science department, made the changes and additions that distinguish the fifth edition from its predecessors. He is assuming responsibility for all modifications from this edition forward.

During a fifteen-year span a writer in government incurs many debts to public officials, reviewers, colleagues, friends, and students. State public officials who contributed to this edition, and earlier versions, include the following: Shannon L. Bybee, formerly with the Gaming Control Board; Andrew Grose, research director, Legislative Counsel Bureau; E. M. Gunderson, justice, Nevada Supreme Court; Russell W. McDonald, formerly Washoe County manager; William D. Swackhamer, secretary of state; and Gordon Thompson, justice, Nevada Supreme Court.

Nevada's congressional delegation also contributed. Senator Howard W. Cannon, Senator Paul Laxalt, and Congressman James Santini responded to requests for information swiftly and generously.

Among many colleagues and friends who helped, special thanks are extended to Russell R. Elliott, Paul S. Hanna, Helma Elizabeth Kuehn, Linda Nagy, William Neeley, Richard Siegel, and Pamela Wilcox.

The cooperative allies named above, and others too, are warmly thanked. Professor Driggs and I absolve them completely of any errors of fact or interpretation that may have made their way into this book.

E.B.

Reno
June 1980

CHAPTER 1

BEFORE STATEHOOD

IN AN AMAZINGLY BRIEF PERIOD of time, the area that became the State of
Nevada went through an astonishing metamorphosis: it progressed from
a virtually unknown wilderness to full-fledged statehood in slightly less
than forty years. Part of a sprawling land mass under the nominal control
of Mexico in the 1820s and 1830s, the area was known only to a few
trappers and explorers. In 1848 the region that is now Nevada became
joined to the United States, since it was a portion of the vast tract ceded
by Mexico at the termination of the Mexican War. In 1850 the national
government established in part of this great expanse of land the Territory
of Utah; as an integral part of that territory, present-day Nevada came
for the first time under control of a formally organized government.
Nevada became a separate territory in 1861 and a state in 1864. So swift a
leap to full partnership in the United States federal system is unusual.

Of the thirteen western states, only California achieved statehood more
rapidly than Nevada; and since California was never a territory at all, it is
not truly comparable. The other western states progressed from territory
to state in the following spans of time: Oregon in eleven years, Colorado
in fifteen, Washington in twenty-one, Wyoming in twenty-two, Montana
in twenty-five, Idaho in twenty-seven, Utah in forty-six, Alaska in forty-
seven, Arizona in forty-nine, Hawaii in fifty-nine, and New Mexico in
sixty-two years. Thus, Nevada, with only a three-year gap between her
designation as a territory and her accession to the Union as a state, moved
from territorial status to statehood far more rapidly than any other western state.

The remarkable acceleration of Nevada's transformation from an
almost unknown region with no governmental structure to full statehood
in forty years is attributable to many forces. Among them are these: the
California gold rush, abrasive relations between the national government
and Utah Territory, the Comstock discovery, and Lincoln's determination to strengthen the Union position by securing more antislavery congressmen. These forces also influenced the governmental pattern that
emerged.

In addition to the speed with which Nevada attained statehood, two other aspects of its history are unusual: both its organized government and its known history are relatively recent. The Indian tribes who lived for thousands of years within present-day Nevada kept no records. The Spaniards, who had legal title to the region until 1821, and the Mexicans, who succeeded to the title and retained it until 1848, made no known explorations of significance nor any lasting settlements. Except for the Indian tribes, there were no permanent residents in Nevada until 1851, and, until Carson County was organized in 1854, no legally authorized local government functioned in the area. Thus, Nevada is a young state both in the span of its recorded history and in the length of its experience with government.

Nevada Before 1849

Before the gold rush to California brought thousands of people streaming across Nevada, the only information about the area was supplied by trappers, explorers, and a few emigrants who traversed it in defiance of orders of the Republic of Mexico, which had forbidden trespass of any kind without a Mexican passport. These early visitors generally described the region as formidable and hostile to settlement.

The first white man to cross what is now Nevada, according to extant records, was Jedediah Smith. In 1826, accompanied by about fourteen trappers, he passed through southern Utah to the Virgin River and entered California by way of southern Nevada; on his return trip, in 1827, he crossed central Nevada, following in a general way the present route of Highway 6. In 1828 a Hudson's Bay Company group, led by Peter Skene Ogden, entered Nevada near the present town of Denio, on the Oregon border. Ogden was the first white man to view the Humboldt River and the first to travel its entire length. In 1833 a group fitted out by Benjamin L. E. Bonneville and led by Joseph Walker came into the territory in search of beaver; the Bonneville expedition, particularly memorable because it was the subject of Washington Irving's *The Adventures of Captain Bonneville, U.S.A.,* is believed to have been the first group of white men to ascend the Sierra Nevada from the east.

Another expedition of importance was the Bidwell-Bartleson party of 1841. As the first band of emigrants to cross Nevada on the way to California, this party inaugurated overland migration through Nevada. Others who had crossed the Great Basin were explorers or trappers who had no intention of making permanent settlements. A second emigrant party, the Walker-Chiles group, traveled to California in 1843. Part of the group, under the leadership of Walker, followed the Humboldt River

> and then turned southward to Walker Lake. They traveled south-
> ward, negotiating the Sierra Nevada Mountains by Walker's Pass,

discovered by Walker in 1834. This party was the first to bring wagons overland to California through the Great Basin, proving that the land of interior drainage was an adequate corridor to California, one in which vehicles could be used.[1]

The first official exploration of the Great Basin was made by John C. Frémont. In 1843–44 he conducted an expedition to ascertain the accuracy of the existing maps of the country by comparing them with the reports of the trappers and with his own observations. He also explored territory not previously visited by the fur trappers and made botanical, geographic, and other scientific observations of the area. In 1844 Frémont came upon Pyramid Lake, which he described as follows:

> . . . we encamped on the shore, opposite a very remarkable rock in the lake, which had attracted our attention for many miles. It rose, according to our estimate, six hundred feet above the water; and, from the point we viewed it, presented a pretty exact outline of the great pyramid of Cheops. Like other rocks along the shore, it seemed to be encrusted with calcareous cement. This striking feature suggested a name for the lake, and I called it Pyramid Lake. . . .[2]

Before Frémont's expedition, knowledge of the geography of the Great Basin was inaccurate, even mythical. ". . . it was not until 1844 . . . that John Charles Frémont . . . made his important pronouncement—the area lying between the Wasatch and the Sierra Nevada Mountains is an interior-drainage basin."[3] His visit and his reports not only furnished scientific data but also stimulated popular interest in the region.

Other parties of both emigrants and explorers came through Nevada during this early period. Probably the best known of the emigrant parties was the Donner group in 1846–47. This unfortunate company, after camping briefly near the present site of Reno, continued its trek toward California and were trapped near Donner Lake in the unusually early and heavy snowfall of October 1846. Of the original company of eighty-seven only forty-seven survived the ordeal.

Thus, until the fourth decade of the nineteenth century, when present-day Nevada became part of the United States, no permanent settlements were made in the region; it was a hunting ground for trappers and a thoroughfare for emigrants on their way to the West Coast.[4] Of permanent occupation, of government institutions, we find nothing.

The 1840s and Settlement of Nevada

Three important events in this decade led to the occupation of Nevada and to the establishment of organized government: (1) the cession by Mexico of vast territories to the United States in the Treaty of Guadalupe Hidalgo in 1848; (2) the migration of the Mormons into the Salt Lake area and later into much of the region that now comprises Nevada; and (3) the discovery of gold in California.

At the same time that the Donner party was trapped at Donner Lake, the Bear Flag War between Mexican authorities and the Americans for possession of the land was going on in California. The Mexican War (1846–48), of which the Bear Flag War was a segment, ended with the defeat of Mexico and the signing of the Treaty of Guadalupe Hidalgo, in which Mexico ceded 1,193,061 square miles of territory to the United States government; this territory included what is now Nevada, Utah, California, parts of Wyoming and Colorado, and the desert Southwest. More than a hundred years after the United States signed this treaty, the Indian Claims Commission ruled that neither Spain nor Mexico had owned the land; that it belonged to the Indians who occupied it; and that they were entitled to compensation for being illegally dispossessed. Monetary restitution for the theft of Indian land began in 1975.

The second important development in the 1840s was the trek of the Mormons to the Great Salt Lake Valley. In March 1849, two years after their arrival, Brigham Young and his group held a convention in Salt Lake City and organized a provisional government for what they called the "State of Deseret." This government was designed to control an enormous portion of the land acquired in the Mexican cession; its boundaries, as defined by Brigham Young, encompassed what is now Utah, Nevada, Arizona, a little of Oregon, part of Wyoming, and part of California. Congress did not recognize this grandiose arrangement. Not until the Compromise of 1850 established Utah Territory and confined its boundaries to a far smaller land mass than the extensive "State of Deseret" did present-day Nevada become part of an organized government.

The third important factor in Nevada's development was the California gold rush, which brought thousands of people through the area and occasioned a need for stations to provide equipment and supplies for the gold seekers.

Organized Government

As part of the Compromise of 1850, Congress admitted California to the Union as a state and established territorial governments in Utah and New Mexico. Formal United States control over Nevada began with the Compromise of 1850, since most of the area that is now Nevada lay within the boundaries of the newly created Utah Territory. The first seat of government of Utah Territory was Fillmore City; in 1856 the capital was changed to what was then called Great Salt Lake City. Brigham Young, leader of the Mormon church, was appointed governor of the new territory and served in that capacity from 1850 to 1857.

In 1851 John Reese and a party of Mormons came into the Carson Valley. They found the land suitable for farming and advantageous because it lay along the route to California. Hence, they decided to remain in the valley. Reese and his company promptly built a stockade to shelter the livestock and for protection against the Indians. This stockade, which has been restored, was the first permanent settlement in what was then western Utah. The community was called Mormon Station until 1856, when the name was changed to Genoa. In addition to being Nevada's first permanent community, Genoa was also the nucleus around which the first indigenous government in the region was formed.

The residents of Mormon Station were too far from the seat of government in Salt Lake City to place much confidence in or feel much identification with the Utah territorial government. Moreover, not all of the settlers were communicants of the Mormon church; some of the non-Mormons were actively antagonistic to the church and did not want to be controlled by a church-connected government.

In November of 1851 the citizens of Mormon Station decided to acquire local control of their own affairs and met to organize a squatters' government. They adopted rules for the peace and good order of the community, regularized procedures for rights in land, set up a permanent committee to govern the area, and drafted a petition to Congress requesting establishment of a territory separate from Utah.

This "government" was not authorized by either the Utah territorial government or the government of the United States, nor did it function to any appreciable degree. One difficulty facing the squatters' government was the new settlers moving into the Carson Valley. These newcomers, indifferent to, possibly unaware of, the problems that had brought the unauthorized government into existence, did not actively support it.

In 1853, despairing of effective local government under Utah control, some of the residents petitioned the California legislature for annexation. No action was taken on the settlers' attempt to be annexed to California, and their petition of 1851 for separate territorial status had been ignored by Congress. Thus, neither of their efforts to secure a change in government severed them from Utah's control. Instead, the settlers' efforts stirred the Utah government into activity and a determination to establish effective control over the dissident residents of western Utah.

Carson County

On January 17, 1854, the Utah territorial legislature created Carson County[5] and provided for appointment of a probate judge who was authorized to organize the new county and to conduct an election to fill the various county offices. Two years before, Utah had created seven counties extending westward from Utah into what is now Nevada; the newly created Carson County was carved from four of the previously established counties.

Brigham Young appointed an influential Mormon, Orson Hyde, as probate judge for Carson County. Hyde arrived at Mormon Station on June 15, 1855, with a party of about forty men, including a federal judge and a United States marshal. Judge Hyde called for a county election, which was held September 20; most of the officers elected at this time were Mormons. The government that Hyde established was essentially theocratic and engendered intense dissatisfaction among the non-Mormons, who, in 1856, made another effort to have the region annexed to California. The California legislature acted upon this second appeal for annexation by sending a resolution to Congress in support of the residents' petition. But this request, like the earlier one, was ignored by Congress.

Efforts to have the Carson County area annexed by California reappeared in reverse in 1968. In that year several communities in eastern California, long offended by that state's policy with respect to water allocation, sought to have themselves annexed by Nevada, claiming that reapportionment had reduced them to political nonentities in California, that California taxes were more burdensome than Nevada's, that Nevada officials showed more concern for the people than officials in California, and that eastern Sierra counties would have greater legislative representation in Nevada than they had in California. Constitutionally, the most interesting argument made by the eastern California residents in support of their plea for annexation was that the act creating Nevada Territory in 1861 described the boundary as the crest of the Sierra Nevada. But Attorney General Harvey Dickerson's opinion was disheartening. He explained that the Enabling Act of 1864, which allowed Nevada to seek statehood, established Nevada's western boundary as the eastern boundary of California. He pointed out that the Enabling Act was the controlling statute, and that years of acquiescence to the border line drawn in the act precluded reopening the question. Despite this discouraging opinion, citizens of Mono County and adjacent regions continued to look for ways to bring their part of California into the State of Nevada.

The separatist influences of 1856 were met by counteraction on the part of Brigham Young, who sent more Mormons into the Genoa (Mormon Station) area to maintain the hegemony of the Utah government and of the church. Dozens of families were instructed to move to Carson County. In the county election of August 1856, these new settlers combined forces with the earlier Mormon inhabitants to elect, once again, a predominantly Mormon slate of officers, much to the irritation of the non-Mormons.

In 1862, several years after Judge Hyde had been recalled from his post in Carson County and had returned to Utah, he wrote a letter indicating that he had not always been happy in his former position as judge and administrator of the county and had, in fact, suffered indignities. Because of the abruptness of his departure for Salt Lake City in 1856, he could not arrange for the orderly disposal of his lands and his mill, and these properties were subsequently appropriated. His letter was a malediction upon the people of Carson and Washoe valleys:

> You shall be visited of the Lord of Hosts with thunder and with earthquakes and with floods, with pestilence and with famine until your names are not known amongst men, for you have rejected the authority of God, trampled upon his laws and his ordinances, and given yourselves up to serve the god of this world; to rioting in debauchery, in abominations, drunkenness and corruption. You have chuckled and gloried in taking the property of the Mormons, and withholding from them the benefits thereof. . . . If perchance, however, there should be an honest man amongst you, I would advise him to leave; but let him not go to California for safety, for he will not find it there.[6]

Hyde went on to say that unless the money he claimed to be due him was paid, he would see that the inhabitants of the area were destroyed.

In January 1857, the Utah Legislature, as part of its preparation for expected conflict with the federal government, attached Carson County to Great Salt Lake County for revenue, election, and judicial purposes; the recall of Hyde had, of course, left Carson County without a resident administrative head. This downgrading of the importance of local government was a further dissatisfaction to many settlers.

Departure of the Mormons

After 1856 relations between the Utah territorial government and the national government progressively deteriorated. President James Buchanan dismissed Brigham Young as governor and, in 1857, appointed Alfred Cumming in his place; Cumming was not a Mormon.

One aspect of the reality of theocratic government is illustrated by the following, possibly apocryphal, dialogue. After Brigham Young had been relieved as governor, the

> conflict in politics in Utah was between the *de jure* government of federal appointees and the *de facto* government of the people of Utah through their church organization, institutions of local government, bishop's and probate courts, and militia. One governor, it is said, irritated at this state of affairs, emphatically declared to Brigham Young that *he* was the governor of the territory. To this Mormon Church President Young is said to have replied, "You may be the governor of the territory, but I am governor of the people."[7]

Difficulties between the national and the Utah government did not subside with Young's dismissal, and President Buchanan ordered troops to Salt Lake City in 1857 to reestablish federal control over Utah Territory. To meet this threat, Brigham Young, still leader of the Mormon church, summoned the Mormons from outlying areas to defend Salt Lake City. A

2

large proportion of the residents in western Utah responded to the summons, leaving their holdings to be disposed of for whatever price they would bring. Their land and buildings passed for small sums of money, in some cases apparently without any exchange of money, into the hands of people coming into the area, most of them from California. The exodus of the Mormons left Carson County with a very small population; Truckee and Washoe valleys were nearly depopulated.[8]

Another consequence of the Mormon departure was a political vacuum lasting nearly four years. From 1857 to 1861 various legal, semilegal, and illegal efforts to establish government in the region failed.

At a mass meeting in Genoa in August 1857, the settlers expressed their displeasure with the inchoate arrangements for their governance. They decided at this meeting to petition Congress for speedy establishment of separate territorial status for Nevada in order to regularize their unofficial governmental arrangements. A territorial government, the settlers argued, would be able to provide security and protection for the inhabitants and for emigrants crossing the area on their way to California. Another reason advanced for the establishment of a territory was that the residents were out of communication with the civil authorities in Utah for long periods of time. The settlers pointed out that this recurring interruption of communication created a very anomalous situation: no debts could be collected, no offenders arrested, no crimes punished. They claimed, as well, that obedience to government could not be enforced and that there was only slight protection of life and property.

The unwanted dominance of the Mormons was also cited in the memorial to Congress. "The Mormons . . . regulate all their business affairs, dealing and intercourse with each other by certain established rules of the church and not by any laws passed by the legislative department of the Territory."[9]

Those attending this protest meeting in 1857 established another squatters' government and selected James M. Crane to go as their delegate to Washington to present to Congress their case for separate territorial status.

Although he was an agent of an unauthorized squatters' government, Crane, by his diligence, commanded enough attention in Washington to feel confident that he was progressing toward the goal of his consitutents. On February 18, 1858, he sent an optimistic letter to the squatters' government in which he reported that Congress was about to create a territorial government in western Utah under the name "Sierra Nevada." Crane believed that Congress would surely pass this act because the new territory would be able to exert a significant control over both the Indians and the Mormons.[10]

Crane's confidence seemed to be justified; on May 12, 1858, a bill to organize the Territory of Nevada (designated by that name instead of "Sierra Nevada" in the bill) was reported.[11] But two days later, following the comment of Congressman George W. Jones (Tennessee), "We certainly do not want any more Territories at this time,"[12] Congress failed to take action and the bill to create Nevada Territory was dropped.

In 1858, the territorial government of Utah, now under Governor Cumming, successor to Brigham Young, made an effort to reestablish control over Carson County. Governor Cumming appointed John S. Child as probate judge. When Child arrived in Carson County he arranged an election, which was held on October 30, 1858. The choice presented at this election was between a Mormon and an anti-Mormon ticket. The winning candidates were on the so-called Mormon ticket; but because of antagonism toward the Mormons and the desire of the residents for separate territorial status, a functioning government did not result.

First "Constitution"

Another attempt at locally organized government began with a mass meeting in Carson City in June 1859. This meeting was called to reopen the question of western Utah's becoming a separate territory. The group sponsoring the mass meeting decided to take political advantage of the continued hostility between the Mormons and the national government and use it as a wedge for acquiring territorial status. The assemblage in Carson City was undertaken before the wealth of the Comstock Lode was realized; thus, it was truly a political movement of the established residents, not of a transient group coming in for gold or silver.

At the mass meeting, a constitutional convention was called for. Delegates to this convention were elected on July 14, 1859, and met at Genoa on the eighteenth. After a nine-day session, the delegates had completed a constitution patterned after the government of California. About half the delegates did not believe that they were authorized to draft a constitution and so were not actively interested in the result.

On September 7, 1859, the constitution framed by this convention was submitted to the people. At the same election the people voted for the officers who were to fill the positions created by the unauthorized constitution. The returns of the election were not preserved. However, evidence exists that Isaac Roop was elected governor and that he did serve; J. J. Musser, president of the convention, attested that the constitution had been adopted by a large majority and that Roop had been elected governor of the purported new territory.[13]

By this time the mineral wealth of the Comstock had been discovered, and many residents were far more interested in silver than in government. When Roop tried to convene the legislature in Genoa on December 16, 1859, only four members attended. Thus, the unauthorized constitution

Home of Orion Clemens, Carson City. (Courtesy of Nevada Historical Society.)

and the unauthorized government it tried to create ceased to offer real promise of becoming the route to independence.

Meanwhile, because of the rapidly increasing population in the Comstock area, Judge Child tried once more to resurrect the Utah government's control over Carson County. He called for another election, which was held on October 8, 1859. No one seemed to pay much attention to the election, and none of the persons elected would accept the positions to which the voters elevated them. Two principal reasons account for the residents' indifference. By the time of this election, the great influx of prospectors in the Virginia City area had shifted the focus of interest to treasure seeking and away from self-government. The second reason, probably of greater significance, was that citizens who wanted self-government ignored the election because they were determined that the kind of self-government they wanted should not be under Utah's supervision.

Territorial Government

Many of the settlers of western Utah, despite their lack of interest in local elections, continued their efforts to seek congressional action establishing Nevada Territory. Judge Crane, the delegate to Congress, died in September 1859. An election was held on November 12, 1859, at which time J. J. Musser, president of the unauthorized constitutional convention, was elected to replace him.

In the same year, 1859, John Cradlebaugh, the federal district judge who later became the first delegate to Congress from Nevada Territory, attempted, without success, to establish law and order in the region. At this time, therefore, three distinct units of government were trying to function in Carson County: the Utah territorial government, the squatters' government of Isaac Roop, and the national government as represented by Judge Cradlebaugh.

Although Musser failed to secure, in 1860, the congressional action creating Nevada Territory that he and his constituents so strongly desired, he won sympathetic attention in Congress. The following year, Congress did pass the act permitting the organization of the new territory, and President Buchanan signed it on March 2, 1861. The willingness of Congress to recognize Nevada as a territory is attributable in part to the energetic promotional activity of Musser, in part to the widening breach between north and south, and in part to the great increase in population due to the discovery of the Comstock Lode. These factors conjoined to cause the creation of a separate territorial government.

On March 22, 1861, President Lincoln, whose inauguration had taken place two days after the creation of Nevada Territory, commissioned James W. Nye of New York as governor of the new territory and Orion Clemens of Iowa as secretary. Governor Nye arrived in Carson City in

July 1861 and soon after issued his proclamation organizing the territory of Nevada, announcing appointments of the various officers, and summoning the territorial legislature to meet in Carson City, which, by an earlier act of the Utah Legislature, had replaced Genoa as the county seat.[14] Nye wrote to Secretary of State William H. Seward on July 19, 1861, that there was "no such thing as law or order existing in the Territory." He said that the greatest demand was for a court system to establish mining rights. Clemens was apparently in pinched circumstances when he was appointed territorial secretary. He wrote to Seward in May 1861, asking for his first quarter's salary and added: "If I could have *two* quarters of my salary advance, I would take my family."[15]

Nevada's first official legislative body, Orion Clemens presiding, met at Abe Curry's Warm Springs Hotel in 1861 to begin the law-making process for the newly created Territory of Nevada. Every legislative session since that time has been held in Carson City. Partisan politics did not torment this first legislature—all the representatives were staunch Unionists. One of the members was William M. Stewart, who would serve in the first Nevada constitutional convention in 1863 and would later represent Nevada in the United States Senate for twenty-eight years. Other prominent members of the first territorial legislature included Samuel Youngs, M. N. Mitchell, and Edward C. Ing, who would be members of the first constitutional convention; James H. Sturtevant, who would serve in the second constitutional convention in 1864; and Isaac Roop, who had earlier been elected provisional governor of a proposed Nevada Territory.

Territorial secretary Clemens's brother Samuel, soon to be widely known as Mark Twain, came to Nevada to serve as private secretary to his brother. Twain later became a reporter of the legislative meetings and of the first constitutional convention for the *Territorial Enterprise,* the leading newspaper in the territory. In addition to lampooning Nevada's constitutional proceedings and its government in general, he engaged in high-spirited exploits after hours; he subsequently became famous for his writings about his Nevada days. He referred to his brother's territorial secretaryship as "an office of such majesty that it concentrated in itself the duties and dignities of treasurer, controller, secretary of state, and acting governor in the governor's absence . . . the title of 'Mr. Secretary' gave to the great position an air of wild and imposing grandeur."[16]

Andrew J. Marsh, reporter for the Sacramento *Daily Union,* is the main source of information about the territorial legislature.[17] He often referred sardonically to that body as "the assembled wisdom." Marsh described his return to Carson City in 1862 for the second territorial legislative meeting as follows: "Once more within the realms of Governor Nye, the land of silver and gold mines, of dust, of loose six-shooters and bad whiskey—one year has wrought wonderful changes in this city. It is as if two Carsons had sprung up . . . for the city has literally doubled."[18] It was a wild environment for legislative meetings. Marsh wrote: "In Carson nobody has been killed for several days, but the usual amusements of drawing bowie knives and snapping pistols have been kept up."[19]

The territorial period is also famous for an organization called the "Third House," a roistering association dedicated to conviviality and to mocking the legislature. Marsh said it was "a peculiar institution of Carson, designed as a burlesque upon the legitimate legislature. Some of its proceedings are quite witty. . . . This august body meets every evening in a rear building, as Mrs. Malaprop would say 'contagious to' a saloon."[20] Mark Twain was a leading figure in the "Third House." The tradition of journalists roasting the legislators has continued to the present; toward the end of each session a "Third House" is held with the press corps burlesquing the lawmakers.

Statehood Movement

A most significant act was passed in the second session of the territorial legislature. Isaac Roop introduced a bill to frame a consitution and establish a state government for the "State of Washoe." Andrew J. Marsh recorded that

> This important measure comes up with startling suddenness, not having been brought about by any "outside pressures" whatever, at least so far as I am at present advised. The general impression of members with whom I have conversed on the subject heretofore has been that "Washoe" has not been sufficiently developed as a Territorial chrysalis to think at present of emerging into a butterfly *State*.[21]

Marsh observed that if Nevada became a state, "it will be a very sensible thing if it adopts its old name of Washoe."[22] "Washoe" was subsequently designated by the territorial legislature as the name for the state. The territorial legislature passed the statehood bill and appropriated $3,000 for salaries and incidental expenses for a constitutional convention if the voters approved.

The statehood act provided for an election in September 1863, at which time the voters would decide whether they favored having Nevada become a state and, if so, would choose delegates to frame a state constitution.

In the September election, the voters selected delegates to a constituent convention. On the question of whether they preferred that Nevada remain a territory or whether they favored the formation of a state government, 6,660 voted for statehood and 1,502 voted against it.[23] Thus, more than four times as many citizens desired statehood as opposed it.

First Convention

In response to this mandate, a constitutional convention was called to order on November 3, 1863, in Carson City by territorial secretary Clemens.

A PROCLAMATION

By James W. Nye, Governor of the Territory of Nevada

To all whom it may concern—

Whereas: By an act of Congress of the United States of America entitled ''An Act to organize the Territory of Nevada,'' approved March 2nd, 1861, a true copy of which is hereto annexed a Government was created over all the country described in said Act to be called the 'Territory of Nevada,' And Whereas, the following named officers have been duly appointed and commissioned under said act as officers of said Government, viz: James W. Nye Governor of said Territory, Commander in Chief of the Militia thereof, and Superintendent of Indian Affairs therein; Orion Clemens, Secretary of said Territory; George Turner, Chief Justice; and H. Horatio Jones and Gordon N. Mott Associate Justices of the Supreme Court of said Territory, and to act as Judges of the District Court for said Territory; Benjamin B. Bunker, Attorney of the United States for said Territory; D. Bayles, Marshall of the United States for said Territory, and John W. North Surveyor General for said Territory: and the said Governor and other officers having assumed the duties of their said offices according to law, said Territorial Government is hereby declared to be organized and established, and all persons are enjoined to conform to [sic] respect and obey the laws thereof accordingly—

Given under my hand and the seal of said Territory this 11th day of July A.D. 1861, and of the Independence of the United States of America the Eighty Sixth—

JAMES W. NYE

The delegates to the first convention had every reason to expect that because an overwhelming majority of the citizens (more than 81 percent) favored statehood, the constitution they were drafting would be adopted. But curiously, the delegates' expectation of success was not realized. The first constitution was defeated by nearly as great a majority of votes (80 percent) as had been cast in favor of statehood!

Records of the deliberations of the first convention reveal many rifts among the delegates on issues confronting them, but the crucial question appeared to be how mines should be taxed.[24] The delegates tried to resolve the problem by providing in the original constitution for taxation of mines and mining property, not taxation only on the proceeds of mines; unquestionably, this provision, emphasized by many opponents of the first constitution as the reason why the voters should reject it, did indeed help to defeat it.

One of the opponents of the mining clause in the convention was William Stewart, a powerful Virginia City attorney who had served as attorney general of California before moving into the territory. However, Stewart decided to support the constitution because of his overriding desire for the removal of the territorial judges, including John W. North whose decision on a large mining dispute case Stewart strongly opposed.[25]

Another major cause of the defeat of the constitution was a political quarrel that split the Union party in Storey County, at that time the most populous county in Nevada. The quarrel broke out at the Union party convention held several weeks before the vote on the constitution. Because the Union party was the dominant political force in the territory, its nominations for the state elective offices would be tantamount to election. The losing faction at the county convention charged that William Stewart had packed the convention with his supporters and had used "strongarm" tactics to get his hand-picked slate of candidates approved.[26] One of those defeated had been John North, a candidate for governor. The losers at the Union party convention in Storey County then proceeded to bolt the convention and choose a different slate of nominees to present to the state convention. When this independent slate was defeated at the state convention by the "regular" nominees, the Stewart opponents announced their opposition to the adoption of the constitution. The antagonism between the rival factions within the party clouded the issue of adoption of the constitution.

It was a mistake to combine on the same ballot the vote on the constitution with the election of the state officers created by that document because "those disappointed in getting nominations for the positions they desired, and their names were legion, became hostile to its adoption."[27] An editorial in the *Virginia Evening Bulletin,* January 20, 1864, supports this position. After expressing regret that the constitution was not adopted, the editor continued: ". . . there is no use disguising the fact that the sole cause of the defeat of the Constitution was the nomination for officers to have been elected on its adoption."

The territorial governor also expressed his ideas on why the document was rejected. In a letter to Secretary Seward dated March 25, 1864, Governor Nye said:

> The reasons why it was not ratified are very obvious to those who were here and cognizant of the circumstances. The Constitution contained quite stringent provisions in regard to the right of suffrage. This arrayed all the disloyal or secession element against it. It likewise contained a provision for the taxing of mines which was unpalatable to the miners (or some of them). Neither or both would have defeated it, but it was submitted at the same time that the election for State officers was held, and the dissatisfaction with some of the State ticket, and the proceedings of some of the county conventions caused its opponents to act in concert, and all combined they were strong enough to defeat it.[28]

Thus, Nye viewed the election of state officials on the constitution ballot as the strongest reason for the defeat.

These elements, plus the dissatisfaction of ranchers and farmers (also referred to by Nye in his letter to Secretary Seward) created a negative reaction, so that in apparent defiance of the logic by which they had voted overwhelmingly in favor of statehood, the electorate roundly rejected the constitution drafted by this convention: only 2,157 voted yes and a very large number, 8,851, voted no.[29] But the territory promptly convened another constituent body, and the second convention drafted the constitution that still serves the state today.

CHAPTER 2

FORMING THE CONSTITUTION

THE SECOND CONSTITUTIONAL CONVENTION, held after Nevada had acquired territorial status, was called to order in Carson City on July 4, 1864. Delegates to the second convention were understandably anxious to avoid the causes that they believed had led to the rejection of the first constitution. Some of their comments, and their efforts to obviate the objections they considered to be decisive to those who had voted no, are valuable to an understanding of Nevada's constitutional development.

A number of statements can be found in the *Debates* indicating that the tax on mines was a cause of the defeat of the first constitution. However, at least one delegate, John A. Collins (Storey), believed that the mining clause was merely a pretext for some of the negative votes. He said:

> . . . when the people had once resolved that the Constitution should not be adopted, they naturally brought to bear every possible argument, and they found that mining clause to be a very strong and efficient one. And I repeat that, but for certain political transactions—and I refer especially to the efforts made to introduce a certain set of delegates into the State Convention—there would not have been much opposition to the Constitution, on account of that mining clause.[1]

But William Wetherell (Esmeralda) expressed the more common view: ". . . no Constitution will be adopted by the people of this Territory with a clause in it making it imperative upon the Legislature to tax the mines. . . . That was the very point upon which was based the condemnation of the old Constitution, in Esmeralda County, last fall."[2]

Another suggestion of particular interest to political scientists was made by Nelson E. Murdock (Churchill), who asserted that the first constitution was defective because it contained too much detail, too much material which rightfully should have been left for the legislative body to decide; for example, it specified the salaries for the state officials. Murdock said: "Now, I voted against the adoption of the former Constitution . . . solely for the reason that I thought it was too legislative in its character."[3] He explained his argument to develop the very sound position that

the legislature should not be bound too tightly by constitutional requirements, that the constitution should be a basic document, not a collection
of pieces of legislation.

During the debates, frequent references were made to opposition to
statehood because of the cost. Thomas Fitch (Storey) tried to discourage
in advance the probable argument that state government would cost too
much. He believed that if, without tying down the legislature excessively,
the power to appropriate could be limited, some of the objections to the
first constitution would be removed. But he warned the delegates that

> we cannot be oblivious to the fact that there is the nucleus of a very
> strong opposition to the Constitution now existing, that it is active
> and energetic, and that a very great effort is likely to be made to
> defeat the acceptance of the Constitution, to defeat the adoption by
> the people of a State Government, on the ground of its cost. The
> parties about to oppose the ratification of the Constitution say that
> the Territory is in no condition to afford the expense; that a State
> Government will cost a large sum of money; that to adopt it will
> necessitate the levying of a large amount of taxes; and that the people
> are too poor, in the present condition of our affairs, to undergo the
> expenses which will be involved.[4]

J. G. McClinton (Esmeralda) advanced a curious reason for the no vote
in his county; he averred that his constituency rejected the constitution
because, instead of requiring a two-thirds vote for amendment, the constitution permitted a majority vote of both houses to start the amendment
procedure. Students of Nevada constitutional history are more likely to
agree with B. S. Mason, also of Esmeralda County, who did not support
McClinton's hypothesis. Mason said:

> I was not aware of any such argument having been used against the
> old Constitution; certainly none such were advanced in my presence.
> I am satisfied that that Constitution was repugnant to a majority of
> the people in our county, from a variety of causes. One objection
> was, that it contained too much legislation, and another was the pov-
> erty of the Territory and its consequent inability to sustain a State
> Government.[5]

Nevada Territory had experienced serious difficulties over the judiciary;
judges were frequently charged with corruption, indifference to duty, and
absence from the bench. By the time of the second convention, the persistent criticisms of the judiciary were becoming acute. Some delegates
believed that the people would now vote in favor of the constitution
because statehood would ameliorate the difficulties related to the courts.
As a state, Nevada could have as many judges as were needed and could
punish incompetent, corrupt, or absentee judges.

An example of the public attitude toward the judiciary, a readiness to
believe "the worst," is shown by the public reaction to repeated attacks in
the newspapers on one of the supreme judges of the territory. He was

accused of accepting bribes and of neglecting his office. No evidence sub-
stantiated these charges, but about 4,000 people are said to have signed a
petition calling for the resignation of the *entire* bench!⁶

Other frequently given reasons for the defeat of the first constitution
were that Nevadans were "too young" a people for statehood and that
there was not enough taxable property to support a state. A. J. Lockwood
(Ormsby), who had also been a member of the first convention, had
opposed the first constitution and was not in favor of drafting a second
because he simply did not believe that it was necessary for Nevada to
become a state. The foregoing comments indicate the major and recurrent
observations made by the delegates to the second convention on why the
first constitution was defeated.

However, it is unwise to accept the comments made by the delegates to
the second convention as an entirely reliable source of information on the
true reasons for the voters' rejection of the first constitution. All that is
revealed by these comments is what the delegates themselves thought were
the reasons. The *Humboldt Register* summarized the problem in an
unscholarly, but probably realistic, fashion by stating that the people just
didn't want *any* constitution. An editorial in the paper stated that there
was no reason to have a constitution at all, and said that "To urge the
adoption of a constitution because it is a good one, and we're not likely to
get another so good when we want one, is miserable nonsense. . . . We
don't want any constitution—and we don't propose adopting one just
because it is good, and handy to have around the house."⁷

Enabling Act

One point about Nevada's first constitutional convention is especially
interesting: it was not legally authorized. A statehood bill for Nevada won
approval in the United States Senate on March 3, 1863. On the same day,
this bill was brought before the House of Representatives on a motion to
suspend the rules and so permit the House to consider Nevada's admission into the Union. The motion to suspend the rules was defeated in the
House;⁸ Congress adjourned the same day, thus precluding any further
discussion in that session on the statehood bill. Therefore, the convention
that framed the first constitution did so without prior congressional
approval. This fact troubled members of the 1863 convention. On the
very last meeting day, Ormsby delegate J. Neely Johnson, an attorney,
asked whether Congress had authorized Nevada to draft a constitution
and was told no. He then offered a resolution stating that if the people
approved the constitution as drafted, it should be sent to Congress
accompanied by a memorial respectfully asking that Nevada be admitted
to the Union. The resolution was agreed to.⁹

Thus, if the voters had adopted the first constitution and if Congress had subsequently agreed to their action, the territory could have been admitted without prior authorization of an enabling act. It is a curious fact of constitutional history that Nevada sought to gain admission to the Union by drafting a constitution in advance of, but hoping for, congressional assent.

Although Nevadans had voted down the first constitution, pressures for statehood continued. Probably the strongest came from the national government, which counted upon Nevada, after if was admitted as a state, to vote in favor of the antislavery amendment to the United States Constitution. Nevada politicians were conscious that they would be important in Washington because their vote on the antislavery amendment and their expected support of the Radical Republican position in Congress were so greatly desired.

During the second constitutional convention, Francis M. Proctor (Nye) referred to Nevada's potentially influential position in the national government. He said:

> . . . there are two objects for forming this State Government. One is the amendment of the Constitution of the United States, for the purpose of abolishing slavery. . . . The other object is, that there is a remote possibility that the election of the President of the United States . . . may be thrown into the House of Representatives, and we are cognizant of the fact that in such an event Nevada . . . would have just as many votes for the President . . . as the State of New York.[10]

Some Nevadans wanted statehood because they were ambitious for state office; others wanted statehood because of the recognition and prestige it would confer upon Nevada. Another argument for Nevada's becoming a state is suggested in a letter written to Governor Nye by the governor of Colorado Territory. He urged Nye to give full support to formation of a state government, on the ground that Nevada, like Colorado, was in great need of representatives in Congress to speak for and protect the mining interest.[11] For these and other reasons, the desire that Nevada should become a state did not die with the defeat of the constitution.

Less than a month after Nevadans had rejected the first constitution, another bill to admit Nevada to the Union was introduced in the Senate. This enabling act was passed by both Houses; it was signed by President Lincoln on March 21, 1864.

The enabling act, which is reprinted in the convention *Debates,*[12] stipulated, among other instructions, that the state must be republican in nature, that there could be neither slavery nor involuntary servitude, that religious toleration must be insured, and that federal property in the state could not be taxed. The enabling act also stated that if, after its ratification by the people, the Nevada Constitution satisfied the president, he could sign it and declare Nevada a state without any further action on the part of Congress. This is precisely what happened.

Composition of the Second Convention.

The second constitutional convention opened in Carson City on July 4, 1864. Thirty-nine delegates had been elected; the number was determined by apportionment among the counties to reflect the population as closely as possible. Storey had ten delegates; Washoe and Roop combined had five; Ormsby, five; Esmeralda, four; Lyon, four; Humboldt, three; Lander, three; Douglas, two; Nye, two; and Churchill, one.[13] Four delegates failed to come to the convention, one from Humboldt, one from Esmeralda, and two from Lander.

Of the thirty-five men who did attend, ten had also participated in the first convention: Nathaniel Ball, Cornelius M. Brosnan, Samuel A. Chapin, John A. Collins, George L. Gibson, James W. Haines, George A. Hudson, J. Neely Johnson, Francis H. Kennedy, and John H. Kinkead. In the pages that follow, the comments of these men concerning the debates in the first convention and their assessment of why the 1863 constitution failed deserve attention. Eleven of the delegates were lawyers, seven were connected with mining, three were in the lumber business, three were merchants, two were editors, two were farmers, two were mechanics, two were connected with mills, one was a banker, one was a physician, and one was a surveyor. Every delegate except two had come to Nevada from California. The two exceptions were George A. Nourse, who had come from Minnesota, and W. W. Belden, who had come from Wisconsin; both men represented Washoe County. One of the former Californians, J. Neely Johnson, had been the fourth governor of California (1856–58) as the candidate of the American party, a nativist group connected with the Know-Nothing movement.

All the delegates were relatively new to the territory. Nineteen of the thirty-five had been residents for less than four years; two had come the very year that the convention was held; and the delegate with the longest residency had been in Nevada only seven years. This brief acquaintance with the territory for which they were framing a constitution made the Nevada delegation unusual when compared with the constituent bodies of her sister states.

Other delegations present telling contrasts. The California Constitutional Convention had seven delegates who had been born in California; the Montana convention included among its seventy-five delegates twenty-seven who had lived in the territory more than thirty-three years; of the forty-five delegates in Wyoming's convention, there were twenty-three with more than ten years' residence; half of the delegates to the Oregon convention had lived in Oregon Territory longer than seven years;

Warm Springs Hotel, site of the first meeting of the territorial legislature.
(Courtesy of Nevada Historical Society.)

and in Washington's delegation of seventy-five members, thirty-seven had been residents of the territory more than nine years.

The curious "newness" of the members of the Nevada convention is further evidence of the rapidity of development referred to in the preceding chapter. However, even though the Nevada delegates had had a brief residency, they did not manifest a casual attitude toward the work of state building, nor did the fact that the delegates were newcomers appear to have an adverse effect upon the document drafted.

The caliber of most of the arguments at the convention, the intensity with which the delegates presented their positions, and the evidence throughout the debates of extensive study and experience indicate that this was a competent group of men and, generally, highly dedicated to Nevada Territory and to the new state they hoped to create from it. During the debates, the delegates made comments that show the variety of their reading. Frequent references were made to Magna Carta, the Bible, Samuel Johnson, Alexander Pope, Robert Burns, Thomas Babington Macaulay, William Blackstone, and the drafters of the United States Constitution.

The members of the convention also showed extensive knowledge of constitutional procedures in other states. Because thirty-three of the delegates had come from California, references to that state's practices were the most common; a startling number of comments were made about California's ruinous taxation and the widespread corruption several delegates had allegedly observed in that state. Occasionally during the debates, unhappy observations were made that the local press was inaccurately reporting the convention proceedings. Sporadically, the delegates showed impatience with someone's prolixity; one participant thought that the convention was "torrents of talk." Sometimes the debate was bitter and antagonistic. But, in general, the convention was dignified and hardworking.

Name

One of the early discussions concerned the name that should be given to the new state. In addition to "Nevada," proposals were made that the state be called "Esmeralda," "Humboldt," or "Washoe." Before the first constitutional convention, the territorial legislature had designated "Washoe" as the name for the new state, but the first convention had disregarded this instruction and had used the name "Nevada" throughout the constitution it drafted. J. Neely Johnson (Ormsby, president of the convention) doubted that the convention had the authority to select any name it wished, as the first convention had done:

> It is true that the late Constitutional Convention did override the act of the Legislature by substituting the name of "Nevada" for "Washoe"; but that cannot be regarded as a precedent, because the

3

Convention was held entirely without authority having previously been given by Congress. The entire action of that Convention depended upon subsequent approval of Congress, for it rested with Congress to say whether we should be admitted under that Constitution or not, and we could just as well have been admitted by one name as by another. The people, however, refused to ratify the action of the Convention, and consequently Congress took no action upon it, but provided for the assembling of a Convention, by the passage of our Enabling Act.[14]

Johnson contended that because the state was called "Nevada" in the enabling act, the delegates had no choice but to continue that name; such an inhibition had not existed for the first convention, but the second convention, meeting by authority of Congress, was bound by the terms of the enabling act.

The delegates did not adopt the proposal to substitute the name "Washoe," preferring to retain "Nevada." No more arguments were heard on the question of the name for the state.

First Constitution Basis for Second

The first substantive debate in the convention began when the proposal was made that the rejected constitution should be the starting point for discussion in the current convention. Some delegates advanced the counterproposal that instead of beginning with Nevada's first constitution, the California Constitution should be the base of discussion; they reasoned that Nevada's problems were very similar to those in California, specifically in the field of mining. Finally, it was argued that because the first Nevada Constitution owed much of its substance to the California Constitution, there was no point in starting all over again. This sensible contention prevailed, and the convention agreed to base its deliberations upon modifications of the first constitution. (The original constitution may be found in *Debates,* pages 24–33). That the Nevada Constitution derives in part from California's reveals an interesting aspect of the evolution of constitutions, since the California Constitution was, in turn, largely adapted from that of New York.

Having determined upon the first constitution as the starting point, the delegates began their discussions of the crucial issues facing the territory, issues on which accommodations had to be made before Nevada could become a state. It is not possible, of course, to summarize all the important matters covered in the more than eight hundred pages of the *Debates;* instead, attention will be focused upon four major topics that have both historical and current significance: (1) problems attendant upon the Civil War, particularly the question of a loyalty oath; (2) education; (3) a railroad subsidy; and (4) taxation. The convention arguments concerning the executive, legislative, and judicial branches will be summarized in later chapters.

Civil War

Because Nevdaa became a state during the Civil War and marks its birth by using the term "Battle Born" on the state flag, it is appropriate to begin analysis of the debates with those discussions in the convention reflecting the environment in which Nevada entered the Union. The debates contain numerous references to the fact that a number of disloyal persons had fled to Nevada. Many of the delegates expressed the greatest alarm that these people would be able to vote. Some delegates argued for permanent disqualification from voting of persons who had borne arms against the Union, particularly if they had served *voluntarily*. Some delegates thought that any decision Nevada might make about who had the right to vote would not be of real consequence if the national government proclaimed a general amnesty following the Civil War. The clause that many wished to see inserted in the constitution—and which finally did become part of Article II, Section 1, in the constitution as drafted—read that no person could vote in Nevada "who, after arriving at the age of eighteen years, shall have voluntarily borne arms against the United States, or held civil or military office under the so-called Confederate States, or either of them, unless an amnesty be granted to such by the Federal Government."

One argument for this clause was made by J. H. Warwick (Lander), who said: "Why, here we are surrounded with rebellion. It is well known that there is no State or Territory in the Union which has become so much a harbor of refuge for secessionists as Nevada and California. As a gentleman who preceded me remarked, it is here they fly as to their city of refuge. In my own county of Lander, I know that treason is blatant in almost every hamlet and village."[15]

Support for Warwick's charge appears in a letter addressed to Governor Nye asking that Nevada troops stationed in Susanville be withdrawn because "four-fifths of them are blatant Rebels" and their commander, Captain Hasselt, had been on intimate terms with local secessionists.[16]

A second method of preserving the purity of the ballot by keeping alleged traitors from voting would have been to insert in the constitution an oath to be required of any person whose right to vote was challenged on account of disloyalty.

Two opposing ideas on the matter of requiring special test oaths for loyalty and the problem of determining from whom such oaths should be exacted can be observed in the comments of John A. Collins (Storey) and E. F. Dunne (Humboldt). Collins said:

> I see no objection to allowing every voter in the district to lodge the names of A, B, C, with the registering officer, as suspected persons. . . . I think if, in my district, I lodge with the Registrar the names of ten men whom I regard as suspected, or whose loyalty I doubt, and who I think ought not to be allowed to exercise the elective franchise,

unless they purge themselves, if I desire it the Registrar should be required to compel them to take the oath.[17]

Dunne, however, feared the consequences of what he saw as an undesirable incitement to eavesdropping and spying comparable with the deplorable practices he believed to exist in certain European countries. He wanted an oath to apply to everyone. He explained:

> I must regard with the utmost abhorrence the last proposition of the gentleman from Storey. It savors too much of the denouncements of a secret police. It is a proposition to allow any man to inscribe on a bit of paper, which he deposits with the Registrar, "I denounce A, B, C, as traitors!" . . . I desire rather to adopt one simple, broad, sweeping requirement, to which no man can take exception—a law which applies to all with equal force—and not a provision under which any man may be able to fasten upon another the brand of disloyalty.[18]

The prolonged and often bitter debate on the test oath brought forth expressions of patriotism as well as of deep antagonism toward the Southern position on seccession, which had precipitated the war. B. S. Mason (Esmeralda County, the only delegate who was a physician), arguing vigorously for the inclusion of the oath, declared: "Why, sir, they said that poor, crazy, old John Brown must be hung; but this day old John Brown stands far higher in my estimation, than that vile old Iscariot, James Buchanan. [Applause]"[19]

Another speech on the problem of traitors and the right of suffrage has not only historical interest but also relevance to current controversies over the proper relationship between the states and the federal government. Lloyd Frizell (Storey) said:

> Those men who are in rebellion in the South are fighting for what they believe to be a principle—the principle of State Rights, or, as they term it, self-government. . . . I will say that that principle is one which strikes at the very root of our liberties, and the foundations of our Government. I hope to God that this war, when it is fought out, will put an end to that principle—a principle for which by the way, I have contended for years, in consequence of the prejudices of early education. I had always heard my father and my grandfather speak in contempuous [sic] terms of Alexander Hamilton, Chief Justice Marshall, John Adams, and others of those statesmen who were endeavoring to make the Federal Government strong; and I had heard them advocating what they called the prinicple of democracy, or States Rights. They held the great leaders of the old Federal party—as it was called in former times, when it was led by such men as Marshall, Hamilton, and other eminent Federalists—in the profoundest contempt, and to a great extent, my own mind was swayed and biased by their teachings. But in the past three or four years of my life I have seen my error. . . . I now see that what I have been cherishing was a heresy. . . .[20]

As he continued in this speech, Frizell expressed great compassion for the

South and voiced a desire to permit or even encourage the former Confederate soldiers and the people of the South to be reunited with the North as full partners in the Union. He pointed out the generosity with which George Washington and Patrick Henry accepted former Tories under liberal and comfortable provisions after the Revolution. He wanted to see the same compassion extended to the misguided Confederates, and cited his own early prejudices as a good example of the possibility of reform and renewed loyalty.

When J. W. Haines (Douglas) was arguing for a test oath in the constitution, he made a number of obscure but harsh remonstrances against some members of the convention, charging them with inconsistent stands on both the test oath and the railroad subsidy. He declined to designate his target. When asked to name names, he replied: "I do not know as it is necessary for any gentleman to take it up who is not hit; there are plenty who are hit."[21] Despite his unwillingness to be specific, it seems obvious that he was attacking the mining interests. He claimed that until the taxation clause had been modified to the pleasure of that industry, "certain delegates" had threatened to withdraw from the convention. Having achieved their objective with respect to taxation, Haines continued, they shifted their position on a railroad subsidy, which they had formerly opposed, and on the test oath, which they had formerly supported.

The gravamen of Haines's argument was that "those people" were grossly self-serving. When their holdings had to bear the same burden of taxation as other property, he maintained, they opposed aiding the railroad; when they achieved a special tax status, they were willing to have public funds expended on a subsidy. When they were hostile to the adoption of the constitution, they supported a test oath; when they eagerly desired the widest possible public support for the constitution, they were satisfied to ignore the risk of giving disloyal persons the right to vote. To these bitter accusations Haines added that, having arranged the taxation clause to their own benefit, these self-serving people opposed the loyalty pledge because they were convinced that certain groups in the territory would vote against the constitution if it embodied a test oath. Therefore, they were willing to "pander" (he used the word several times) to disloyal elements so that the constitution, which they now heartily endorsed, might win approval by the voters.

Haines was not alone in his fear and antagonism. The vote eliminating the test oath carried by nine votes, nineteen to ten. James H. Sturtevant (Washoe) said of his no vote: ". . . I do not believe in throwing out any inducements to gain the copperhead influence, even though we needed help ever so badly."[22]

The settlement of the vigorously debated test oath remains in the present constitution as it was originally passed. It is a part of Article II,

Section 6, and states simply that the legislature has power "to prescribe by law any other or further rules or oaths as may be deemed necessary as a test of electoral qualifications." Thus, the question of oaths was left to the legislature. Certainly this decision was a triumph for Josiah Earl (Storey), who, among others, had kept insisting that only the legislature should determine the best method for securing purity of the ballot. Earl had cautioned: ". . . do not let us fill up the Constitution with legislative provisions."[23]

Having finally decided to strike out the test oath, the delegates passed Article II, "Right of Suffrage," by a vote of twenty-five to four. Section 1 stated that no person who had voluntarily borne arms against the Union or held office under the Confederacy could vote unless the federal government granted an amnesty. This portion of Section 1 was removed from the constitution by amendment in 1914.

Education

During the debates on Article XI, "Education," great concern was expressed that religious or sectarian instruction would somehow or other creep into the public schools. The delegates, greatest worry about the schools was focused upon this problem. Their concern shows in two places in Article XI; Section 2 of that article, modified in 1938, contains an injunction that any public school in which instruction of a sectarian character is permitted may be deprived of its share of public funds. The same fear is shown again in Section 9 of the article on education, which states: "No sectarian instruction shall be imparted or tolerated in any school or university that may be established under this Constitution." As if these two statements were not enough, Section 10 was added to the constitution in 1880. That section reads: "No public funds of any kind or character whatever, State, county, or municipal, shall be used for sectarian purposes." Thus, the Nevada Constitution reflects a profound anxiety about the danger of religious influences in the schools.

A second educational problem bothering the delegates was whether attendance in the public schools should be compulsory. One argument against compulsion was that many people lived far away from a school, and it would be unfair to require parents to get their children to schools from great distances. Despite their recognition of this transportation problem, some of the delegates argued for compulsory attendance on the ground that a properly functioning democracy requires people who can read and write. All citizens manage the affairs of their own government through their right to vote, and they must have some education in order to make intelligent choices. Because a democracy presupposes an educated citizenry, several delegates argued that the only way to insure such a citizenry was to make school attendance compulsory.

Others opposed compulsion because it appeared dictatorial and undemocratic; several negative references were made to Prussian education. The problem was finally resolved by agreement of the convention on Section 2 of Article XI that the legislature may pass laws that "will tend to secure a general attendance of the children in each school district upon said public schools."

As is so often the case, the key problem proved to be financing—how to support the public schools and the university. The solution eventually adopted provided for a special tax of one-half mill on the dollar on all taxable property, this tax to be used for the common schools and for the university. This section has been changed since to read as it does now in Article XI, Section 6.

During the debate on the best ways to provide adequate revenue for education, several delegates referred to the bad condition of the public schools, the need for more schools, and the need for repairing schoolhouses. Albert T. Hawley (Douglas), however, did not feel that the schoolhouses of Nevada were in bad condition, As a nostalgic reminder of costs at that time, Hawley's comment is worth quoting:

> . . . in the extreme southern district of the county, they have built a frame school house, at a cost of five or six hundred dollars, and it is now completed. . . . In the Genoa precinct, a brick schoolhouse to cost about $2,000, is building. It will be ready for occupancy in January, and only four hundred dollars remain unpaid of the entire cost. . . . I think our schools are in very creditable condition. Moreover, we have received from the public school fund three or four hundred dollars to expend in supporting our schools, and we do not owe any teacher a dollar.[24]

In general, the discussions on a state university strongly favored establishing such an institution. The delegates showed thorough familiarity with the Morrill Act of 1862, which required that instruction be provided in agriculture, mechanic arts, and military tactics to qualify for federal assistance. Although they planned to create the departments required to secure federal aid, their discussions on forming a mining department, understandably, generated the greatest interest.

John A. Collins (Storey) thought it important to frame special financial provisions for the maintenance of the university. His comment shows remarkable prescience: ". . . I am confident the Board of Regents will have great difficulty in getting funds. It is always the case that institutions of this character are embarrassed for the want of funds. . . ."[25] The deliberations of 1864 reveal the same kind of problem that is still apparent today: most people want the finest educational opportunities for their children, but they disagree, sometimes violently, over how to raise the money.

Railroad Subsidy

Nearly 100 of the 829 pages recording the constitutional debates are on the question of a subsidy for a railroad through Nevada. Although various proposals were made for assisting the railroad, only two received attention. The first provided that the state could lend its credit to the Central Pacific Railroad to an amount not exceeding $3 million when tracks had been laid to a distance of eighty miles east of the Sacramento River, but that this loan could be made only after an affirmative vote by the people. The second proposal was that the state, on terms prescribed by the legislature, could issue bonds to an amount not exceeding $1.5 million at a rate of interest not exceeding 7 percent. These bonds were to be issued to the company that first completed a railroad connecting Virginia City with the Sierra Nevada.

A great deal of rancor marked the discussions on the highly controversial subject of subsidizing a railroad. The arguments in favor of aiding a railroad company centered upon the expected economic benefits to the prospective state; although acknowledging that the railroad would benefit the mining interests primarily, several delegates contended that a railroad would also improve the entire economy of Nevada. The main opposition focused upon the current poverty of the territory; those against the subsidy felt it would be most unwise to bankrupt the new state for the benefit of a very wealthy and highly subsidized railroad.

On July 13, Leland Stanford, former governor of California and president of the Central Pacific Railroad, appeared at the convention and was invited to speak on the subject of the Central Pacific. He discussed the financing of the railroad and the problems of railroad construction, particularly construction over the mountains. He said he knew that Nevada wanted to help the Central Pacific Railroad, and the best way to do so would be to assist in the most costly part of the construction over the mountains. He contended: "The people of California do not need a railroad to Nevada so much as the people of Nevada need a railroad to California."[26] Stanford expressed opposition to the clause in the first constitution that provided that bonds not to exceed $3 million could be issued to the first company that would complete a railroad connecting Nevada with either the navigable waters of California or the navigable waters of the Mississippi. Stanford felt that if such a clause were repeated in the new constitution, the wording would indicate a doubt that the Central Pacific Railroad was the only railroad with a feasible route. He said he preferred no assistance to assistance indicating any possibility that another railroad company might come into the state.

Thomas Fitch (Storey) was deeply distressed at the thought that Nevada might decline to help the railroad:

The Capitol about 1872. (Courtesy of Nevada Historical Society.)

. . . after the consummation of this mighty work, which will be the boast of the nineteenth century, the pride and glory of the age, a work grander than the aqueducts of Rome, more stupendous than the pyramids of Egypt, more wonderful than the Sphynx [*sic*] in the desert sands, I should be sorry if it should be said . . . that in the community which was most benefited by it, the community which was raised from a state of comparative indigence to wealth by that road . . . their representatives . . . had absolutely declared that the people of Nevada, whether they wished it or not, should not be allowed to aid that road in the hour of its direst necessity.[27]

Charles E. DeLong (also from Storey) did not view the railroad as being in dire necessity. He commented: "According to Governor Stanford's own showing, if we give this aid it would not help the road a pin, yet he would like it, because it would be an indorsement of the enterprise, that is all. While it would distress us terribly to raise the amount, it would scarcely help the railroad at all."[28] Later in the debate, having given a resumé of aid totaling $21 million to the Central Pacific from the federal and various city governments, DeLong added: "Now, in the face of all this, how can they ask poor, little, old, sage-brush Nevada to burden herself by giving more aid, when it would be of little or no practical benefit to the road?"[29]

There was some discussion whether the question of aid to the Central Pacific Railroad or any railroad should be left to the legislature. J. W. Haines (Douglas) spoke as follows:

If such a question is left to the Legislature—the gentleman from Lander has seen how it has worked in the California Legislature, and possibly in other legislative bodies—the moment the question is left to them, if it were necessary, there would be a hundred thousand dollars brought here to corrupt the Legislature, and I venture to say that the gentleman has never seen any Legislature yet that was not more or less liable to be corrupted by the influence of money.[30]

The suggestion that legislatures could be suborned by railroad money was not just a gratuitous insult to legislative bodies or to railroad companies. In several western states similar claims had been made concerning the influence and control of legislatures by the railroads.

A justification for Haines's fear that railroad money could be corruptly used in Nevada may be found in a later occurrence in Nevada's history. In 1877 widespread protests were voiced over the rates imposed by the railroad for shipments to Nevada. Charges for a carload of coal oil, for example, shipped from New York to San Francisco were $300; from New York to Reno, $536; from New York to Winnemucca, $716; from New York to Elko, $800.[31] Nevadans were clearly victims of discrimination. At least one protester against such unfair treatment of Nevada claimed that his protest brought banishment, which he attributed to the railroad. F. E. Fisk wrote a letter in 1881 detailing how he was driven from Nevada for

opposing the railroads. Part of his letter reads: "I know the inside work-
ings of the railroad companies. I know that members of the Ninth Legislature were bought, body and soul, and money was paid for votes almost
openly."[32]

Although this alleged episode occurred more than ten years after
Haines warned the convention about the susceptibility of some legislators
to railroad pressures, it does illustrate the kind of situation he feared. It is
unclear whether the delegates' anxiety about such possibilities of corruption made them decide against aiding the railroad; but, after many caustic
exchanges, they determined upon this wording for Article VIII, Section 9:
"The State shall not donate or loan money or its credit . . . except [to]
corporations formed for educational or charitable purposes." So ended
the long fight over a railroad subsidy.

Taxation

More than 130 pages of the records of the convention are taken up with
the ever-troublesome problem of taxation. One question was technical:
Could the mines be taxed, since the enabling act stipulated that unappropriated public lands were to remain at the disposition of the United States
and that no taxes could be imposed upon such property? The first constitution had provided for taxation of mines and mining property. J. Neely
Johnson (Ormsby, president of the convention) again drew a distinction
between the present and the former convention on the right to tax mining
property:

> I think I have enunciated distinctly the proposition that under this
> Enabling Act, the Legislature would not have the power to tax the
> mines, as the property of the Federal Government, but that in the
> former Convention, before the Enabling Act was passed, I felt satis-
> fied they had that power. Since the passage of the Enabling Act,
> however, containing inhibitory language, I do not think they could
> do it.[33]

James A. Banks (Humboldt) supported Johnson's conclusion; he held
that the circumstances under which the first convention met permitted the
taxation of the mines, "yet they are not sufficient under the present circumstances. . . . This body is convened, as has been stated by our worthy
President, under an Enabling Act. . . ."[34] The discussions on this topic
were intended to insure the legality of the proposed new constitution and
its unequivocal clarity concerning what would and would not be taxed.

It has been mentioned that many people believed the first constitution
had been defeated because of the clause providing for taxation of all
property, "including mines and mining property." Whether or not this
clause was responsible for the rejection of the constitution, there is no
question of its significance to the delegates. The lengthy debates on taxation of mines clearly revealed the bitter division of feelings in the territory over what some delegates saw as greedy self-serving by the mining

interests and other delegates saw as necessary protection of the largest revenue producer in Nevada.

Several delegates objected to the proposal that only the proceeds of mines should be taxed; they felt that assessments should be at a uniform rate, without special favor to any commercial activity. Charles E. DeLong (Storey, a lawyer) argued for a tax only on the proceeds of mines. George A. Nourse (Washoe, also a lawyer) commented that if DeLong would add to his proposal that "farms, and saw-mills, and other property shall be taxed only on their net proceeds, there will be some degree of fairness in his proposition." DeLong: "And lawyers' offices?" Nourse: "Yes, and lawyers' offices. [Merriment.]"[35]

But such "merriment" did not characterize the bulk of the debate. A. J. Lockwood (Ormsby) said:

> . . . there is a strange inconsistency in the action of some of the members of this Convention. They were so liberal in their views and feelings a few days ago, that they proposed to vote away three millions of dollars to the Pacific Railroad Company, when the great State of California, whose wealth, compared with that of this Territory, is as a mountain to a mole hill, only proposes to pay the interest on a million and a half of the bonds of that company.[36]

According to Lockwood, the people who wanted to give money to the railroad inconsistently opposed a levy on the mines. He held that both the benefits of statehood and the benefits of a railroad would accrue to the mining industry, which persistently showed itself unwilling to pay its fair share of the costs of government. It was the mining interests who most wanted Nevada to become a state, he argued; yet no state government could function without the revenue that would come from the taxation of mines.

Lockwood said that the miners wanted the agricultural areas to pay for what would benefit only the mines. "I am in favor of taxing the mines, because I want to make those gentlemen who are rolling in wealth in San Francisco, pay something for the support of our government, for the support of our common schools, and for the support of our courts."[37] Later in the discussion he said that the industrial and agricultural interests were satisfied with the government as it was and that the people who were demanding the change should be at least equal partners in the financial support of the new government they were so eager to establish.

E. F. Dunne (Humboldt) expressed the opposite position: he did not wish the mines to be taxed at all. In reply to the argument that if mines were not taxed, the burden of government would be thrust entirely upon the agricultural interests, he said: ". . . what is that interest without the mines? Impose a tax which shall encumber the mining interest, which shall destroy it, or thwart its development, and you thereby strike a ruinous blow at the agricultural interest."[38]

Apparently answering the charge that the pressure for statehood came essentially from the mining groups, Dunne declared his opposition to a state government because he "believed that it would be suicidal policy to tax the mines, and when I found that there was only twenty-five millions of taxable property other than mining property, with which to carry on the State Government, I concluded that it was unwise and impolitic in every sense, for us to attempt the organization of a State Government."[39]

Some delegates said that they would have no objection to taxing the proceeds of mines, but that if mining property were subject to taxation, the mines would not be worked and Nevada would then have no revenue of any consequence at all.

At the conclusion of the twelfth day of the convention, July 16, a vote was taken on an amendment, the crucial part of which read: ". . . secure a just valuation for taxation of all property, real, personal, and possessory, excepting mines and mining claims, the proceeds of which alone shall be taxed. . . ."[40] The vote was twenty-three yes, ten no; none of the ten who voted no listed his occupation as mining. This vote shows that the delegates believed the taxing of mining property as provided in the first constitution was a mistake; it was a clear victory for the position of the miners and others who had opposed the first constitution mainly because of the clause which permitted taxation of mining property, whether productive or not. The final vote on Article X, "Taxation," was taken on July 20; twenty delegates voted yes, ten no.[41]

Article X, which occupied so large a part of the convention's time, has since been modified by seven amendments. Section 1, comprising the entire article in the constitution as drafted, was amended to add the material on patented mines, the portions making Nevada a "free port," the prohibition on inheritance and estate taxes, the motor vehicle exemption clause, and the special assessment rate for open-space property. The other change, enacted in 1936, was the addition of Section 2 in its entirety.

One more taxation problem deserves comment: the poll tax. This tax, of $2 to $4, was to be levied upon male residents between the ages of twenty-one and sixty. The central argument in the convention pertained to including in the poll tax clause a provision that would allow the legislature discretion in making payment of the tax a prerequisite for voting. Making payment of a tax a condition for voting bothered many delegates. Josiah Earl (Storey) said: ". . . it savors too much of a property qualification."[42] He observed that he had known times when he could not have paid the stipulated sum; he expressed fear that worthy citizens might be deprived of their right to vote; and he deplored any connection between payment of a tax and voting. J. Neely Johnson (Ormsby, president of the convention) wanted the tax retained to insure the purity of the ballot box; he foresaw no evil consequence from making payment of the tax a requirement of voting and asserted that the people most likely to object to such payment "are generally that class of men who would be likely to spend more in a day for rot-gut whiskey than would suffice to pay the whole of their tax."[43] Nelson E. Murdock (Churchill) did not oppose the tax itself, but the disenfranchisement of the poor as a consequence of their inability to pay; he also feared that purchase of votes could ensue by offers to pay a man's poll tax in return for his vote.

As it came from the convention, the controversial poll tax clause was included in the constitution, as part of Article II, Section 7. This section was amended in 1910. The amendment eliminated the connection between paying the tax and the right to vote, and also the requirement that one-half of the tax be applied to state, one-half to county purposes. The stipulation that the receipts from the tax be expended on public roads was also added in the 1910 amendment. The Twenty-fourth Amendment to the United States Constitution, ratified in 1964, prohibits collection of a poll tax as a requirement for voting in primaries or general elections for president, vice-president, or members of Congress. In the 1966 election, Nevada voters adopted an amendment proposed by the legislature and repealed the poll tax clause entirely; the vote was a decisive 86 percent in favor of repeal.

One other discussion in the convention is of interest. As it appeared in the first constitution, and as it was originally drafted by the second convention, the clause on imprisonment for debt stipulated that only in cases of fraud could a person unable to pay his debts be jailed. On the next-to-the-last day of the convention, Cornelius M. Brosnan (Storey) moved to add that persons could also be imprisoned for inability to pay a judgment against them in cases of libel or slander. In the quotation that follows, his sincerity is evident, as is the depth of his conviction:

> . . . the reckless and malevolent may permeate every avenue of society, circulating vile falsehoods and base accusations against their neighbors, with impunity, smiting down perhaps the best citizens, in the days of their usefulness, by the villainous shafts of slander, or the empoisoned arrows of the pen. The man of malevolent heart may squat toad-like at the ear of his neighbor, as the devil did in the garden at the ear of Eve, infusing the poison of his own malicious heart, by uttering falsehood and scandal against that neighbor's friend, and yet for him who is maligned there is no redress. . . . the penniless, characterless, ruthless, merciless ruffian . . . not having the wherewith to respond in compensating damages, goes forth free, and laughs with impunity not only at the wrongs he has perpetrated against his neighbor, but also at the powerlessness of the law. . . . You allow the vulture of slander to prey upon his vitals, as did that other foul bird upon the liver of the chained Prometheus. . . . let us at least place the slanderer and the libeller upon the same platform with the defrauder, the cheat, and the swindler.[44]

It is pleasing to record that, following this speech, the convention unanimously adopted Brosnan's amendment; and to this day, anyone convicted of slander or libel in Nevada may be imprisoned if he cannot pay damages.

Adoption of the Constitution

The last day of the convention, July 27, 1864, was spent in tidying the document, eliminating discrepancies, and removing contradictions; there was very little substantive argument. The final day was a day of revising, with one notable exception. George A. Nourse (Washoe) expressed again his displeasure with the taxation arrangements and said that he opposed the constitution because of "odious and unjust discrimination between different kinds of property."[45] He said that he would vote against the constitution, and indeed he did so; joining him in this negative vote was Israel Crawford (Ormsby). The final convention vote on the new constitution was nineteen yes and two no.[46] Thirty delegates signed the constitution. Since both Nourse and Crawford were among the signers, as was Dunne, who had frequently expressed antagonism toward the constitution, their signatures cannot be interpreted as approval, but only as an indication of their offical participation in the drafting.

Following convention acceptance of the new document, preparations were begun for the all-important popular vote, to be held September 7, 1864. Proponents of the new constitution must have believed that animosity among rivals for state offices had been a factor in the defeat of the first constitution, for this time no candidates for state office were on the ballot to becloud the issue; they were elected at a separate time, on November 8, 1864. Thus, the voter, free of any confusion between his choice of officials and his choice on the constitution, could focus his attention entirely on the latter.

The constitution was emphatically supported. The yes vote was 10,375; the no vote was 1,284, a majority of 9,091 in favor of the constitution. The vote of the two largest counties, Storey and Washoe, was as follows: Storey, yes 5,448, no 142; Washoe, yes 1,055, no 115. Only Humboldt County returned a preponderance of no votes; yes 320, no 544.[47]

Nevadans expressed their pleasure in the successful adoption of the constitution and their desire for speedy recognition as a state by wiring the entire text of the document to Washington at a cost of $3,416.77. It was the longest telegram ever sent up to that time.[48]

By the terms of the enabling act, President Lincoln had been authorized to admit the new state without further reference to Congress. So, by presidential proclamation, Nevada was admitted to the Union on October 31, 1864.

CHAPTER 3

THE CONSTITUTION

NEVADA'S CONSTITUTION—drafted more than one hundred years ago, defeated when first presented to the voters, and then decisively adopted when presented in its second form—has served the state quite well. Promulgated on October 31, 1864, the constitution contains about 17,000 words and has been amended eighty-six times (1978); fifty-three other proposals for amendments have failed.

Despite the changes made and the changes contemplated, the Nevada Constitution is above average when compared with the majority of state constitutions on the basis of brevity and effectiveness. This observation should preclude neither thoughtful proposals for making it a better document nor criticisms of the parts of the constitution that do not work well, are obsolete, or are in illogical order. Constitutions embody the fundamental principles of government and so should not lightly be changed; but neither should stagnation be permitted in the name of reverence for history.

Only nineteen states, including Nevada, still function under their original constitutions. Massachusetts, whose constitution dates from 1780, has the oldest living constitution. It contains approximately 36,000 words and has been amended about 115 times. To appreciate the prudence and economy of the drafters of the Nevada and Massachusetts constitutions and the durability of the documents they drafted, we need only look at the records of Georgia or Louisiana. Georgia has had eight constitutions, its latest adopted in 1945. It contains 500,000 words and more than 1,000 amendments. Louisiana has been governed under eleven constitutions, the most recent of which was enacted in 1974. Its tenth constitution had 256,000 words and was amended 759 times. Such wordy and frequently changed documents do not reflect the central purpose of constitutions, which is to provide the broad and underlying principles of government, not the details.

In the 1970s, Nevada citizens were given the opportunity to vote on numerous constitutional amendments: seven on the 1970 ballot, eight in

4

1972, three in 1974, ten in 1976, and five in 1978. Such piecemeal treatment of constitutional change may force political leaders to consider making a more coherent and thorough analysis of the state's constitution than is presently provided by the barrage of often unrelated amendments hurled at the voters every other year.

Constitutional Revision and Amendment

Two methods, not counting violent overthrow of government, are available for bringing about changes in constitutions: revision and amendment. Revision entails rewriting the constitution so that it is essentially a new document; it is this procedure that Louisiana has employed eleven times and Nevada not at all.

In the period since 1965 more than half of the states have considered revising their constitutions. Twenty-two states have undertaken serious studies designed to modernize their basic documents. This notable burst of activity was caused partly by the antiquated character of state constitutions, but mainly by the imperatives of reapportionment. When the states were forced to alter their legislative patterns in conformity with the "one man, one vote" ruling of the United States Supreme Court, most of them had to change their constitutions, since provisions for area representation, no longer permissible, were usually stipulated in the constitution, as was the case in Nevada. In contemplating changes in the clauses describing the representative pattern, most of these states decided to look over the whole cluttered patchwork of their constitutions with an eye to making the entire document clear and consonant with modern times.

Some attention has been given in Nevada to revising the constitution; the most recent attempt was made in 1955, and the subject was brought up again in 1968. However, neither the legislature nor the public gave enough support to these proposals for them to be taken seriously. In an earlier day, 1876–90, the desire for revision was earnest. A proposition calling for a constitutional convention appeared on the ballot in four elections. The measure was defeated by strong majorities in the elections of 1876, 1884, and 1888, although many of those voting did not bother to cast a ballot on the important question of a new constitution; about 39 percent, 45 percent, and 66 percent of those going to the polls each election failed to express a position on calling a convention. In the general election of 1890 the call for a convention apparently won, but some strange performances in the legislature and some allegations of defective ballots caused the issue to be dropped, even though Acting Governor Frank Bell stated in his annual message (15th session, 1891) that there was no doubt that the proposal to call a convention for revising the constitution had won a majority of the votes cast, and that it was the duty of the legislature to put the wishes of the people into effect.

If Nevadans ever decide that a new constitution should be written, the following process will be required: (1) a two-thirds vote of the elected membership in each house of the legislature favoring revision of the constitution; (2) support of the revision by a majority of those voting at the next election at which legislators are chosen; (3) a call by the legislature at its next session for a constitutional convention, to be held within six months.[1] On the basis of court decisions in other states, a new constitution drafted by such a convention would undoubtedly have to be approved by the voters in an election before it could go into effect, even though the constitution is silent on the matter. The procedure is intentionally lengthy; since legislators are elected every other year, about two years would normally elapse between the legislative vote for revision and the popular vote. This deliberately protracted method for revising the constitution is not, however, a hopeless barrier to creating a new constitution if the people of the state really want to do so.

The attitude of the public in Nevada, and in other states also, has usually been a hindrance to constitutional revision. Coupled with a widespread public indifference to authorizing so radical a change in the governmental pattern, active hostility to such a change often existed in rural areas. Before reapportionment was forced upon them, most states had, in varying degrees, overrepresentation of the nonurban areas. Consequently, one of the major pressures for drafting new state constitutions came from the desire of the growing cities to secure greater representation. Rural districts could hardly support a revision of the constitution that might work against their interests.

For example, prior to 1966, when Nevada was required to apportion both houses of the legislature to reflect population in each chamber, the senate was composed of seventeen members, one from each county. Fifteen of the seventeen represented relatively small populations, about 25 percent of the total population of the state according to the 1960 census; only two senators, one from Clark and one from Washoe, represented the remaining 75 percent. Since a two-thirds vote of both houses is required to begin the process leading to revision of the constitution, support in the Nevada senate for a revision that might lead to a change in apportionment of the senate was obviously unlikely. The Nevada assembly had thirty-seven members, of whom twenty-one were from Washoe and Clark counties (nine and twelve, respectively), which contained about 75 percent of the state's population. As in the senate, the two populous counties did not command the necessary two-thirds vote; neither house of the Nevada legislature, then, could initiate revision of the constitution short of some dramatic crisis in government. Reapportionment in Nevada, as in most states, resulted from a judicial decision; it did not stimulate interest in constitutional revision, nor was it widely applauded in the state.

The second method for changing constitutions is the more familiar process of amendment. The Nevada Constituion stipulates that only a *majority* vote of the elected members in each house is needed to propose an amendment, whereas a *two-thirds* vote is required for revision of the constitution. The proposed amendment is then referred to the next elected legislature; consequently, nearly two years would intervene between the first and the second legislative consideration of the proposed amendment. If the newly chosen legislature also approves the proposal by a majority of the elected members, the amendment goes on the ballot; if the voters then approve it, the amendment becomes part of the constitution. Again, we note a deliberately cumbersome but not a hopeless procedure, as the fact that it has been successfully used more than eighty times attests.

All states provide that proposals to amend their constitutions may originate in the legislative body; the same arrangement exists at the national level.

Initiative, Referendum, and Recall

Most of the states restrict to the legislature the power of originating amendments to the constitution. But Nevada and sixteen other states also permit the amending process to be started by initiative petition, a method allowing the voters rather than their elected representatives in the legislature to start the movement to change the constitution. The initiative in Nevada, then, can be used for amendment as well as for proposing ordinary legislation. Twenty-one states in all allow the initiative to originate statewide legislation.

Initiative and referendum are two devices that have been adopted in several states with the commendable intent of making citizens more active in the process of government. As drafted, the Nevada Constitution did not provide for the initiative or the referendum. The constitution was amended in 1904 to add the provisions for the referendum;[2] amendments in 1912, in 1958, in 1962, and in 1972 established the initiative and the conditions for its use.[3]

To begin the process of proposing a law or an amendment, an initiative petition is circulated. For the petition to be valid, two requirements must be fulfilled: (1) 10 percent of the number of voters who cast a ballot in the preceding general election in thirteen of the seventeen counties must sign the petition, and (2) the total number of these signatures must equal 10 percent of the number of all the voters in the entire state who cast a ballot at the preceding general election. This latter provision prevents a few voters in the thirteen least populous counties from proposing a law or an amendment without the concurrence of at least 10 percent of all the voters. The requirement that signatures be obtained in thirteen counties

Statue of John W. Mackay, a benefactor of the university who made a fortune on the Comstock (sculpture by Gutzon Borglum; located at the University of Nevada, Reno). This photograph, taken probably in 1908, is particularly interesting because the plate remained undeveloped in the camera of the late Senator Key Pittman and was not discovered and printed until 1965. (Courtesy of Nevada Historical Society.)

prevents the voters of Washoe or Clark county from securing the necessary number of signatures entirely within either county. The Nevada Constitution has the same provision for starting an initiative whether the petition proposes an ordinary law or proposes an amendment to the constitution.

The requirements that an initiative must bear signatures of 10 percent of the voters in thirteen of the counties who cast a ballot in the preceding general election does not seem to be in harmony with the United States Constitution as interpreted by the Supreme Court in *Moore v. Ogilvie* (1969). In that case, the Court rejected a nearly identical system in Illinois and ruled that requiring signatures from a specified number of counties dispersed political strength, discriminated against residents of populous areas, and unreasonably inflated the voting power of residents of sparsely populated areas. If the initiative-petition arrangement of Nevada were challenged in court, it is unlikely that it would be upheld. In the 1975 session of the Nevada Legislature the assembly briefly considered a proposal to change Nevada's law by dropping the clause stipulating that signatures must be obtained in thirteen counties. But no action was taken.

An initiative petition proposing a *law* or a modification of an existing law is presented to the legislature, which is required by the constitution to consider it before any other measure except appropriation bills. If the legislature passes the initiative and it is approved by the governor, it becomes a law. If the petition is rejected by the legislators, or if they fail to act on it within forty days of the beginning of the session, the initiative must go on the ballot. Should the voters approve, it becomes law. An initiative measure that is approved by vote of the people attains temporary invulnerability to change: for a period of three years after the vote, the measure cannot be annulled, repealed, amended, set aside, or suspended by the legislature.

Use of the initiative route to make a law is illustrated by Nevada's experience with "right to work," an occasion for hectic voter participation in the legislative process. An initiative petition providing that no person could be required to belong to a union in order to get or hold a job reached the ballot in 1952. It was passed[4] by a margin of 50.6 percent. Labor, not a strong political force in this state, immediately began collecting signatures for an initiative petition to repeal the just-passed "right to work" law. The repeal initiative appeared on the ballot in 1954 and was defeated in a close vote by 51.3 percent. Once more labor supporters set to work. They circulated two initiative petitions. The first proposed an amendment to the constitution establishing the union shop—that is, requiring that all workers must belong to a union after they have been hired. The second petition would have repealed the "right to work" law. At the 1956 election, the amendment was defeated by 56 percent and the initiative by 54 percent. Fearing that labor would continue to seek repeal of the "right to work" law by presenting one initiative petition after another at each election, supporters of "right to work" succeeded in passing an amendment in 1958 that tightened requirements for initiative petitions. Prolabor forces lost ground in each of these elections. The 1958 result showed 61.9 percent favoring more restrictive initiative provisions. The new amendment changed the existing law that 10 percent of the voters must sign such petitions to a law establishing that 10 percent of the voters in thirteen of the counties (but totaling 10 percent of the state's voters) must sign. This revision eliminated the opportunity to obtain the necessary signatures in only Clark or Washoe counties, where labor is organized. Despite continued efforts by labor to repeal the "right to work" law, Nevada remains (1980) one of nineteen states that do not permit union membership to be a condition for getting or holding a job.

An initiative petition proposing an *amendment* to the constitution does not go to the legislature. Instead, it is placed on the ballot at two successive general elections; if approved in both elections, it becomes part of the constitution. Before 1962, when a constitutional amendment changed the requirements, an initiative petition, whether it proposed a law or an amendment, went to the legislature.

The theory and practice of the initiative are worthy of close study. In Nevada, by use of the initiative petition, a law can be made in the absence of any action by the legislature or, indeed, in the face of opposition by the legislature; an amendment to the constitution can be effected without any legislative involvement in the process at all. Whether this bypassing of the legislature is a serious violation of representative government, which entrusts lawmaking to the elected representatives of the people, or is, instead, a commendable involvement of the voters in the operation of their government is debatable; sound arguments can be made for either position. Some critics of the initiative claim that most people don't take the time to inform themselves on at least some of the proposals and therefore often vote blindly on them. Then, too, the voter is only given the option of approving or disapproving an initiative proposal as it is written on the petition.

Nevada's constitution has been amended three times by using the initiative process. The first time was in 1958, when supporters of the "right to work" law were successful in amending the constitution by way of the initiative route in order to make it more difficult to use the device of the initiative petition.[5] The second time was in 1960, when the voters, who had just voted in 1958 to have annual sessions of the legislature, promptly reversed themselves, initiating an amendment to return to biennial sessions and voting yes on the new amendment. The third time was in 1962, when the voters approved two substantive changes in Article XIX. The first change deprived the legislature of its power to take action on a constitutional amendment proposed by initiative petition and provided, instead, for voter approval only, as described above. The second change substituted, for the requirement of 10 percent of the *qualified* voters, the requirement that 10 percent of those who actually *voted* in the preceding general election in thirteen counties could propose an initiative. A possible fourth amendment via the initiative procedure came before the voters for a second time in the general election of 1980, after being approved by 77 percent of the voters in 1978. The proposed amendment, Question 6 on the 1978 ballot, was copied from the famous Proposition 13 initiative overwhelmingly approved by the California electorate in June 1978. If approved a second time, the Nevada amendment would roll back property assessments to 1975–76 levels and limit the tax to one percent of market value.

In trying to determine the value of the initiative, it is important to distinguish between its use to originate a particular law and its use to amend the constitution. The latter use can be construed as a violation of the theory of amendment, which is an intentionally sluggish process that traditionally begins with the legislative body. However, both the initiative and the amendment provisions are part of the Nevada Constitution and, of course, are of equal constitutional validity. In 1960 the Nevada Supreme Court held in *Wilson v. Koontz,* 76 Nev. 33, that constitutional amendment by initiative process is valid; and the 1962 amendment of Article XIX reaffirms this judgment. However legal it is, use of the initiativie method to amend is not in the usual spirit of amending a constitution.

Although both the initiative and the referendum are designed to stimulate voter involvement in the legislative process, they are exercised for different reasons. The initiative is used when some particular law is desired by the people and the legislature has failed to enact it. The referendum, on the other hand, is used when a law already passed by the legislature has aroused public controversy and the people want to express their position on the questioned law; or it is used when the legislature desires special endorsement by the public of a particular law. Thirty-eight states, including Nevada, provide a referendum on statewide legislation. In Nevada, when 10 percent of the number who voted in the last general election sign a referendum petition requesting that a law be submitted to a vote of the people, said law must be placed on the next statewide election ballot. If a majority disapproves, the law is void. If a majority approves, the law not only is upheld but attains a most unusual status; it cannot be changed without direct vote of the people.

Nevada is among the minority of states that employ both initiative and referendum as devices of "direct" democracy. Thirty-eight states have some form of referendum; twenty-one have the initiative for originating ordinary laws, and seventeen permit originating an amendment by initiative petition. Neither of these procedures is available for use with respect to federal legislation.

Nevada is one of twelve states that provide for recall, a process added to the constitution in 1912. All elected state and local officials are subject to removal during their terms through the recall procedure. (Members of Nevada's congressional delegation can be removed only by action of their colleagues in the respective houses.)

In Nevada, a recall petition must be signed by not less than 25 percent of the number of registered voters who voted at the preceding general election in the unit of government that elected the official whose recall is sought. Thus, if a mayor were the unhappy official involved, 25 percent of the registered voters in his city who voted at the last election would have to sign the petition; were a governor involved, 25 percent of the registered voters of the entire state who voted at the preceding general election would have to sign the recall petition. Twelve states, including Nevada, provide for recall of officials, but this device for getting rid of unsatisfactory officers has rarely been used at the statewide level; only one governor, Frazier of North Dakota, has been removed at a recall election.

In Nevada, notice of intention to file a recall must be given to the official against whom the recall is directed. The notice is good for sixty days and the petition must be filed within that period. This law, enacted in 1975, prevents a surprise filing and a drawn-out proceeding. The recall petition must state, in two hundred words or less, the reasons for wanting to remove the official. Unless he resigns within five days after the petition is filed, a special election must be held within twenty days of the filing of the petition; on the ballot must be set forth the charges against the official and his reply to them (also limited to two hundred words). The recall ballot may list, in addition, the names of other candidates for the office held by the person whose recall is being attempted; whoever receives the most votes, whether the officer who is the object of the recall or any other candidate, serves the remainder of the term for which the official was originally elected. To prevent political harassment of a newly elected officer, no recall may be started until he has served for six months, except for legislators, against whom a petition may be filed after ten days of a legislative session. A second recall petition may not be filed against an official who survived a recall election unless the petitioners pay all the expenses of the first election.

In 1970 the voters approved a constitutional amendment that made the recall procedure more difficult by requiring the signatures of 25 percent of those voting in the preceding general election to start a recall. Before this change, the requirement had been that 25 percent of the voters who voted for a supreme court justice in the jurisdiction concerned (state, county, district, or municipality) must sign the recall petition. Because jurists run as nonpartisans and are usually unopposed, fewer voters cast a ballot in this category than for president, governor, or other national or statewide offices. The amendment, in effect, requires more names on recall petitions, thus making them harder to complete.

Declaration of Rights and the Fourteenth Amendment

Nevada's "Declaration of Rights" (Art. I) substantially repeats the first ten amendments of the United States Constitution; even the terminology is similar, in places identical. Among the familiar federal protections that Nevada extends to residents of the state are guarantees that trial by jury, the writ of *habeas corpus,* and freedom of assembly will be preserved, and that excessive bail and cruel or unusual punishment will be prohibited. One reason why Nevada, and other states too, repeat these guarantees of fundamental liberties is that the Bill of Rights in the national Constitution was drafted out of fear of encroachments by the federal government; it is to that government that the Bill of Rights addresses itself, or so, at least, was the pre-Civil War exegesis. Thus, for example, the First Amendment forbids *Congress* to pass laws respecting the establishment of a religion. State governments, in repeating this promise in their own constitutions, were making their own guarantees to their own residents in order to insure that this freedom and all other protected rights would not be diminshed or destoryed by *state* action.

If the foregoing were an adequate summary, we could assume that a citizen is protected by the federal Constitution from invasion of his rights by the federal government and protected by his state constitution from invasion of his rights by his state government. What, then, of national rights that are not protected from state invasion in a particular state's constitution? What about free speech if a state constitution doesn't include it? Has an indigent defendant charged with a crime a *right* to be provided with counsel in a state trial if his state constitution does not require it? Can a person's property be entered and possible contraband seized and used as evidence against him if the state in which the action takes place does not prohibit such a performance? To what extent can the national government demand that certain protections be given to suspected violators of *state* laws?

These questions have been partially answered by the United States Supreme Court in many decisions in cases that raised the issue of a federally protected right allegedly being abridged by state action. Some of the federal rights have, by Court decision, become protected from state infringement even when the state concerned had not included such protection in its own constitution. But prior to the adoption of the Fourteenth

Amendment to the United States Constitution in 1868, the Bill of Rights was considered applicable to the national government only.[6]

Since the passage of the Fourteenth Amendment, and because of the broadening scope of its applicability as described by the Supreme Court, the need for explicit guarantees of some of the basic rights in state constitutions may have changed to a certain degree; but the Illinois Constitution, effective as recently as July 1971, contains a Declaration of Rights very similar to Nevada's, thus suggesting that states may continue to set down citizens' rights as defined and protected by the state.

The Fourteenth Amendment requires that every *state* must extend to every person within its jurisdiction the equal protection of the laws, and it forbids a *state* to deprive any person of life, liberty, or property without due process of law. The impetus for the amendment was to insure that the newly freed slaves would not be victims of discriminatory state laws. But its meaning has been widened by the Supreme Court to encompass far more than racial discrimination; the Fourteenth Amendment and the commerce clause share the distinction of being the most litigated parts of the national Constitution. The courts have not yet settled the question of whether the Fourteenth Amendment "incorporates" the protections of the Bill of Rights in their entirety and so makes all of them inviolate from state interference, regardless of the presence or absence of the guarantees of such federally protected rights in any individual state constitution.

Suppose a state constitution has no clause protecting free speech. In such a circumstance, the absence of a specific clause protecting free speech would not subject a person to punishment by his state for exercising the right. The Supreme Court has determined that the protection of free speech and free press in the First Amendment is applicable to state as well as federal action because of the Fourteenth Amendment, which forbids any state to deprive any person of "liberty."[7] Since the protections of the *First* Amendment have been "incorporated" by the Fourteenth to make them applicable against the states, what about the protections of the rest of the federal Bill of Rights? Should all residents in all states have the complete protection of the Bill of Rights? Just parts of it? Only those rights a state chooses to protect? Is there room for variation in practices among the states?

For example, the Fourth Amendment forbids unreasonable search and seizure. The Supreme Court, in 1914, adopted a rule that illegally seized material—that is, material obtained without a valid search warrant—could not be admitted as evidence in a *federal* court.[8] The Court reasoned that the constitutional protection against unreasonable search and seizure was of no value if improperly seized evidence could be used in court to convict the accused. The Supreme Court left the matter of admission of such evidence in state courts to be determined by each state, because the administration of criminal justice is primarily a state, not a federal, function. But many cases reached the Court from many states in which improperly secured evidence was used to convict, and the Supreme Court began to show increasing uneasiness about the fairness of such convictions. Finally, in 1961, the Court ruled that illegally seized evidence could not be used against a defendant in a *state* court,[9] just as it had decided nearly fifty years earlier that federal courts could not admit such evidence.

How far will the Supreme Court extend its supervision of state criminal proceedings? A conviction based on improperly seized evidence can no longer be obtained in any state court. But what about a conviction based on a *confession* in a case where illegally seized evidence was admitted in the trial, but the *state* court rules that the evidence was not essential to the conviction, did not prejudice the case against the defendant, and was not the basis of the finding of guilt? Must states provide an attorney during interrogation of a suspect? Or must states assure the accused, during custodial interrogation, that the protections of the Bill of Rights are available to him?

The first instance, that of illegally seized evidence used in a trial but held by a state court as not essential to attaining a conviction, arose in a Connecticut case.[10] Connecticut has a law that if an error occurs in a trial but does not materially injure the accused, the conviction need not be reversed. Two men were found guilty of painting swastikas on a synagogue; the paint and the brush used for this defacement were seized by the police, who did not have a warrant to do so. The illegally seized material was admitted in evidence in the trial; but conviction was based on the defendants' confession. On appeal, the Connecticut supreme court held that though the paint and the brush were illegally obtained, their admission as evidence at the trial was "harmless error" which did not materially injure the accused; so the conviction was valid.

Without the Fourteenth Amendment, such a case as this and the two defendants' rights cases summarized below would presumably begin and end within a state; but because of that amendment, the Connecticut case was carried to the United States Supreme Court on the ground that a federally guaranteed right had been transgressed by the state. In a five-to-four decision, the closeness of which further shows that the application of the Bill of Rights against state action is still unsettled, the Court held that illegally seized evidence could not be admitted in a state court and that its admission in this case had actually damaged the accused.

The four dissenting justices, however, believed that the state must be allowed to determine its own standard of what constitutes "harmless error," and that in the absence of evidence of unfair practices or unproved charges in a state trial, the state's own rules of procedure should prevail. The dissenters did not believe that the Fourteenth Amendment could properly be construed in such a way as to prevent a state from applying its own conclusion that illegally seized evidence did not prejudice the outcome of the trial.

In July 1976 the Supreme Court moved toward the position of the dissenters in the Connecticut case. It ruled, six to three, that prisoners whose only challenge to their convictions was that illegally seized evidence had been used against them by the state could not appeal to a federal court unless they could prove that they were denied a fair trial. Thus, a state prisoner appears to have only one opportunity to argue against improperly obtained evidence, and that opportunity will occur at his trial in state court.

Escobedo and *Miranda*[11] are the two fundamental cases that define the demand upon the states to provide federal constitutional protection to suspects in state custody and the two that aroused the most consternation among many state law enforcement officers. Escobedo confessed to a murder after requesting and being denied an attorney during police interrogation; the Illinois court ruled that the confession was voluntary and the conviction valid. The United States Supreme Court overruled the decision and held that a person being interrogated must be informed of his right to remain silent, and that when the investigation has begun to shift to a particular suspect who is in custody, he must be permitted legal help. A central question arising from the *Escobedo* decision was whether it was police refusal to permit counsel after the suspect had specifically asked for his lawyer that caused the conviction to be overturned. That is: must the person being interrogated ask for his lawyer and be refused as the condition for casting out a confession subsequently obtained?

This question led to the *Miranda* case, in which a suspect, identified by witnesses, confessed to a kidnaping and rape. Again the United States Supreme Court overruled a state court decision finding the defendant guilty and held that protections of the Fifth and Sixth amendments were applicable in state courts. The Court demanded that a suspect be informed (1) that he has a right to be silent, (2) that statements made by him during interrogation may be used against him, and (3) that he has a right to have an attorney; the Court also stated that if the suspect waived any of these rights, the waiver must be voluntary and made with comprehension of the possible consequences. Thus, the question whether the suspect needed to ask for legal help was answered—he must be informed by the police of this right.

Both these cases, like the Connecticut case, have been somewhat narrowed by subsequent decisions. All three were determined by five-to-four votes, and public response to them showed the same close division. Public reaction was heightened by the circumstance that guilt or innocence was not involved; the matter was one of appropriateness of procedure. But for present purposes—contemplating stresses in the federal system—these cases exemplify an unresolved conflict of federal-state relations: a continuing disagreement over whether a disputed power belongs to the federal government or is reserved to the states.

Some people believe that by such broadening of the application of the Fourteenth Amendment as is illustrated in the foregoing cases, the Supreme Court is improperly extending national control into areas that should be subject only to state regulation, and that the Court is thereby diminishing state authority and blurring the lines of the federal division of powers. Others believe that the great guarantees of the Bill of Rights are so precious a part of our heritage that they should surround the individual and defend him from state as well as national invasion.

Instances of harsh practices in some states (but not Nevada, which has a good record for protecting suspects' rights) have frequently stirred the public conscience and have led some people to approve of federal action to stop these evils. They believe with Justice Douglas that, because of the Fourteenth Amendment, the federal government is legally obliged to prevent infringement by the state of any part of the Bill of Rights. This view of the scope of the Fourteenth Amendment has never commanded a majority of the Supreme Court, but Douglas said: ". . . happily, all constitutional questions are always open."[12]

Despite the opinion of Justice Douglas that all of the federal Bill of Rights should be protected against state interference, the United States Supreme Court has not applied the first right of the Fifth Amendment, that guarantees indictment by a grand jury in serious criminal cases, against the states. Thus, most of the individuals accused of serious state crimes in Nevada are brought to trial on the basis of information furnished by the district attorney at a preliminary hearing before a justice court. (In 1977, only 2½ percent of criminal cases in Washoe County went before the grand jury.)

Another serious constitutional problem with which the United States Supreme Court has wrestled in recent years is the question of whether or not the death penalty is "cruel and unusual punishment" and so forbidden by the Eighth Amendment. The Supreme Court ruled in *Witherspoon v. Illinois*[13] in 1968 that the death sentence could not be carried out if persons having doubts about capital punishment were excluded from the jury. Then in a 1972 case *(Furman v. Georgia),*[14] the Court stated that the death penalty constituted cruel and unusual punishment in cases where it was invoked in an arbitrary and capricious manner. The 1973 Nevada Legislature reponded to this latter decision by passing a law providing execution for every person convicted of capital murder, as defined in the statute. This automatic use of the death penalty was struck down, however, in Supreme Court decisions in 1976 and 1977.[15] In *Roberts v. Louisiana* (1977), the Court stated: "It is essential that the capital sentencing decision allow for consideration of whatever mitigating circumstances may be relevant to either the particular offender or the particular offense."[16]

In view of the foregoing decisions of the United States Supreme Court, the 1977 legislature passed a law providing for a separate penalty hearing in cases in which defendants have been found guilty of first-degree murder. At this penalty hearing, the jury or panel of judges may impose the death penalty only if it finds at least one *aggravating* circumstance which outweighs any mitigating circumstances. Nevada's first execution under this new law was carried out in 1979.

Another constitutional question that has turned out to be highly emotional in Nevada and many other states concerns abortion. The United States Supreme Court stirred up a fury with its decision in *Roe v. Wade*[17] that states could not prohibit an abortion in the first third of a pregnancy; could regulate in the second third if necessary to preserve maternal health; and could forbid abortion in the last third unless it was necessary to preserve the mother's life. The case was decided on the Fourteenth Amendment and a "right to privacy" protected by it. In *Roe,* the normal presumption in favor of the validity of legislative acts fell before the Court's interpretation that the Constitution prohibited state activity in the area under consideration. In 1973 Nevada modified its laws on abortion to conform with the *Roe* requirements (NRS 442.250). But the 1975 legislative session showed its dissatisfaction with the Supreme Court by passing a resolution requesting Congress to pass a "human life" amendment that would close out liberal abortion policies, recognize the sanctity of human life, and assert that the unborn have some fundamental rights protected by the Constitution.

Rights of Minorities

Unmet needs of minorities and the poor have led to serious disturbances in many states. President Johnson's Commission on Civil Disorders analyzed the causes of the outbreaks and recommended ways of eliminating or reducing the despair and hatred leading to murders, riots, and loss of confidence in political solutions.[18] Another presidential commission investigated violence and found ghetto slums disproportionately responsible for violent crimes. Indicating the government's failure to grapple with needs of minorities or the poor, the commission stated:

> To be a young, poor male; to be undereducated and without means of escape from an oppressive urban environment; to want what the society claims is available (but mostly to others); to see around oneself illegitimate and often violent methods being used to achieve

material gain; and to observe others using these means with impunity—all this is to be burdened with an enormous set of influences that pull many toward crime and delinquency. To be also a Negro, Puerto Rican, or Mexican-American and subject to discrimination and segregation adds considerably to the pull of these other criminogenic forces.[19]

Tensions leading to violent outbreaks in other states have existed in Nevada in recent years but have not become explosive, with the exception of some racial clashes at Las Vegas high schools. State civil rights legislation makes it unlawful to discriminate in public accommodation or employment on the basis of race, color, religion, or national origin. The state's first fair-housing law was passed in 1971 after much parliamentary maneuvering.[20] It prohibits discrimination by lending institutions as well as by public conveyors of real property. This measure, though tardily enacted, puts Nevada in compliance with the United States Supreme Court decision of 1968, *Jones v. Mayer,*[21] which prohibited both public and private discrimination in the sale or rental of real property.

Blacks, Indians, and welfare recipients have been the groups in Nevada least likely to receive helpful assistance from lawmakers. But the 1975 session of the legislature made significant increases in welfare payments. Efforts made by disadvantaged people to improve their position have not resulted in any notably hostile acts, although other states have suffered violence when people who found their lot insupportable believed that the political and economic system did not provide them with an orderly way to improve their situation. Political energies of minorities in Nevada have been directed to effecting changes within the existing system; the use of "confrontation politics" has been rare.

About 5.7 percent of Nevada's population is black. Woodrow Wilson (Clark County), elected in 1966, was the state's first black legislator. In the legislature Mr. Wilson concerned himself particularly with welfare measures and was active in securing passage of the state's first fair-housing law (1971). Assemblyman Wilson commented that legislative attention to welfare in the 1971 session was inadequate; he thought that the bills passed were "repressive, discriminatory, and vindictive" and that the "Legislature was irresponsible and did not respond adequately to the need."[22]

Tensions that arose in early 1971 caused some legislators to be hostile toward welfare recipients, many of whom are black. The state stopped benefits for over 1,000 recipients who, it claimed, were ineligible because they had failed to disclose full information about their other income. A federal district judge ordered reinstatement of the welfare recipients because procedure had been faulty—no hearing to allow former recipients to refute charges of falsifying outside income. The National Welfare Rights Organization led extensive demonstrations against the Welfare

Division in Las Vegas. Suspicions that many on welfare do not deserve
public support exemplify a long-standing characteristic of "pioneer"
communities—a lack of interest in the dependent needy.

Indians compose just under 2 percent of the state's population. They
are late-comers to the organized protest movement and have concentrated
on securing federal payment for the lands taken from their ancestors and
on maintaining their rights, notably with respect to Pyramid Lake, north
of Reno. Washoe Indians received a settlement of $5.5 million from the
federal government in 1975 as compensation for land taken from the
Indians by settlers along the California-Nevada border. Northern Paiutes
were awarded $20 million for lands from which their ancestors had been
driven. The poverty and despair of many Indians is becoming a political
as well as an economic and social issue. Indian leaders are beginning to
organize to achieve recognition of their claims, a recognition denied them
as a weak and fragmented minority.

The Equal Rights Commission, established in 1961, is designed to
investigate charges of discriminatory practices in employment and housing based on race, religion, sex, or national origin and to promote good
community relations. It is composed of five members appointed by the
governor and serving at his pleasure. Members are chosen to reflect religious, racial, and ethnic groups; they serve without pay. An executive
director, appointed by the governor upon recommendation of the commission, is responsible for directing the commission's activities. The
largest single cause of complaint concerns discrimination in employment.

One of the most controversial and hotly-debated issues considered by
the Nevada Legislature in the 1970s was the federal Equal Rights Amendment (ERA) which would prohibit discrimination based on sex. Although
strongly supported by Governor Mike O'Callaghan and Attorney General
Robert List, the ERA was voted down by the state senate in 1973 and
1975. After being passed in a disputed vote by the senate in 1977 (see
Chapter 5), the lower house defeated the amendment by a vote of 25-14.
The legislators then placed the measure on the 1978 general election ballot
for an advisory, non-binding referendum. The almost 2-1 defeat of the
ERA in the referendum for all intents and purposes marked its death knell
in Nevada.

Declaration of Rights and the Convention

Certain of the comments made during the constitutional convention are
of value in understanding Nevada's "Declaration of Rights." Section 4 of
Article I guarantees religious toleration and concludes with the statement
that the liberty of conscience secured by that section does not "excuse acts
of licentiousness." John A. Collins (Storey) considered that adding a religious toleration clause to Article I would be a tautology. He pointed out

5

that the enabling act required such a clause to be part of the ordinance of
the Nevada Constitution and that, in obedience to the enabling act, the
convention had already included in Section 2 of the ordinance the stipulation that "perfect toleration of religious sentiment shall be secured."
Charles E. DeLong (Storey), nevertheless, argued for inclusion of a clause
forbidding licentiousness. He explained that, despite its repetitious quality, Section 4 "shuts up the bars . . . against polygamy."[23] The delegates,
agreeing with him, voted to incorporate the clause.

Section 5 of Article I stipulates that the writ of *habeas corpus* shall not
be suspended unless rebellion or invasion makes such suspension necessary for public safety; this section of the Nevada Constitution is copied
verbatim from the United States Constituion. The writ of *habeas corpus*
is probably the most revered of the safeguards of the citizen against arbitrary action by government. It requires, upon a court order so directing,
that a person held in custody be brought before the court to ascertain
whether his detention is lawful.

Even President Lincoln, who suspended the writ during the Civil War,
was denounced for his action by critics who argued that only Congress
could authorize suspension of the writ of *habeas corpus*. This national
controversy was briefly revived during the Nevada convention. When
delegates were ready to vote on the *habeas corpus* section, Francis M.
Proctor (Nye) moved to add to the section the stipulation that when public necessity required the suspension of the writ, it could be abrogated
"only by the Legislature, who shall be the judges of that necessity."[24]
Several voices called out, "No! No!" and the amendment died for want
of a second. Proctor was the only Democrat at the Nevada convention;
every other delegate listed himself as a member of the Union party.[25]
From the convention's response to Proctor's suggested amendment, it
appears that the delegates did not want to embarrass President Lincoln by
specifying that the writ of *habeas corpus* could be suspended only by
legislative decision.

As originally drafted, the free speech and free press clause, Section 9 of
Article I, ended with the statement: ". . . the jury shall have the right to
determine the law and the fact." George A. Nourse (Washoe) objected to
these words. He said: "It strikes me as being the most absurd thing in the
world, that twelve men, drawn from the different walks of life, should be
empowered to determine nice questions of law. . . . By this absurd proposition, you take away the proper occupation of a Judge and leave him
merely to exercise the functions of a chairman of a town meeting."[26] The
convention agreed with him, and the words were deleted.

Another part of Section 9 is worth noting. If a person is charged with a
libel and the jury decides that the libelous statement "is true, and was
published with good motives, and for justifiable ends," the libeler will be

acquitted. It is not enough in Nevada to show that the information that damaged another is true; the accused libeler must also prove that he made the information public with proper motive.

The section describing treason (19) was a subject of intense disagreement among the delegates. The first constitution had not required the testimony of two witnesses to convict a person of treason. Because of the tensions of the Civil War, the delegates were conscious that, in response to public pressures, they might be expected to define treason loosely and punish it harshly; but the argument expressed by Charles E. DeLong (Story) prevailed. He said: ". . . persons are not apt to be charged with, or tried for treason, except in times of war, or of peril to the commonwealth; and in such a time, when the public mind is greatly excited . . . it is but a proper measure of precaution to require at least two witnesses to convict a man of this infamous crime."[27] DeLong's addition was adopted by the convention; so the Nevada description of treason is identical with that of the national Constitution. Treason consists in levying war against the state, or in adhering to or aiding the enemy. To convict a person of treason requires two witnesses to the same overt act, or the accused person's confession in open court.

Nevada's provision for the right of trial by jury (Art. I, Sec. 3) is another interesting reflection of the period in which the constitution was drafted. Historically, decisions of a jury had to be unanimous. But the delegates were painfully aware of the frequency of "hung" juries, particularly in the extensive litigations over mining rights. Several references were made in the convention to jurors being bribed and to the difficulty of getting a unanimous verdict. Many of the delegates, therefore, wanted to change the traditional requirement of unanimity and permit a verdict to stand in a civil suit if three-fourths of the jurors agreed.

J. H. Warwick (Lander) commented:

> . . . I certainly think that a three-fourths verdict would be more apt to secure justice to all parties than a unanimous verdict would be likely to do. I suppose that there is no gentleman either exercising any judicial functions or engaged in practising [sic] law in Nevada, but is fully aware of the manifest injustice which time and again litigants are subjected to, and the sometimes immense expense to which they are put, on account of there being some improper persons on the jury. Perhaps, while the party thinks that he has carefully guarded every avenue of approach, he finds that still, by some means or other, some one man out of the twelve has been secured to the adverse interest, and he loses the verdict.[28]

Samuel A. Chapin (Storey) felt the same way:

> We are . . . mostly immigrants here. We are from all parts of the world, unknown to each other. We have our juries sitting upon cases where millions of dollars are at stake, and we are obliged to take men for such juries who are unknown to us, whose integrity has never had

a test; and we know that it has been proved, time and again, that some of those men can be approached—that they can be bribed to stand out—and verdicts have, in that manner, been prevented in cases where the greatest injustice has thereby been done.[29]

Some members of the convention pessimistically feared that the three-fourths rule would not stop bribery of jurors by wealthy litigants, who could be expected merely to bribe four jurors instead of just one. Even so, the three-fourths rule in civil cases was finally adopted. Unanimous verdicts are required in criminal cases, however.

The delegates were unsure of the permanent validity of the three-fourths rule; so they stipulated that the legislature, by a two-thirds vote of the elected members of both houses, could pass a law requiring a unanimous verdict of the jury in civil cases.[30]

Structure of the Constitution

Nineteen articles comprise the Nevada Constitution. Article XVII, "Schedule," is mainly of historic interest; it was included to insure that Nevada's transition from territory to state would be orderly. Two articles, II and XVIII, are both titled "Right of Suffrage." For clarity and ease in locating information, Article XVIII should be put with Article II. Certain other parts of the constitution are also out of order. Section 13 of Article I requires that "Representation shall be apportioned according to population." The proper location for the material in this section would be Article IV, Section 5, which describes the composition of the legislature. Also included in the latter section should be Article XV, Section 6; this section establishes that the legislature may not exceed seventy-five members. This reordering would consolidate the details on the legislative body. Article II, Section 9, provides for recall of public officials and would more logically be located in Article VII so that all the rules on how to be rid of unworthy public servants would be in one place. Some other parts of the constitution would benefit by such reorganization. These proposals for change are not substantive; but if they were made, it would make understanding the constitution easier by putting all the material on a subject in one place.

Comparison With the United States Constitution

State constitutions are longer and are amended more frequently than the United States Constitution. The latter is about 7,200 words long, has existed since 1789, and has been amended only twenty-six times. It is, thus, only half as long as the Nevada Constitution, has been in effect seventy-five years longer, and yet has needed modification less than half as many times as the state's constitution. If the Georgia Constitution is the subject for such comparison, the contrast with the federal Constitution is glaring. But in varying degrees all the states show such a contrast. Why?

The answer is that United States federalism tends to make state constitutions obsolete, so that they must be frequently amended; federalism is also responsible for their greater length. Our system divides the power of government between the nation and the fifty states; the powers that may be exercised by the national government are granted to it in the Constitution or are powers that are logically corollary to or implied by the Constitution. The remaining powers of government belong to the states. It is easy to see the problems for drafters of state constitutions; they are tempted to put down in the constitution all the powers the state can exercise; they are tempted to write in detail and in specifics instead of in generalizations. Details of government become obsolete as the economy is altered, as new inventions are developed, as populations shift. These and other changes affect society and, therefore, the government process. Thus, state constitutions become out of date and have to be changed because they contain too much transitory material.

Another contributor to the length and detail of state constitutions is the activity of interest groups who wish to have laws for their own benefit become part of the constitutions, making them less vulnerable to change than ordinary statute law, i.e., law passed by the legislature. Farm groups, taxpayers' associations, labor organizations, and many others have sought, often successfully, to include in state constitutions stipulations benefiting them; Nevada's "free port" law is a good example of such special-interest provisions. (Art. X, Sec. 1). This amendment was added to the constitution in 1960. By ordinary act of the legislature, Nevada had previously exempted from taxation personal property moving in interstate commerce through the state or in storage in Nevada with a final destination outside the state. The law had fostered a thriving warehouse business. Fearful that questions could be raised about the constitutionality of exempting such property from being taxed, supporters of the exemptions succeeded in having the provision made part of the constitution, where it is more immune from attack and can only be revoked or modified by the amendment procedure.

Finally, most state constitutions reflect a distrust of the legislature, a distrust manifested in provisions that confine, often stringently, the scope of legislative action. The desire to confine the legislature may be observed in the detail with which many state constitutions describe state and local government and in the restrictions upon the legislature's power to tax and to contract public debts.

Thus, federalsim as a system of government, the pressures of interest groups, and distrust of legislatures combine to make state constitutions lengthy, detailed, obsolete, and frequently in need of change.

CHAPTER 4

POLITICAL PARTIES AND ELECTIONS

WITH FEW EXCEPTIONS, Nevada has been a two-party state throughout its history. Exceptions to political control by the two major parties occurred in the 1890s when the Silver party was dominant, in the 1912 presidential election when the Progressive (Theodore Roosevelt) and Socialist electors outpolled the Republicans, and in the 1924 presidential election when the Progressive (Robert LaFollette) electors ran a close second to the Republicans.

The Four Political Periods

On the basis of the number of elections for statewide partisan offices[1] won by the Republican, Democratic, Silver, and Silver-Democratic parties, the political history of Nevada can be divided into four periods (see Table 4.1). The first period from 1864 through the 1890 election was dominated by the Republican party, which won 78 percent of the elected positions. Nevadans showed preference for the Democratic presidential electors only once (1880) during this period and generally aligned themselves with the party of Lincoln, which had put together a strong coalition of interests in the postwar period.

TABLE 4.1

PARTY VICTORIES IN STATEWIDE PARTISAN ELECTIONS

Office	1864–1890			1892–1906				1908–1930		1932–1978	
	Rep.	Dem.	Silver	Rep.	Dem.	Silver	S–D	Rep.	Dem.	Rep.	Dem.
Pres.	6	1	0	1	0	1	2	3	3	5	7
U.S. Sen.	8	1	2	1	1	5	0	3	7	3	15
U.S. Rep.	11	4	0	0	0	2	6	9	3	4	20
Governor	5	3	0	0	0	2	2	3	3	4	8
Lt. Gov.	5	3	0	0	0	2	2	2	4	4	8
Sec. State	8	0	0	2	0	2	0	0	6	0	12
Treas.	6	2	0	0	0	1	3	3	4	0	12
Contr.	8	0	0	1	0	1	2	3	3	6	6
Att. Gen.	6	2	0	0	0	2	2	0	6	2	10
Total	63	16	2	5	1	18	19	26	39	28	98

SOURCE: *Political History of Nevada,* issued by Secretary of State William D. Swackhamer. Carson City: State Printing Office, 7th ed., 1979.

During the second period covering the elections from 1892 through 1906, the issue of the free coinage of silver dominated Nevada politics because of the overriding importance of mining in the state. The Silver party drew support from both Republicans and Democrats in the first two elections of the period when it won all but two of the statewide positions. The Silver party and the Democrats in Nevada combined in 1896; that coalition then dominated the last five elections of the period, with popular President Theodore Roosevelt being the only Republican presidential candidate who carried the state (1904). In 1896 the national Democratic party had, in effect, offered the members of the Silver party in Nevada an appeal which they found impossible to refuse: a plank in the platform calling for the free coinage of silver and the selection as presidential candidate of William Jennings Bryan, who strongly supported the plank and was famous for his "cross of gold" oration. Nevada voted differently from the rest of the nation in seven presidential elections prior to the 1980 election and four occurred during this period: first in 1892 when for the only time the state supported a minor party candidate (General James B. Weaver, the national Populist party candidate, to whom the Silver party electors were pledged) and three times (1896, 1900, and 1908) when the state supported the losing campaigns of William Jennings Bryan.

In the third period, from 1908 through the 1930 election, the elected positions were fairly evenly divided between the two major parties. Although the Democrats won 60 percent of the statewide elections during this period, the Republicans won 53 percent of the high-visibility presidential, congressional, and gubernatorial elections.

The fourth period, 1932 through the 1978 election, revealed Democratic dominance in statewide elective positions by about the same margin (76 percent) that the Republicans had achieved during the first period. The Democrats became the majority party in the nation during the 1930s, and Nevada supported Franklin Roosevelt and Harry Truman in the first five presidential elections of the period. However, the Republicans carried five of the next seven presidential elections in Nevada in the face of a strong Democratic registration margin. The Democrats were victorious in five times as many congressional (Senate and House) elections as were the Republicans during the fourth period, perhaps at least partially because of the tendency of Nevadans to re-elect their representatives in Washington for many terms.

Voting Requirements

All states now require United States citizenship as a qualification for voting. The original Nevada Constitution limited voting to white males; the limitation regarding color was overruled by the Fifteenth Amendment to the United States Constitution, which declared that a state could not deny the suffrage "on account of race or color," although the word "white" was not actually removed from the Nevada Constitution until the election of 1880. The restriction of the franchise to males was voted out in Nevada in 1914, and women voted for the first time in 1916, four years before the Nineteenth Amendment to the United States Constitution required that sex discrimination be abolished.

In 1971 the Twenty-sixth Amendment to the national Constitution, making eighteen-year-olds eligible to vote in all elections, was ratified by the necessary three-fourths of the states. Before this amendment was ratified, forty-six states, including Nevada, set twenty-one as the minimum age for voting; Georgia and Kentucky had previously allowed voting at age eighteen; Alaska, at nineteen; and Hawaii, at twenty. The history of the effort to make eighteen the minimum age throughout the country shows that Congress, state legislatures, and public officials supported the reduction of the voting age and that the public, or part of it, did not. In seven states, voters rejected proposals to give the vote to eighteen-year-olds. The Nevada legislature did not ratify the proposed Twenty-sixth Amendment but arranged for a public referendum on the matter at the municipal elections in June 1971. The measure passed by a mere 1,565 votes and was decisively supported only in Clark County; it lost in Washoe. Fewer than half (49.3 percent) of the registered voters of Nevada went to the polls to cast a ballot on this basic question of who should be eligible to participate in government. With the adoption of the Twenty-sixth Amendment, the states that voted against lowering the voting age were required, of course, to comply with the new law. State legislatures, which are the agencies for ratifying amendments to the national Constitution, did, in large part, ratify the amendment even when the voters in their state had voted against it. Some observers suggest that public office holders were already conscious of a new constituency.

States have always been concerned to restrict the right to vote to bona fide residents. Until the United States Supreme Court, in *Dunn v. Blumstein,*[2] threw out "durational" residency as a condition for voting, all states required that a person live in the state for a relatively long period of time before he could become a voter. Thirty-three states had had a one-year residency requirement; Nevada and fourteen other states had permitted voting after six months' residence; and New York and Pennsylvania permitted it after three months.

In striking down existing residency requirements, the Court said that each state had a legitimate interest in limiting the ballot to people who actually lived in the state. Bona fide residence could be established by requiring voters to register. Since checking voter registration and preparing lists of eligible voters takes time, the Supreme Court allowed states to close registration a reasonable period before an election to allow these procedures to be accomplished. By 1975 all states had changed their laws to comply with the *Dunn* decision. Eighteen states simply abolished all residency requirements. The rest set a minimum number of days to qualify for voting, ranging from Florida's sixty to Wisconsin's ten; Nevada and twenty other states established by act of the legislature a thirty-day minimum residency. Because the Nevada Constitution required a six-month residency, voters in this state were asked to approve an amendment in 1976 that would reduce the requirement to thirty days and thereby make the constitution fit the actual procedure. This they declined to do: 52 percent voted against the change. So the constitution continues to require a six-month residence for voting, but the fact is that a person may register to vote in this state after residing here for only thirty days. Thus, even though the amendment was voted down, Nevada could not continue to abide by its six-month provision, since the Supreme Court's *Dunn* decision is controlling.

Primary Elections

Prior to the 1910 election, candidates qualified for the general election ballot in Nevada either through nomination by a party convention or by a petition with a specified number of signatures. Wisconsin was the first state to adopt a direct primary system in 1903; such a law was enacted in Nevada in 1909. Although the national constitutional amendment mandating direct election of United States senators did not become effective until 1913, the Nevada direct primary law called for senate candidates to be nominated at the same primaries as candidates for other state offices.

Nevada's regular state primary election is held on the Tuesday following the second Monday in September of the even-numbered years. Nevada and the majority of states have a *closed* primary law, which means that only those who are registered members of a party which has qualified for the ballot may vote for partisan offices. Under the *open* primary system, used in eleven states, a person can wait until he or she goes to the voting booth before deciding in which party's primary to vote. In three of the open-primary states—Alaska, Louisiana, and Washington—a *blanket open* primary system allows the people to vote in two or more party primaries, as long as only one vote is cast for each office.

Supporters of the *open* primary argue that it is more democratic than a system which forces people to declare party preference when registering to vote and so works against their right to change their minds. (Party registration may be changed in between elections, but most voters don't bother to make such a change.) Those who support the *closed* primary argue that it promotes party responsibility and prevents "raiding" by members of the other party.

Prior to 1976, Nevada delegates to the national presidential nominating conventions of the two major parties were chosen at the respective state conventions, often without any reference to which candidates the individual delegates favored. The 1973 Nevada Legislature passed a law providing for a presidential primary. The statute stipulates that delegates to the Democratic and Republican conventions are to be divided among the various candidates according to the popular votes each received, with any candidate receiving at least five percent of the total vote cast in each primary sharing in the apportionment.

Registration and Voting Patterns

In Nevada, and in many other states, voters' party preferences as expressed by registration figures often are not correlated with voting habits. In the period recorded in Table 4.2, the number of voters registering as Democrats sank from 63 percent in 1966 to 57.6 percent in 1972. There was even a dip in the gross number of Democratic registrants between 1966 and 1968. This decrease was probably due to dissatisfaction with President Lyndon Johnson and to the effect of the Wallace candidacy in 1968; in that year miscellaneous registrations rose 36 percent.

TABLE 4.2

REGISTRATION AND VOTING, 1966–78

Year	Demo-crats	Repub-licans	Misc.	Total Registered	Total Votes Cast	Percent of Reg. Voters Voting	Percent of Voters Reg. as Demos.
1966	116,643	58,281	8,939	183,863	139,355	76.1	63.4
1968	111,390	65,302	12,119	188,811	156,217	82.7	58.9
1970	112,248	67,713	12,972	192,933	150,078	77.8	58.2
1972	133,278	80,199	17,568	231,045	185,400	80.2	57.6
1974	139,192	79,229	17,990	236,948	172.355	72.7	58.7
1976	149,397	83,474	18,181*	250,953	206,423	82.2	59.5
1978	158,576	90,371	18,751*	267,698	192,445	71.9	59.2

*Includes Independent American and Libertarian parties.
SOURCES: *Official Returns of the General Election* (Carson City: Secretary of State, 1976, 1974, 1972, 1970, 1968, 1966); compilation and percentages by Bushnell; 1978 data supplied by William D. Swackhamer, secretary of state.

Republicans rose steadily both in number of registrants and in percentage of total registrations from 1966 through 1972. In 1974 and in 1976, probably as a consequence of "Watergate," Republicans lost ground to the Democrats. Democrats remained the majority party throughout the period. An example of Clark County and of Democratic party dominance is illustrated by a statistic of 1976: there were more registered Democrats in Clark County alone (84,145) than there were registered Republicans (83,474) in the entire state of Nevada.

Even though the Democratic party has maintained registration superiority over the Republicans, some important statewide elections have been won by Republican candidates in recent years. Paul Laxalt won the governorship in 1966 and was elected to the United States Senate in 1974; David

Towell won a surprise victory in the congressional election of 1972; Robert List was elected attorney general in 1970 and 1974, prior to winning the governorship in 1978; and the Republican candidate for president was victorious in 1968, 1972, and 1976.

How can these Republican victories in the face of the heavy Democratic registration edge be explained? Many Nevadans do take pride in voting independently of party. Undoubtedly, the personal appeal of a particular candidate such as Paul Laxalt can help to overcome the minority registration status of the Republicans. Perhaps a more important factor is that a substantial percentage of the registered Democrats in the state is conservative. In each of the elections cited above, the Republican candidate was viewed as clearly more conservative than the Democratic opponent.

The fact that many Nevadans cast their votes on the basis of their attitudes toward "liberal" and "conservative" as distinct from "party" considerations is not peculiar to the state. American parties, unlike, for example, their British counterparts, are not clearly distinguishable as liberal or conservative either at the national or at most state levels. Instead, both major parties have liberal and conservative wings which vie with each other for command within the party. That a conservative Republican and a conservative Democrat hold more opinions in common than either shares with his own party's liberal wing is a truism of current politics; the converse is equally true.

Although Nevada's population is clustered in the Reno and Las Vegas areas, the voting pattern in only one of the two large counties supports the political aphorism that urbanization usually increases the strength of the Democratic party, while the Republican party is usually strongest in rural sections. Las Vegas and Clark County exemplify this aphorism; Reno and Washoe County do not.[3]

Clark County is a good example of the hypothesis that urbanization strengthens the Democratic party; in 1978 Democrats had 70 percent of the registrations for the two major parties. Furthermore, Clark County Democrats normally vote for their party's candidate; the ultimate in political dominance occurred in 1976, when the Democrats swept all the state legislative contests and thus held all the county's thirty-three seats in the 1977 legislature.

Reno and Washoe County, unlike the Las Vegas area, do not support the hypothesis that urbanization tends to favor the Democrats. Although the Democratic party always had a registration superiority during the 1966–78 period, it was more modest than in Clark County, averaging about 55 percent of the two-party registration. For major statewide offices during the period, Washoe voters chose the Republican candidate in three of four elections for governor, in three of four elections for the United States Senate, and in all three elections for president.

Two other aspects of voting behavior should be noted. Proportionately fewer Clark than Washoe residents register and proportionately fewer actually go to the polls. Thus, the most populous county's percentage of state voting isn't as high as its percentage of the state's population.

Despite the superiority of the Democratic party in registration and election victories in recent years, Nevada does not give evidence of becoming a one-party state. The Republicans have done well in many races, and most statewide elections have been competitive.

Campaign Finance

The Federal Election Campaign Act of 1974 applies to presidential and United States Senate and House elections in Nevada. No person may contribute more than $1,000 a year to any candidate for federal office, and every contribution over $100 must be disclosed.

The Nevada Legislature followed the lead of Congress and enacted a campaign disclosure and spending limitation law during the 1975 session. However, the United States Supreme Court declared the spending limitations in congressional elections unconstitutional in *Buckley v. Valeo* in 1976. On the basis of the *Buckley* decision, the Nevada Supreme Court declared the campaign spending limitation in the 1975 Nevada law unconstitutional.[5] The federal and Nevada supreme courts' opinions held that such limitations interfered with the freedom of speech guarantees of the First Amendment. The United States Supreme Court indicated that such limitations were permissible if combined with public funding of the campaigns, as in the case of the presidential elections, for the candidate would then have the option of refusing public funding and avoiding the limitations. Since this decision, a few states have provided for partial public funding of state election campaigns in order to be able to limit expenditures.

The 1977 Nevada Legislature amended the 1975 campaign finance law so that the disclosure of campaign contributions and expenditures sections were salvaged. However, by early 1980 conflicting opinions had been issued by the Legislative Commission, acting upon the advice of legislative counsel Frank Daykin, and by Attorney General Richard Bryan as to which contributions had to be reported. The commission ruled that only contributions received after the candidate filed for office had to be reported, whereas Bryan's opinion stated that the law provides that all contributions are to be reported regardless of when received.[6] Both the commission and the attorney general agreed that under the law only expenditures made after June 10 had to be reported; however, Bryan called upon the 1981 legislature to amend the law to require the reporting of expenditures made earlier in the year.[7]

The costs of campaigning have increased greatly in recent years because of heavy reliance on expensive television advertising by the candidates for major statewide offices and even state senate races in the large multi-member districts in Las Vegas and Reno. In the gubernatorial election in 1978, each of the major party candidates spent about a million dollars. With single-member districts in the assembly, it is still possible for candidates to use shoe leather rather than heavy spending to get their messages across and win.

"None of These Candidates"

The "none of these candidates" ballot option was introduced and guided through the legislature in 1975 by Assemblyman Don Mello of Washoe County. The option is available to the voters in both primary and general elections for offices which are elected statewide. The ballot listing received national attention in the September 1976 primary when two "live" candidates for the Republican nomination for Nevada's lone seat in the lower house of Congress were soundly defeated by "none of these candidates." In such cases, the leading live candidate goes on the final ballot albeit at a severe disadvantage because of the disapproval evidenced by the party faithful.

In Nevada's second presidential primary, held May 27, 1980, 33.5 percent of the Democratic voters displayed their dissatisfaction with both President Carter and Edward Kennedy by casting their ballots for "none of these candidates." Although Carter led with 37.5 percent of the votes cast, the combination of the 29 percent for Kennedy and the votes for the "none" category emphasized the president's weakness among Nevada Democrats.

The experience with the new ballot listing in the 1976 and 1978 elections does not bear out the claim of its supporters that giving the voters an opportunity to register a protest vote would increase voter turnout (see Table 4.2). However, the national attention which the option has received and the large number of Nevadans who have voted for "none of these candidates" augur well for its continuance and perhaps expansion to other elected offices at the local and district level.

Short Ballot

The short ballot was developed (1) to focus the voter's attention on the major offices of state government by eliminating from the ballot such offices as superintendent of public instruction, or state printer, or secretary of state; and (2) to make the governor's power commensurate with his duty to run the state by giving him the authority to appoint more of the members of his "official family." Alaska, Pennsylvania, and Hawaii elect only a governor and a lieutenant governor; New Jersey, New Hampshire, Maine, and Tennessee, only a governor. Michigan, in its recent constitution, reduced the number of elected officials from eight to four: the governor and the lieutenant governor, who are elected on the same ticket as an executive "team;" the attorney general; and the secretary of state. In states with a short ballot, other administrative posts are filled by executive appointment or, occasionally, by legislative selection. The trend in state governments is to have the governor and lieutenant governor run as a team and to reduce the number of elected administrative officials, thus making the governor more responsible and more accountable to the public for the outcomes of his term in office.

Because fears have been expressed that reducing the number of elective offices might lead to dictatorial or oligarchic procedures, it is instructive to review the practice of the federal government. At the national level only the president and the vice-president are elected; the president appoints the cabinet and is fully responsible for each man's conduct of his department. In the majority of states a governor has no control over his "cabinet," neither in their selection nor in their performance. He cannot dismiss an incompetent or even a corrupt member of "his" administration; that member was elected by the people and is *politically* the equal of the governor. The unfairness in denying the removal power to a governor lies in the fact that a taint may fall upon his administration, a taint that may attach to him although he is powerless to discharge the person causing it.

This difficulty may be illustrated by comparing the power of the president to the power of most governors in a hypothetical case. Suppose the United States secretary of the treasury were performing in some bizarre fashion and exhibiting a careless attitude toward public funds. The president could and would dismiss him forthwith or bear the full responsibility for his own appointee's conduct in office. If an elected state treasurer were misbehaving in such fashion, the governor would be essentially helpless. He may deplore, he may inform, but he may not dismiss, even though the misconduct of the official could unfairly bring the whole administration into disrepute.

Probably the most convincing argument for the short ballot is that most people simply cannot become informed on the qualifications for such diverse and numerous offices as secretary of state, treasurer, controller, attorney general, university regents, and supreme and district court judges. When choices must be made for all these offices and also for a mayor and other city officials, county commissioners, district attorneys, county assessors, a representative in Congress, usually one of the senators, and every four years a president, it is easy to see why voters become overwhelmed.

In a recent Nevada election the voter was confronted with forty-six different decisions on one ballot! It seems fair to suggest that no voter can be sufficiently informed to make forty-six intelligent choices. His inertia, when he is confronted with so many offices and candidates, may cause him to vote only for the major offices, to make random choices, to vote a straight party ticket, or, most distressing of all, to stay home.

One more matter concerning the length of the ballot deserves consideration. The voters give relatively little attention to constitutional amendments and other propositions on the ballot compared with the attention they give to the "top of the ticket." This phenomenon is sometimes called "fall off." During the period 1970–78 Nevada voters had to make decisions on thirty-three constitutional amendments. These proposed amendments varied in importance, in comprehensibility, and in the efforts interested persons had made to persuade the public to pass or defeat them. Twenty-three of the amendments were passed.

TABLE 4.3

VOTE ON CONSTITUTIONAL AMENDMENTS, 1970–1978

	1978 Election	1976 Election	1974 Election	1972 Election	1970 Election
	1) 88.5	1) 87.4*	1) 87.2	1) 81.9	1) 78.9
	2) 87.4	2) 85.2	2) 84.9*	2) 81.5	2) 75.3
	3) 88.9	3) 87.0*	3) 83.4	3) 82.2	3) 77.6
Percentage of ballots cast on amendments	4) 92.7	4) 86.1*		4) 80.0*	4) 77.8*
	5) 95.2*	5) 84.6		5) 78.4	5) 79.2*
	6) 92.6	6) 83.5		6) 76.0	6) 73.8
		7) 83.6		7) 79.0*	7) 74.6
		8) 84.8			
		9) 83.5			
		10) 81.0*			
Highest percentage of ballots cast	98.6 (Governor)	97.8 (U.S. Senator)	98.3 (U.S. Senator)	98.0 (President)	98.4 (U.S. Senator)

*Indicates defeated amendments. Question 5 in 1978 was not actually an amendment; it was a referendum "advisory" to the legislature on whether ERA should be ratified.

SOURCES: Compiled by Eleanore Bushnell from data in *Official Returns of the General Election* (Carson City: Secretary of State, 1976, 1974, 1972, 1970); 1978 data supplied by William D. Swackhamer, secretary of state.

An average of 83 percent of those voting in the five elections surveyed in Table 4.3 voted on the amendments; an average of 98.2 percent voted for the leading office on the ballot. Although in a presidential election year Nevada ordinarily casts the highest vote for candidates for the presidency, in 1976 the highest vote was recorded in the United States Senate contest. In only eight of the twenty-eight presidential elections in the state's history has someone other than a presidential candidate scored the top vote; the most recent instance, prior to the 1976 election, was in 1936.

An interesting aspect of the 1978 election was the relatively high vote on two constitutional amendments and the advisory referendum. The latter vote on ERA showed the highest percentage of ballots cast on any issue in the period covered; interest was also high on questions 4 and 6, which would remove the tax on inventories and reduce the property tax, respectively.

Some states, including Nevada, that have not adopted the short ballot hold elections for state offices in years different from the election years for the presidency; this arrangement at least permits voters to concentrate on the statewide candidates in the election of 1978, for example, and on the presidency in 1980. But it still requires close attention and prior study to make knowledgeable choices among the candidates and propositions on the state ballot. In the 1978 election, Nevada voters had the following offices to fill: United States congressman, governor, lieutenant governor, secretary of state, treasurer, controller, attorney general, justice of the supreme court, state board of education, university regents, state senators, state assemblymen, and district judges. Having selected these important officials, the voter then had to decide on five constitutional amendments and the advisory referendum.

The short ballot has been recommended for Nevada, and four recently adopted constitutions (Alaska, Hawaii, New Jersey, and Michigan) provide for it. For fixing responsibility squarely on the governor and for focusing the voter's attention on a few key offices, the short ballot is eminently desirable. It leaves determination of the fundamental goals of society just where it belongs—with the voter. It relieves him of making choices he is not qualified to make. And it establishes the governor's authority as more nearly equal to the responsibility with which he is entrusted.

Opponents of the short ballot fear that it takes away some of the citizen's power and control. They also point out that certain groups in each community do know about and do make an intelligent decision on such specialized offices as attorney general or controller; they argue that these groups should not be deprived of their choice. There is no trend in Nevada at this time toward adoption of the short ballot.

Influence of Nevada on National Politics

With only three electoral votes, Nevada has not been an important factor in presidential elections, even though it consistently supported the winning candidate from 1912 through 1972 before backing a loser in 1976. Also, the state's lone congressman hasn't normally attracted much attention in the 435-member House of Representatives. One notable exception to the usual anonymity was Francis G. Newlands, who served five terms in the lower house of Congress from 1893 to 1903. Newlands gained national prominence by sponsoring a bill that provided for federal construction of irrigation systems—a matter of great significance to the growth of Nevada. More recently, Congressman Jim Santini was elected as a member of the "Watergate class" of 1974 and played a key role in the

6

passage of the "in lieu of taxes" measure, under which the national government makes payments of millions of dollars to Nevada counties with substantial federal land. In his third term Santini became chairman of the Interior Subcommittee on Mines and Mining, a key position for Nevada's interests.

It is within the United States Senate, however, that Nevada has had its greatest impact. Republican William Stewart, one of Nevada's original senators, served a total of twenty-eight years and was considered one of the foremost experts on mining legislation in the upper house. Stewart's total years in the upper house of Congress have been exceeded by only one Nevadan—John Jones, a Republican, who was elected to five consecutive six-year terms by the Nevada Legislature in the last three decades of the nineteenth century. Jones, along with Stewart, was an important leader in the ill-fated movement to gain passage of a law providing for free coinage of silver.

In the twentieth century, Nevada's most powerful United States senators have been Democrats, who have amassed considerable seniority and thus attained important committee and subcommittee chairmanships. Key Pittman served for almost twenty-eight years before his death shortly after being re-elected in 1940. He was chairman of the Senate Foreign Relations Committee and president pro tempore of the upper house in the 1930s. Another powerful Nevada senator was Patrick McCarran, elected in the Roosevelt landslide of 1932, who served for twenty-two years. McCarran was chairman of the Judiciary Committee and its Subcommittee on Internal Security; his name is in the history books because it is attached to acts providing for registration of Communist organizations and the national-origins quota system for controlling immigration.

Alan Bible was elected to fill McCarran's seat when the latter died in 1954. Bible served twenty years and became known as "Mr. National Parks" because of his key subcommittee chairmanships on the Appropriations and Interior committees which had jurisdiction over national parks and recreational areas. Bible also served as chairman of the Senate Select Committee on Small Business during his latter years in Washington.

Howard Cannon was re-elected to a fourth term in 1976 and became the Nevadan with the fourth longest service in the upper house of Congress in the fall of 1980. Cannon attained national recognition during the "Watergate" epoch by reason of his chairmanship of a usually obscure committee, Senate Rules and Administration, which ordinarily handles mundane housekeeping and procedural chores. To this committee came three important "Watergate" assignments: (1) to prepare the rules under which Richard Nixon would be tried by the Senate if the House impeached him; (2) to hold hearings on the fitness of Gerald Ford to serve as vice-president in 1973; and (3) to hold hearings on the fitness of Nelson

Rockefeller for the same office in 1974. Mr. Ford's appointment by then-President Nixon to the vice-presidency following Spiro Agnew's forced resignation from the post placed upon Senator Cannon's committee the first hearing in United States history on an appointed vice-president. The hearings were televised. Senator Cannon and the committee were widely praised for the way they conducted themselves in the ground-breaking inquiries on Ford and later on Rockefeller. In January 1978, Cannon became chairman of the Commerce, Science, and Transportation Committee; he is also known around Washington as "Mr. Aviation" because of his chairmanship of the aviation subcommittee of the Armed Services Committee.

Another member of Nevada's congressional delegation who has received national attention is Senator Paul Laxalt. The former Republican governor became an outspoken leader of the conservative wing of his party, was the national chairman of Ronald Reagan's campaigns for the presidency in 1976 and 1980, and held memberships on two committees that are important to Nevada—the Committee on Appropriations and the Committee on Energy and Natural Resources. In 1974, Laxalt defeated Democrat Harry Reid for the United States Senate seat vacated by Alan Bible, a Democrat. Reid was expected to win because he was the incumbent lieutenant governor and lived in populous Clark County; in addition, it was a year for the Democrats, thanks to "Watergate." But Laxalt won an upset victory by 624 votes, the only new Republican senator to replace a Democrat. Because of the closeness of the vote, Reid demanded a recount, the result of which showed Laxalt to be the victor by 612 votes. In a courteous nonpartisan gesture, retiring Senator Alan Bible resigned his seat in December 1974 in order that newly elected Senator Laxalt could be appointed to the "vacancy" and so gain valuable seniority in the Senate.

Ten years earlier Paul Laxalt had been a central figure in the only other statewide recount in Nevada history, one that also concerned a United States Senate seat. In 1964 Howard Cannon, the incumbent senator, defeated Laxalt by forty-eight votes. The far-reaching consequences of this election illuminate the political process in Nevada.

Because of the narrowness of his loss, Laxalt demanded a recount. When, as a result of the recount, Cannon's margin was increased to eighty-four votes, Laxalt appealed to the Nevada Supreme Court for a ruling on certain paper ballots judged invalid and so not counted. The court dismissed the suit for want of jurisdiction, and Laxalt promptly conceded.

The Cannon-Laxalt contest, closest statewide election since 1914, when another incumbent Democrat, Senator Francis G. Newlands, won reelection by just forty votes, was unique. Because Laxalt's challenge occasioned the first statewide recount in Nevada history, the statutes describing recount procedures had never before been tested.[8] They proved to be silent on whether a canvass by the Nevada Supreme Court is necessary to validate a recount of election returns (a regular election is official only after a canvass by the court). No such canvass followed the Cannon-Laxalt recount, but the secretary of state issued a supplementary certificate of election showing Cannon to be the victor by eighty-four votes. The supreme court did not canvass the votes of the Laxalt-Reid recount in 1974. Thus, pending any legislative action, a precedent appears to have been established: a recount in Nevada is certified by the secretary of state without the necessity of validation by the supreme court.

A second significant result of the Cannon-Laxalt race of 1964 was that, because of unanswered questions over the invalidation of certain paper ballots, a bill was passed by the 1965 legislature establishing a uniform ballot. It requires that all ballots and ballot labels be in a form approved by the secretary of state and that they be uniform throughout the state.

Third, the appeal to the Nevada Supreme Court resulted in the unequivocal ruling that the jurisdiction of the United States Senate to judge a disputed senatorial election is supreme and exclusive.[9] The court also expressed its doubt that the statute endowing the court with original jurisdiction in a contested election was constitutional. Justice Gordon Thompson, speaking for the court, pointed out that the Nevada Constitution explicitly designates the subjects over which the court shall exercise original jurisdiction; a disputed election is not one of those subjects. The court suggested that the legislature direct its attention to resolving the question of constitutionality. The 1965 legislature followed this suggestion and moved hearings on contested elections down to the district courts; it also excluded contests over United States Senate or House elections from being heard in court, thus following the lead of the Nevada Supreme Court that such disputed elections must be settled by the legislative body concerned.

As mentioned above, a key factor in attaining positions of influence in the Congress is the much-maligned seniority system. Although both parties in Congress have secret-ballot elections in their respective caucuses to select committee chairmen, the members of the Democratic caucus in the Senate have consistently elected the members of their party with the longest continuous service on a committee as the chairman. The Democratic caucus in the House of Representatives did unseat three senior chairmen in 1975, but returned to the seniority system in electing the chairmen of all other committees in the three following congresses. The seniority system has helped Nevada gain more power than most other states in the United States Senate especially, because of the tendency of Nevadans to re-elect their senators to several terms.[10]

Various interest groups keep track of how congressmen vote on bills of concern to the group and rate congressmen on the basis of the number of

Nevada's congressional delegation in 1980: From left to right, Congressman James Santini, Senator Howard W. Cannon, and Senator Paul Laxalt. (Courtesy of Senator Cannon.)

favorable votes they give to group-supported measures. For the selected
roll call votes during 1978, Senator Howard W. Cannon pleased the liberal Americans for Democratic Action group 30 percent of the time and
the conservative Americans for Constitutional Action group on 43 percent of the votes. Senator Paul Laxalt received only a 5 percent rating
from ADA but was a favorite of the ACA with an 81 percent score. Congressman Jim Santini, who has a much more conservative voting record
than had been expected when he was first elected in 1974, also had a 5
percent rating from ADA in 1978 and fell in between Cannon and Laxalt
with a 65 percent rating from the conservative ACA.[11]

The generally conservative voting behavior of the Nevada congressional delegation is also verified by its support of the "conservative coalition," which *Congressional Quarterly* defines as a "voting alliance of
Republicans and southern Democrats against northern Democrats in
Congress."[12] During 1979, Senator Cannon voted with the coalition on 62
percent of the relevant roll calls, the second highest support record among
northern Democrats. Senator Laxalt's 80 percent support figure placed
him fourteenth among thirty-eight Republican senators, while Congressman Santini's 69 percent agreement with the conservative coalition
ranked him ninth among all the northern Democrats in the lower house.[13]

Traditionally, Nevada's representatives in Washington have been zeal-
ous in the support of mining and monetary policies which are important
to the state's economy. In the last fifty years, one of their primary concerns, of course, has been to defeat proposed laws which might interfere
with the well-being of the state's primary industry, gambling. Their generally conservative voting behavior probably mirrors the political conser-
vatism of most of Nevada's citizens; members of the Nevada
congressional delegation have been especially opposed to an enlarged federal role in intergovernmental activities.

CHAPTER 5

THE LEGISLATIVE BRANCH

ATTEMPTS TO ALLOCATE, and thereby limit, power have characterized the political process in the United States since colonial times. When the founding fathers met in Philadelphia, their desire to restrict the authority of government led, among other things, to efforts to distinguish the various powers of government and then place them in separate branches. A concomitant effort was directed to restraining each branch from exercising a power designated as belonging to another branch. If a given power clearly belongs in the category "executive," few would question its being assigned to the president or, at the state level, to the governor; few would contest the assignment of an agreed-upon "legislative" power to the Congress or to the state legislature. But serious difficulties spring from efforts to place government powers in categories that are truly logical. Political power is not always plainly "executive," or "legislative," or "judicial," and cannot, therefore, be assigned to the indisputably appropriate authority. Another difficulty stems from a confidence that an orderly government pattern will result merely because powers have been separated and allotted to specific branches—a confidence that is frequently illusory.

The drafters of the United States Constitution, fresh from obnoxious experiences under the British crown, were notably desirous of fostering political liberty by limiting the powers of government. One way to limit power is to trisect it so that one power may act to offset another. Probably the most immediate and important force in determining the founding fathers' adoption of separation of powers was the actual colonial experience with government. They were also influenced in their choice by Locke and more directly by Montesquieu, who, "through a glass, darkly," thought he observed a separation of powers in the British pattern of government and admired what he thought he saw. Whatever the priority of the forces leading to their decision, the drafters tried to describe executive, legislative, and judicial powers and place them in three separate departments of government.

The United States Constitution embodies, by obvious implication, the doctrine of separation of powers: "All legislative powers herein granted shall be vested in a Congress. . . ."; "The executive power shall be vested in a President. . . ."; "The judicial power . . . shall be vested in one Supreme Court." The Constitution does not expressly announce that the national government is dedicated to the theory of separation of powers, but the intention of the framers clearly emerges from the language they used.

State constitutions, sometimes implicitly and sometimes explicitly, follow the national pattern and separate the reserved powers of the state into legislative, executive, and judicial compartments, each theoretically having its assigned task: making the law, administering the law, and enforcing the law. The Nevada constitution separates power explicitly. Article III reads as follows:

> The powers of the Government of the State of Nevada shall be divided into three separate departments—the legislative, the executive, and the judicial; and no person charged with the exercise of powers properly belonging to one of these departments shall exercise any functions appertaining to either of the others, except in the cases herein expressly directed or permitted.

Thus, Nevada attempts a distinct separation, an attempt not restricted to the period in which the constitution was drafted. For example, the Legislative Counsel Bureau, an agency of the legislature, submits its budget directly to the legislature and not to the budget director, an official of the executive branch, through whom the budgets of other agencies are submitted and by whom such budgets are ordinarily trimmed down before they reach the legislature.

But it is no longer common to expect the three powers of government to be truly separate; the realities of political life have tended to blur such lines of separation as ever did exist. Rather than worrying about the blurring of "separation of powers," citizens should probably see that power is adequately checked. As Kenneth Culp Davis points out: "The principle whose soundness has been confirmed by both early and recent experience is the principle of check. We have gone far beyond Montesquieu. We have learned that danger of tyranny or injustice lurks in unchecked power, not in blended power."[1]

Structure of the Legislature

Of the fifty states, only one, Nebraska, has a unicameral legislature; the other forty-nine, like the national government, have two-house legislative bodies. Nebraska has another political distinction: its legislature is nonpartisan. However, the political preferences of candidates are commonly known, and behavior in the legislative body is often group, though not party, centered.

The legislative building in Carson City, first used by the 1971 session. (Courtesy of Nevada State Highway Department.)

In all fifty states the upper house of the legislature is called the senate. The lower house is called the house of representatives in forty-two states, the general assembly in one, the house of delegates in three, and the assembly in four. Nevada joins Wisconsin, New York, and California in using the title assembly; since the Nevada Constitution was based on that of California, and it in turn had been based on the New York Constitution, derivation of the title in Nevada has a clear history.

The Nevada Legislature meets every other year in the odd-numbered years; efforts to establish annual sessions will be discussed later. Legislative meetings convene in Carson City on the third Monday in January. Special sessions may be called by the governor, and in those sessions the legislature may consider only the business brought to it by him.

Nevada's senate, since the reapportionment of 1965, is composed of twenty members; the lower house, the assembly, has forty members. In the legislature immediately preceding court-ordered reapportionment, the senate had seventeen members, each county having only one seat; the assembly had thirty-seven members, each county being guaranteed at least one seat without respect to population. The United States Supreme Court reapportionment decisions virtually eliminated geography as a consideration in determining seats in a bicameral state legislature.

Wide differences exist among the states with respect to the size of the legislature; population is not the determining factor. New Hampshire, forty-first state in the nation with respect to population, has the largest legislative body, 424 members. Minnesota has the largest senate—sixty-seven seats—while Nevada and Alaska, with twenty senate seats, have the smallest. The size of the lower houses ranges from New Hampshire's 400 to Nevada and Alaska's forty. The unicameral legislature of Nebraska has forty-nine seats.

Another aspect of legislative bodies concerns how many people each legislator represents. In Nevada a senator speaks for about 24,400 people and an assemblyman for about 12,200. A California senator represents the most people—nearly 500,000, and a Wyoming senator the fewest—11,000.[2] Representation in the lower houses ranges from 250,000 people for each legislator in California to 1,400 for each legislator in Vermont. These figures suggest the degree of "ownership" a citizen may feel towards his spokesman and also how much access he might have to that spokesman if he expects proportional attention to his needs and opinions.

The size of the Nevada senate has ranged from a low of fifteen in the period between 1893 and 1903 to a high of twenty-five in the six years from 1875 to 1881. In the first session of the legislature, in 1864, the senate was composed of eighteen members, allotted on an approximately proportional basis; for example, Storey County, the most populous county in the new state, had four senators.[3]

Apportionment of Seats

The original constitution stipulated that the decennial national census should be the "basis of representation in both houses of the Legislature."[4] However, the legislature did not abide by this constitutional provision and in 1915 passed an apportionment measure patterned after the representation in Congress, providing for one senator from each county. An amendment incorporating this "little federal plan" into the constitution was not proposed by the legislature and approved by the voters until 1950; thus the legislature had explicitly defied the constitutional provision on apportionment for many decades. Prior to 1962 the United States Supreme Court had ruled that the apportionment of state legislatures was a "political question" to be decided by the political branches, i.e., the legislature and executive, and had refused to intervene in challenges to the basis of apportionment within a state.

The apportionment of the Nevada assembly followed the national pattern rather than the state constitutional mandate from the time of statehood in 1864, with each county being allocated at least one member of the lower house. Also, even though the population had increased dramatically in the Reno and Las Vegas areas during the 1940s, rural area legislators, who dominated both houses, refused to give Washoe and Clark counties their constitutionally-mandated proportion of assembly seats. The 1951 apportionment act gave the two urbanized counties only 19 of the 47 assembly seats, even though Washoe and Clark contained over 60 percent of the people in Nevada, according to the 1950 census.

TABLE 5.1

NEVADA LEGISLATURE BEFORE COURT-ORDERED REAPPORTIONMENT

County	Population (1960 Census)	Percent of State's Population	Senate	Assembly	Percent of Seats in Legislature
Clark	137,016	44.6	1	12	24.0
Elko	12,011	4.2	1	2	5.5
Washoe	84,743	29.8	1	9	18.5
Remaining fourteen counties	61,508	21.4	14	14	51.8
TOTAL: 17	285,278	100.0	17	37	99.8

SOURCE: Compiled by Bushnell from data contained in U.S. Department of Commerce, Bureau of the Census, Final Report PC (1)–A30 Nevada, p. 7, 1971.

By the time of the next reapportionment in 1961, apportionment cases from other states were pending in the courts. Additionally, there were rumors that the United States Supreme Court, under the leadership of Chief Justice Earl Warren, might change its longstanding position and intervene in such cases.[5] With federal intervention a possibility, the 1961 Nevada Legislature came very close to reapportioning the assembly on the basis of population *after* allocating one seat to each county. The number of seats in the assembly was reduced, however, from 47 to 37, so that the rural counties would have a larger percentage of the seats than they would have had if the size had remained the same. (The ten seats which were cut would otherwise have been awarded on a population basis to Clark and Washoe counties.) The legislators from the small-population counties felt safe in giving up their majority of the assembly seats because of the 15 to 2 margin they continued to hold in the senate (see Table 5.1).

In its 1962 *Baker v. Carr*[6] decision involving the apportionment of the Tennessee legislature, the United States Supreme Court decided that federal courts could review a charge of unfair apportionment and grant relief if they found that the malapportionment of legislatures had caused violations of constitutional rights. This ruling caused a nationwide convulsion; the impact of *Baker v. Carr* on the law and politics of the states was extraordinary. Within two years of the decision, reapportionment action had taken place in forty-two states. *Baker* was followed in 1964 by the bombshell decision, *Reynolds v. Sims.*[7] In *Reynolds,* the United States Supreme Court ruled that the "little federal plan" was unconstitutional— that senates cannot be patterned on the federal system and be composed of an equal number of senators from each county without regard to population. Chief Justice Warren, speaking for the court, held

> the federal analogy inapposite and irrelevant to state legislative districting schemes. Attempted reliance on the federal analogy appears often to be little more than an after-the-fact rationalization offered in defense of maladjusted state apportionment arrangements. The original constitutions of 36 of our States provided that representation in both houses of the state legislatures would be based completely, or predominantly, on population.[8]

Nevada was one of the states referred to as providing originally for population-based apportionment in both houses.

The full force of this ruling on Nevada and several other states can be recognized in the unequivocal statement of the court that "the Equal Protection Clause requires that the seats in both houses of bicameral state legislature must be apportioned on a population basis."[9]

Following *Baker v. Carr,* suit was filed in federal district court by two residents of Clark County challenging the apportionment formula of the assembly as well as of the senate. After the United States Supreme Court decision in the *Reynolds* case, the federal district court in Las Vegas issued an order convening a three-judge panel to meet in June 1965. Unless the Nevada legislature reapportioned itself in substantial conformity with the *Reynolds* decision by April 15, 1965, the three federal judges would undertake the task.

The 1965 session of the legislature, although duly warned of impending judicial intervention unless it acted, seemed paralyzed by the specter of reapportionment. Six measures relating to legislative approtionment were introduced, but only one was passed. It requested Congress to propose an amendment to the United States Constitution permitting one house of a state legislature to be apportioned on factors other than population if the voters of the state approved. This measure was, obviously, an attempt to avoid revising the state's representative pattern; its passage suggests that the 1965 legislature was satisfied with the existing equal membership in the senate from each county. Thus, the 1965 session failed to act and so brought the federal district court into the business of the legislature. In *Dungan v. Sawyer*,[10] the court ruled that Nevada's legislature was invalidly apportioned and must be changed in compliance with the *Reynolds* "one man, one vote" directive.

This change was accomplished at a special session of the legislature, October 25 to November 13, 1965. Truculent but despairing, the legislators adopted a plan based substantially upon population. However, the still rural-dominated houses did give the small-population counties one more senator and two more assemblymen than they deserved, at the expense of Clark County. The federal district court accepted without enthusiasm the apportionment adopted by the special session, stating that it was constitutional but was "not the fairest and best plan that the Nevada Legislature could possibly enact."[11]

Reapportionment of the Nevada and other state legislatures in the mid-sixties was examined with great interest by students of the political process for signs of changes in voting patterns and for evidence that urban groups, now enfranchised on a "one man, one vote" basis would conspicuously affect electoral outcomes and, among other things, bring gains to the Democratic party. The expected reapportionment-created changes did not materialize in most areas of the country, at least partially because Republican strength in suburban areas tended to counter the increased representation of the Democrats in the urban areas. Large multi-member districts in the Nevada Assembly seemed to favor the Republicans in the 1968 and 1970 elections as they captured almost all the seats in the Reno area, thus enabling the GOP to control the lower house.

In reapportioning the seats after the 1970 census, the legislature did not change the number of seats in each house and in contrast to 1965 gave fair representation to Clark County (see Table 5.2). As a consequence of the 1971 apportionment, Clark County, with about 56 percent of the state's population, achieved a 55 percent majority in both houses of the legislature—eleven of twenty senators and twenty-two of forty assemblymen. Never before in Nevada's history has one county had control of one house of the legislature, let alone both houses.

TABLE 5.2

COMPARISON BETWEEN THE 1966 AND 1971 APPORTIONMENTS

| | SENATE | | ASSEMBLY | | Percent of Population 1971 | Percent of Seats in Legislature |
	1966	1971	1966	1971		
Clark districts	8	11	16	22	55.9	55.0
Washoe districts	6	5	12	10	24.7	25.0
Rest of state	6	4	12	8	19.3	20.0

SOURCE: Compiled by Bushnell from data contained in U.S. Department of Commerce, Bureau of the Census, Final Report PC (1)–A30 Nevada, p. 7, 1971, and A.B. 825, 1971.

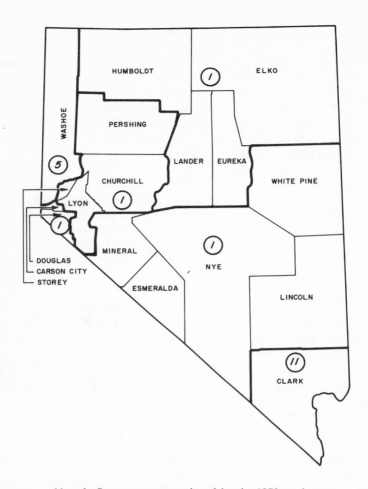

Nevada Senate as reapportioned by the 1973 session

Senatorial District	Number of Senators
Elko, Eureka, Humboldt, Lander, and Pershing counties	1
Esmeralda, Lincoln, Mineral, Nye, and White Pine counties	1
Churchill, Lyon, and Storey counties; Carson City enumeration districts 2 and 11	1
Douglas County and Carson City less enumeration districts 2 and 11	1
Clark County (11)	
District 1: Bunkerville, Goodsprings, Henderson, Logan, Mesquite, Moapa, Nelson, Overton, and Searchlight (townships)	1
District 2: North Las Vegas Township excluding enumeration districts 243A, 243C, 243E, 245, 259, 260, 261, and 263	2
District 3: Las Vegas Township excluding enumeration districts 15, 17, 18A, 19, 20, 21, 22, 23, 24, 25, 26, 27, 28, 29, 30, 31, 32, 33, and 34	7
District 4: The enumeration districts excluded from districts 2 and 3	1
Washoe County	
District 1: Bald Mountain, Gerlach, Reno, Sparks, and Verdi townships excluding city of Sparks	4
District 2: Wadsworth Township, city of Sparks, and enumeration districts 55A, 59, 60, 61, 62, 63, and 64 in Sparks Township	1
Total	20

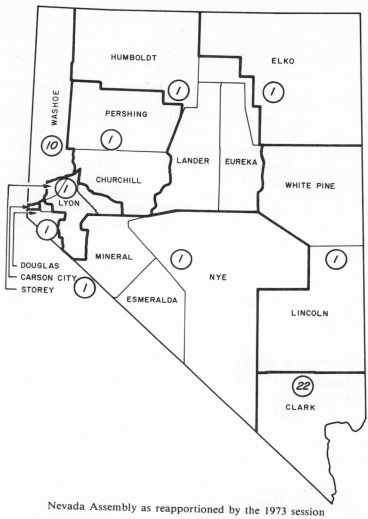

Nevada Assembly as reapportioned by the 1973 session

Assembly District	Number of Assemblymen
Elko County, less Carlin Township	1
Eureka, Humboldt, and Lander counties, plus Carlin Township of Elko County	1
Lincoln and White Pine counties	1
Esmeralda, Mineral, and Nye counties	1
Pershing and Churchill counties, less Churchill enumeration districts 12B, 13, 14, and 18	1
Lyon and Storey counties, plus Churchill enumeration districts 12B, 13, 14, and 18	1
Douglas County and Carson City enumeration districts 1, 2, and 3	1
Carson City, less enumeration districts 1, 2, and 3	1
Clark County	22
Washoe County	10
Total	40

Source: Both the senate and assembly maps are used by kind permission of Arthur J. Palmer, Director of the Legislative Counsel Bureau.

With the *Dungan* decision and the subsequent elections held in accordance with it, small-county dominance of the legislature came to an end.
The fears expressed by some people in the rural areas did not come to
pass, as the legislatures of the late sixties and seventies continued to treat
the small-population counties fairly.

The major change made by the 1971 legislature was the decision to
eliminate multi-member districts in the assembly. The arguments that
single-member districts would provide stronger voter identification and
interaction with the district representative and would considerably reduce
the costs of campaigning in the large urban areas carried the day in the
assembly but did not win the support of the majority of senators. The
counter arguments of some senators were that voters would have more
influence if they were constituents of more than one senator and that
"multiple-member districts . . . promote a community-wide approach and
form a desirable balance to the single-member assembly approach."[12]
Perhaps a more pragmatic consideration for the senate's retention of
multi-member districts was the fact that several of the incumbent senators
in Clark and Washoe counties lived in the same residential areas as some
of their colleagues.[13] Thus several senators would have lost their seats if
single-member districts had been instituted.

Characteristics of the Nevada Legislature

Qualifications for office of Nevada senators and assemblymen are identical. The constitution provides that the legislators "shall be duly qualified electors in the respective counties and districts which they
represent;"[14] whereas state law stipulates that a legislator must be 21
years of age at the time of election and have been a resident of the state
for one year preceding the election.[15]

The legislature sets its own salary and per diem (daily expense allowance), but the constitution requires that salaries be cut off after sixty days
of a regular session and twenty days of a special session.[16] The 1977 legislature passed a law stipulating that a legislator "elected on or after March
7, 1978," should receive a salary of eighty dollars a day. Given the constitutional prohibition against a salary increase taking effect during the
term of office of a legislator who participated in such a decision, senators
who were elected for four-year terms in 1976 received a salary of only
sixty dollars a day during the 1979 session while all other legislators were
paid the new rate of eighty dollars a day. In 1980, legislative salaries in
other states varied from a low of $200 for a single session in New Hamp-
shire to a high of $51,110 for two annual sessions in California. Because
the Nevada Legislature was consistently in session well over a hundred
days during the 1970s, the legislators placed an amendment on the ballot
in 1976 to extend the period during which they could draw pay from sixty

to one hundred days. The amendment was decisively defeated, with 70 percent of the voters opposing it.

The legislators draw per diem for the entire length of a regular or special session and also receive travel and telephone allowances. A new legislative building, first occupied in 1971, provides office space for each legislator and is a great improvement over the former situation in the state capitol building, where the legislator's only "office" was a desk on the floor of the chamber.

The terms of office of the two houses in the Nevada Legislature are similar to those of the majority of states, with four years for the senate and two years for the assembly. Many experts view the two-year term as too brief, especially when the legislature meets for only about four months during such a term. Four states provide four-year terms for both houses, and twelve states have two-year terms for both; the unicameral Nebraska legislature serves for four years.

In contrast to the normal procedure of filling vacancies in elective offices by gubernatorial appointment, the Nevada Constitution states that the relevant county commissioners "shall appoint a person of the same political party" as the party which elected the senator or assemblyman to fill a vacancy.[17] Such an appointment is valid only until the next election at which county officials are selected. With some assemblymen and senators now representing two or more counties, the number of county commissioners participating in such an interim appointment could be large. For example, if there were a vacancy in the central Nevada senatorial district, the county commissioners from Esmeralda, Lincoln, Mineral, Nye, and White Pine counties would meet together to fill the position.

In 1971 the Citizens Conference on State Legislatures published the results of a fourteen-month study on how well equipped legislatures are to do their work. The study rated Nevada thirteenth in the nation, praising the state for the new legislative building, for creating an Interim Finance Committee (discussed later in this chapter), and for requiring that bills show how much they will cost in tax dollars.[18] The state was found wanting because it did not regulate lobbyists or define and prohibit conflicts of interest; the action which has been taken in each of these areas is also discussed later in the chapter.

Regular and Special Sessions

Nevada is one of the minority of fourteen states which meets in regular session only every other year. Most students of the legislative process believe that annual sessions of state legislatures are preferable, with at least a budget session needed each year. One Nevada lawmaker has stated that making a budget for a biennial appropriation requires using crystal balls instead of solid, reasonably predictable financial estimates.

7

Nevada has had one experience with annual sessions. In 1958 a constitutional amendment providing for yearly sessions was approved by 59 percent of the voters. However, before the ink had dried on the new amendment, and before the annual session authorized by it had met in 1960, an initiative petition to revoke the just-authorized amendment was successfully circulated. At the 1960 general election the voters approved the return to biennial regular sessions by about 58 percent of the ballots cast on the issue. Another attempt by the legislature to gain voter approval of annual sessions was soundly defeated by the electorate in 1970, with the proposed amendment receiving the support of only one-third of the voters.

A special session is substantially different from a regular session: it is called by the governor and the legislature may transact only such business as is laid before it by the governor. Twenty-six states have arrangements allowing the legislature to call itself into special session and thirty-five states permit the legislature to decide the subjects on which action may be taken when in special session.

Nevada has had thirteen special sessions. The first was in 1867, when the occasion was the need for additional revenue; the thirteenth was in 1968, when the main issue was approval of a bistate compact with California concerning Lake Tahoe. Five of the thirteen special sessions were called between 1957 and 1968, with the main problem being additional money for the public schools in the face of rapid population growth in the state. The passage of the School Support Tax by the 1967 legislature and the creation of the Interim Finance Committee at the next session are mainly responsible for the fact that no special sessions were necessary in the 1970s.

The original constitution placed limits of sixty and twenty days on the lengths of regular and special sessions, respectively. However, by the middle of the present century the legislators often found themselves unable to complete their important business within the sixty-day period; thus, they adopted the practice of stopping the clock at 11:59 p.m. on the sixtieth day and continuing to operate for a few more days, with all succeeding action recorded as occurring on the sixtieth day. Concerned about possible challenges to the constitutionality of legislation passed during the extra days, the legislature proposed and the people approved in 1958 a constitutional amendment removing the time limits on the length of the sessions, but retaining the aforementioned limits for salary purposes.

Organization of the Legislature

The presiding officer of the Nevada senate is the lieutenant governor, who is, of course, chosen by the people. He need not be of the same party as the governor. The lieutenant governor, like the vice-president of the

United States, can vote only in case of a tie in the senate. But because the Nevada Constitution stipulates that a majority of *elected* members, namely eleven senators, is required to pass a bill, and because the lieutenant governor is not a member of the senate, it has become a custom for him to cast a vote to break a tie only on a motion, on a senate resolution, or on a concurrent resolution; not on passage of a bill. This custom was dramatically challenged by Lieutenant Governor Robert E. Rose during the 1977 legislative session.

Armed with an opinion by the legislative legal counsel that the lieutenant governor could break a tie on the final passage of a bill or joint resolution, Rose maneuvered to cast such a vote on the ratification of the Equal Rights Amendment. With the senate evenly divided on the issue, two senators abstained from voting, with a resultant vote of ten in favor and eight opposed, a result that fell short of the constitutionally-required majority of eleven. With no tie to break, Rose had apparently been thwarted; however, he called attention to a little-used senate rule requiring each legislator who is present on the floor of the chamber to cast a "yea" or "nay" vote unless receiving unanimous consent to abstain. The lieutenant governor proceeded to cast two "nay" votes for the abstaining members and then broke the resultant 10–10 tie with a vote in favor of the Equal Rights Amendment. A possible court suit challenging Rose's actions was dropped when the assembly defeated the amendment.

Like his counterpart at the national level, the actual floor leader of the senate is the majority leader, who is elected at the caucus of the majority party prior to the beginning of the session. By custom the majority leader selects the chairmen and majority party members of the standing committees, with the formal approval of the caucus. In recent years seniority and continuity have been important, although not always decisive, factors in the appointment of senate chairmen.

The senate minority leader and memberships on standing committees are determined by the faction which controls a majority of the votes at the minority party caucus. For example, during the 1975 and 1977 legislative sessions, Carl Dodge was the senior member among the three Republican members of the upper house. However, the two senators from Reno banded together to deny Dodge a seat which he had long sought on the powerful Finance Committee.

The Speaker is the presiding officer of the assembly and is usually the most powerful person in the lower house. Unlike the Speaker of the House of Representatives on the national level, the Speaker of the Nevada Assembly is seldom elected to a second consecutive term. In fact, only three persons have been elected to consecutive terms in the history of the state: Lem Allen in 1895, 1897, and 1899; William Kennett in 1935 and 1937; and Keith Ashworth in 1973 and 1975. The method by which the

Speaker is selected probably contributes to the general lack of continuity in the position. Those aspiring to the speakership trade promises of chairmanships and memberships on important committees for support in the election in the majority party caucus. The other two important leadership positions in the lower house, the majority leader and the Speaker pro tem, are also used as bargaining chips in putting together a coalition. Normally, the winning candidate is the one who receives the support of the majority of the members of the majority party. (There have been instances, such as in 1931 and 1953, when a dissident group from the majority party combined with members of the minority party to elect a different person as Speaker than the one favored by the majority party caucus.) Prior to the 1979 legislative session, twelve of the twenty-six Democrats threatened to vote with the fourteen Republicans on organization unless some changes were made in the proposed committee chairmanships and membership assignments. Enough of the proposed changes were accepted by the majority faction so that the Democrats were reunited and subsequently kept control of all the chairmanships.

The minority party caucus chooses the assembly minority leader and usually the latter plays a major role in determining the minority party committee assignments. However, the majority of the minority party caucus has on occasion dictated the committee assignments.

Party Control

The two major parties are not far apart in the number of times they have controlled the two houses during the sixty regular legislative sessions. Through the 1979 session, the Republicans had organized the senate for thirty-seven sessions, with the Democrats organizing the upper house for eighteen sessions. During the same time, the Democrats controlled the committee chairmanships in the assembly twenty-nine times and the Republicans organized the lower house for twenty-six sessions. For five consecutive sessions, 1893–1901, both houses were controlled by the Silver party, Nevada's most colorful single-interest party. The party was formed in response to falling prices for silver and an act of Congress that had stopped the minting of silver dollars. Nevadans and other westerners connected with mining called this law the "Crime of '73;" they felt that neither the Republicans nor the Democrats cared very much about their plight and so formed a party of their own. The entire membership of the Nevada Assembly in 1893 belonged to the Silver party, which had temporarily replaced the Democratic party and had cut into Republican strength.

Each of the major parties had a long period of dominance in one of the legislative houses between the 1930s and 1960s. The Democrats controlled the assembly from 1931 through 1968, while the Republicans held the majority of senate seats from 1937 through 1964. During the 1965 session, the senate was composed of eight Republicans, eight Democrats, and one Independent (who happened to be a disaffected Democrat). The Independent bargained with both parties and finally threw his vote to the Democrats in return for important committee assignments. The Democrats have dominated the senate since the reapportionment of 1965, reaching a high point of seventeen of the twenty members during the 1975 and 1977 sessions. The Republicans used their dominance in the large nine-member Reno assembly district to gain control of the assembly for the 1969 and 1971 sessions, but the Democrats regained control after reapportionment and single-districting in the 1972 election. The peak of Democratic strength in the lower house was reached in the 1977 session, when the party held a 35–5 majority.

TABLE 5.3

COMPOSITION OF THE NEVADA LEGISLATURE, 1967–79

Session	SENATE		ASSEMBLY		PERCENT REPUBLICAN	
	Dem.	Rep.	Dem.	Rep.	Senate	Assembly
1967	11	9	21	19	45.0	47.5
1969	11	9	18	22	45.0	55.0
1971	13	7	18	22	35.0	55.0
1973	14	6	25	15	30.0	37.5
1975	17	3	31	9	15.0	22.5
1977	17	3	35	5	15.0	12.5
1979	15	5	26	14	25.0	35.0

SOURCES: *Official Returns of the General Election* (Carson City: Secretary of State, 1976, 1974, 1972, 1970, 1968, 1966); 1978 data supplied by William D. Swackhamer, secretary of state. Percentages by Eleanore Bushnell.

Strictly partisan issues have been rare in Nevada legislative politics in the twentieth century. Perhaps one of the reasons for the normally non-partisan approach lies with the generally conservative nature of Nevada politics during the past sixty years. Most Republican and a large number of Democratic legislators in recent years have been conservative in their political views, and it is likely that they are reflecting the viewpoints of voters who elected them.[19]

Legislative Procedures

The steps in the enactment of a bill in the Nevada Legislature vary in some respects from the procedures of Congress. In contrast to the provision of the United States Constitution that all revenue bills must originate in the House of Representatives, any bill (except for a bill of impeachment) may originate in either house of the Nevada Legislature. In order to prevent the attachment of non-germane "riders," the Nevada Constitution states that no bill may embrace more than a single subject.[20]

Nevada is the only state which gives the introducer of a bill the privilege of designating the committee to which the bill will be referred; however, there are rare occasions when another legislator will move an amendment to send the bill to a different committee. In most state legislatures, the presiding officer or the majority leader decides to which committees the bills are assigned. If a bill involves an expenditure of state funds in Nevada, it must also be considered by one of the "money" or appropriations committees: Senate Finance or Assembly Ways and Means.

The Nevada Constitution mandates that the final vote on the passage of a bill or joint resolution must be taken by "yeas" and "nays" and recorded.[21] Both legislative chambers now have electrical voting, which is much more efficient than the roll-call procedure. The constitution further requires that final passage must be by a majority of all members *elected* to the house instead of the congressional requirement of a majority of those present and voting. With current (1981) membership of the two Nevada chambers, eleven votes in the senate and twenty-one votes in the assembly are required for passage, regardless of how many legislators are actually present.

Lobbying

During a legislative session, Carson City becomes the temporary home for representatives of a large number of interest groups. Lobbyists who have proven their effectiveness in influencing the votes of legislators often represent several businesses or interests. Campaign contributions are also likely to insure access to legislators for groups or individuals; some groups, such as teacher organizations, gain support in the legislative halls because of the large number of campaign workers they can provide for legislators who vote the "right" way on issues important to the group membership.

Because of the comparatively small cadre of full-time lobbyists involved prior to the 1970s, the legislators resisted efforts in the 1960s to require individuals they viewed as their friends to register and declare the interests they represented. Public interest groups and reform-minded legislators finally succeeded in getting a registration bill passed in 1973.[22] Approximately 350 lobbyists registered in 1975, the first session for which the act was effective.[23]

In the aftermath of the Watergate scandals and the approval by the California voters of an initiative measure which severely restricted the expenditures of lobbyists, a number of veteran Nevada lobbyists decided in 1975 that it was in their interest to cooperate with reform-minded legislators in strengthening the 1973 lobbying act. (Otherwise, they feared that the public interest groups would sponsor an initiative ballot measure which would be much tougher.) The 1975 law required that lobbyists register with the secretary of state and file periodic statements of expenditures during a legislative session.[24]

A number of representatives of state agencies and local governing boards are also likely to be "working" the halls or waiting to testify in committee rooms during a legislative session. These individuals, including both elected and appointed officials, may be present to speak on behalf of legislation proposed by an agency or a local government body, or they may be at the legislative building to oppose "unfriendly" legislation. These representatives from the public sector often provide the lawmakers with expert testimony on a complex bill; therefore, their input is not only welcomed but is often considered indispensable.

The relationship between most professional lobbyists and Nevada legislators has been close over the years, with integrity being an important factor in the positive rapport. Thus, if a lobbyist is to be effective, he or she needs to be scrupulous about the accuracy of information given the legislators so that mutual trust can be established.

Reform Legislation

In addition to the registration of lobbying act, the Nevada Legislature enacted a conflict-of-interest law in 1975; however, the Nevada Supreme Court, by a vote of 4-1, struck down the law in April 1976 as unconstitutionally vague.[25] The 1977 legislature enacted a more tightly drawn statute with a code of ethical standards as a "guide" for the conduct of public officers and employees who are forbidden to vote or otherwise participate in a matter "in which he has a financial interest without disclosing the full nature and extent of his interest."[26]

An additional provision of the law forbids members of the legislative branch from participation "in the consideration of a matter with respect to which the independence of judgment of a reasonable person in his situation would be materially affected by his acceptance of a gift or loan, his private financial interest, or his commitment in a private capacity to the interest of others."[27] Two separate ethics commissions, one for the executive branch and the other for the legislative branch, were set up by the conflict-of-interest law and charged with informing the attorney general or the appropriate district attorney of noncompliance with the disclosure requirements.

Minorities and Women in the Legislature

Nevada did not have a black legislator until the 1966 election, when Woodrow Wilson, a Las Vegas Republican, won an assembly seat. Joe Neal, a Las Vegas Democrat, elected to the senate in 1972 after the 1971 legislature had carved out a black district in the upper house, is the first, and to date (1980), only black senator in Nevada's history. A total of five black legislators, all men, have served in the legislature; all were elected from Clark County, where the largest percentage of blacks reside; four of the five are Democrats.

The first woman elected to the Nevada Assembly was Sadie D. Hurst of Washoe County, a Republican who served in the 1919 regular session and

Sadie D. Hurst observing Governor Emmet D. Boyle signing the resolution for ratification of the Nineteenth Amendment. (Courtesy of Nevada Historical Society.)

in the 1920 special session, which ratified the Nineteenth Amendment. Prior to the 1980 elections, a total of forty-two women had served in the assembly. Two assemblywomen each served six consecutive terms in the lower house: Maude Frazier from 1951 through 1961, and Eileen Brookman from 1967 through the 1977 session; both were Las Vegas Democrats. Miss Frazier also served briefly as lieutenant governor in 1962, a position to which she was appointed by Governor Grant Sawyer when the office became vacant upon the death of Rex Bell. The largest number of women to serve in the assembly came from Nye County, which chose nine female legislators between 1920 and 1944 and has elected none since. Helen Herr, a Democrat from Clark County, became the first woman elected to the senate in 1966; twice re-elected, she lost in her try for a fourth term in the 1976 primary. Two women joined Senator Herr for the 1975 session, Mary Gojack and Margie Foote, both Washoe County Democrats; Democrat Jean Ford (Clark) was elected to the upper house in 1978 after serving two terms as a Republican assemblywoman. The seven women serving in the 1975 and 1977 sessions hold the record to date (1980) for the most women serving in the legislative branch at one time.

Special Services

All states have legislative-service agencies, which provide a number of services to the legislature. Nevada's agency, established in 1945, is called the Legislative Counsel Bureau; most states use the term "council." The Nevada bureau has four divisions; legal, audit, research, and fiscal analysis. Included in the work of the bureau is a bill-drafting service to insure that bills are cast in correct form. All states provide such a service; it includes presession bill drafting. Referring to the quality and quantity of the work done by the Nevada bureau, Senator Clifton Young, of Reno, said, "They are the unsung heroes of a successful legislative session."[28]

Every state has some arrangement for providing reference assistance or has established reference libraries for the legislators. This need is met in Nevada by the state library in Carson City, which assists the legislature with research and reference problems, as does the Legislative Counsel Bureau.

Thirty-three states conduct a legislative postaudit, which assures the legislators that the money they appropriated was spent as the legislature intended. In some states, including Nevada, the responsibility for conducting the postaudit belongs to the legislative service agency, which reports directly to the legislature.

The legislative fiscal analysts attend the presession budget presentations of the various government departments and agencies and often make different recommendations from those contained in the governor's budget request. Fiscal analysts are also assigned as staff assistants to the appropriations and taxation committees of the two houses during a session and to the Interim Finance Committee between sessions; their advice is often crucial in the final decisions of the committees.

The director of the Legislative Counsel Bureau and the heads of the four divisions are appointed by the Legislative Commission, which also appoints and oversees the activities of the legislative study committees that operate between sessions. The Legislative Commission is composed of twelve members of the Nevada Legislature—six senators and six assemblymen—and generally meets monthly between the regular sessions.

The Legislative Counsel Bureau is specifically entrusted with furthering interstate cooperation by participating in the Council of State Governments and the National Conference of State Legislative Leaders; it is also directed to encourage the maintenance of friendly relations with the national government. Specific duties of the four divisions of the bureau may be found in the *Nevada Revised Statutes;*[29] additional duties may be prescribed by the Legislative Commission.

Another of the Legislative Counsel Bureau's duties concerns the Interim Finance Committee. Established in 1969, this committee is composed of the members of the assembly Ways and Means Committee and the members of the senate Finance Committee. The purpose of the Interim Finance Committee is to deal with financial problems arising between legislative sessions and thereby to avoid the need for special sessions to meet financial crises. In its inaugural year it faced a severe test arising from Nevada's failure to establish the Work Incentive Program. All the other states had this program. The 1969 legislature, whose indifference to welfare was marked, did not provide funds for WIN. Subsequently, the federal government informed the state that other federal welfare programs might be terminated at a loss to Nevada of from $1.5 million to as much as $2.7 million. So a request for $100,000 to start the program was made to the Interim Finance Committee, thus raising the general constitutional question of whether the committee could grant funds at all and the more profound question of whether it could grant money to initiate a program as distinct from supplying money to an established program. Some argued that if the Interim Finance Committee could allot money for projects that had been ignored by the legislative money committees or had been rejected on the floor or in committee, then a potentially dangerous extralegal legislative body would be created.

At its first meeting, December 15, 1969, the committee refused the request of $100,000 to fund jobs for needy mothers under WIN. Before the meeting, two state senators had said they didn't care if all federal money in aid of welfare were cut off; some legislators had doubted that the federal government would really stop supplying welfare funds. After the December meeting, the Legislative Counsel gave an opinion that (1) the Interim Finance Committee had been lawfully established, (2) it was not authorized to fund new programs, and (3) WIN was merely a continuance of the established Aid to Dependent Children program. Because of this third provision and a letter from the Health, Education, and Welfare Department stating that it would be obliged to impose sanctions if the state did not act, the committee agreed in January 1970 to provide the $100,000.

The Interim Finance Committee is activated in the following way. A state agency, finding that money exceeding the amount provided by the legislature is needed, submits a request for funds to the Board of Examiners. If the board decides that the request is justified, it recommends the amount to be granted to the director of the Legislative Counsel Bureau, who notifies the chairman of the Interim Finance Committee. The committee makes its own independent evaluation and is not bound by the recommendations made to it. A separate vote is taken among the senate and assembly members, and a majority of both groups must vote yes for the request to be approved. Such a "concurrent majority" requirement is unusual for committee voting but is, of course, the standard procedure in two-house legislative bodies.

Action was taken by the 1971 legislature to remove doubts about the power of the Interim Finance Committee to provide money. The 1971 law prohibits funding salary increases for state employees; it also forbids funding programs rejected by the preceding legislature or raising the allocation for existing programs unless the lack of such funding would result in forfeit of a federal grant.

The Constitutional Convention and the Legislature

Reference has been made to a suspicious attitude toward legislative power, common in Nevada both now and in the past, and to the consequent effort to circumscribe that power. Two comments made at the constitutional convention show that such distrust existed in Nevada even during her formative period.

In a debate over limiting the bonding capacity of the state, a proposal was made that such a specific matter should be left to the legislative body. George A. Nourse (Washoe) did not agree. "Why not leave all these things with the Legislature? We do not leave them with the Legislature because the province of the Constitution is to restrict legislative powers, which otherwise would be unlimited. And we propose to restrict the power of the State to incur debts, which would otherwise be unlimited."[30]

Like Nourse and many of his contemporaries, many people nowadays believe that a constitution's essential function is to confine legislative power as strictly as possible. They fear that, left to its own devices, a legislature would behave in a disastrously reckless fashion, particularly where money is concerned.

Legislatures have also long been the target of wicked shafts of humor, as the following remark by E. F. Dunne (Humboldt) suggest. In supporting a clause he thought would reduce the amount of business the legislature would transact and so limit the length of the sessions, he said: "The fact is, that whenever the Legislature is in session, the people wait with fear and trembling for it to adjourn, and then they thank God that it is over. [Laughter.]"[31]

So much for the abuse to which legislative bodies find themselves subjected.

CHAPTER 6

THE EXECUTIVE BRANCH

ANALYSIS OF GOVERNMENT POWERS may be attempted in at least two ways. The first, mentioned in the preceding chapter, employs the theory of separation of powers, with its probably misleading supposition that the powers of government can be distributed into distinct categories. The second method attempts to locate and define power by regarding the legislature as the policy-making organ and the executive and judicial branches as the policy-enforcing organs of government. Neither theory has produced a fully satisfactory explanation of the complexities and interrelationships of the political process.

An examination of the Nevada executive and the Nevada judiciary as separate organs of government will reveal something of the functions of these two branches and their relationships to each other and to the legislature; it will also indicate the constitutional base of the power exercised by each.

The Governor

Although governors of the states are small-sized replicas of the president of the United States, they do not have as much power within their states as the president does within the entire country. The reason for this difference stems in part from the abhorrence of executive power engendered by the behavior of some of the colonial governors. By the time the United States Constitution was drafted, this hatred had dwindled in the face of the shocking reality of legislative irresponsibility and executive impotence that existed in the period when the Articles of Confederation were in effect. So the national Constitution does not reflect hatred of executive power to the same degree as did the state constitutions enacted ten or more years earlier, while the Revolution was in progress.

The state constitutions drawn up during the Revolution exacted punishment for the sufferings of the colonists under the colonial governors by reducing the scope of executive power to a very narrow range. The governor was sometimes made little more than an agent of the legislature. Distrust of executive power still lingers. For example, in four states (1976) the governor had only a two-year term; eight states prohibit an incumbent governor from running for a second consecutive term; Nevada and eighteen other states limit the governor to two terms in office. All but six states force him to share executive power with other elected officials, such as the attorney general, secretary of state, and treasurer.

The current trend, however, is to increase the power of the governor in order to make it more nearly commensurate with his responsibility. Reorganizations of state governments in recent years are directed toward streamlining government by combining state agencies and giving the governor tighter control over their operations. Also, most of the states, recognizing the value of placing financial responsibility in the hands of the governor, have given him the duty of budget making. Reducing the number of elected executive officials is another way to clarify the governor's responsibilities and to lay them more squarely upon him.

Qualifications of the Nevada Governor

Article V, describing the executive, remains substantially unchanged from the form in which it was drafted by the constitutional convention of 1864; modifications in the executive branch have been accomplished by legislative action and have not usually required constitutional amendment. The governor is elected for a four-year term and is limited to two terms. The two-term restriction was added in 1970; the original constitution had not limited the length of time that a governor could serve, but no Nevada governor was ever elected to a third term in office. Governor L. R. Bradley in 1878, Governor Charles H. Russell in 1958, and Governor Grant Sawyer in 1966 attempted to win third consecutive terms; however, none was successful. Only five governors have served two full terms in office: the three who unsuccessfully sought third terms and Governors Emmet D. Boyle (1915–22) and Mike O'Callaghan (1971–78).

The constitutional amendment limiting the governor to two four-year terms further provides that a person succeeding to an unexpired term of two or more years is eligible for only one four-year term following his fulfillment of the unexpired term of his predecessor. The Nevada amendment parallels the Twenty-second Amendment of the United States Constitution, which places the same restriction upon the president's eligibility for reelection.

The governor of Nevada must be at least twenty-five years old and a qualified elector of the state; he must have been a resident for two years. The same requirements are prescribed for the office of lieutenant governor. The governor's annual salary is set by the legislature, although the constitution states that the salary may not be increased during a term of office. Thus, when the 1977 legislature raised the salary to $50,000, the increase did not become effective until after the gubernatorial election of 1978. The governor is supplied by the state with an official residence and

Robert List, Nevada's Twenty-Fourth Governor, 1979–.
(Courtesy of Governor List.)

an automobile; expenses for maintenance of the mansion are provided by legislative appropriation.

In case the office of governor becomes vacant, the lieutenant governor assumes the powers and duties of the executive. Five Nevada lieutenant governors have succeeded to the governorship upon the death or, in one instance, the resignation of the elected governor. Of these five, four where candidates for election to the governorship following completion of the unexpired terms of their predecessors; two were successful: Reinhold Sadler in 1898 and Vail Pittman in 1946. The constituion provides for succession of the president pro tempore of the senate if the offices of both the governor and the lieutenant governor become vacant. By act of the legislature, the succession beyond the president pro tempore is Speaker of the assembly and then secretary of state.[1] At the federal level, the Speaker of the House of Representatives is next to the vice-president in the line of succession, followed by the president pro tempore of the Senate.

When the president of the United States travels outside the country, the office travels with him; he is president wherever he may be. But the Nevada Constitution provides that the powers and duties of the governorship devolve upon the lieutenant governor not only when the office is vacant or the governor is incapacitated, but also when he is absent from the state.[2] Problems in the exercise of gubernatorial powers can develop when the governor and lieutenant governor are of opposite parties and are political rivals.

Exactly what "absent" means became a matter for court determination in late 1965. A controversy erupted between Democratic Governor Grant Sawyer and Republican Lieutenant Governor Paul Laxalt over the need for a grand jury to investigate charges leveled against the Highway Department. Laxalt believed an investigation was necessary and announced that he would summon a grand jury the first time he was acting governor. Sawyer was out of the state for five hours one day; Laxalt requested a district judge to impanel a grand jury, and Sawyer revoked the request upon his return. This political exchange would have no lasting importance had it not resulted in a Nevada Supreme Court decision[3] defining the circumstances in which a lieutenant governor may act when the governor is absent from the state. The court ruled that the constitution presupposes an effective absence from the state "measured by the state's *need* at a given moment for a particular act by the official then physically not present."[4] It found no pressing need for the impaneling of a grand jury. Thus, a governor's absence is not construed as authorizing *nonemergency* action by the lieutenant governor. Attorney General Richard Bryan cited the 1965 decision in an advisory opinion in late 1979 in which he stated that Lieutenant Governor Myron Leavitt was not entitled to receive a salary for days in which Governor Robert List was absent from the state, unless as acting governor he had taken some significant and required action.

Chief Executive and Chief of State

The Nevada governor has considerably less power over the executive branch than does the president of the United States because other *elected* executive officials in the state are not responsible to him. Whereas the president selects his attorney general, the governor may be faced with the prospect of working with an attorney general who is of the opposite party and who may have designs on the governorship. Local district attorneys and law enforcement officers are similarly independent of the governor's control, so that there is reason to question whether the governor has adequate authority to perform his constitutional duty "to see that the laws are faithfully executed."[5]

TABLE 6.1

PARTY CONTROL OF THE EXECUTIVE BRANCH, 1962–78

	1962	1966	Election 1970	1974	1978	Percent Democratic Victories
Governor	D	R	D	D	R	60.0
Lieutenant governor	R	R	D	D	D	60.0
Attorney general	D	D	R	R	D	60.0
Secretary of state	D	D	D	D	D	100.0
Treasurer	D	D	D	D	D	100.0
Controller	R	R	R	R	R	0
Percent Democratic administrators	66.7	50.0	66.7	66.7	66.7	

SOURCES: Compiled by the authors from data contained in *Official Returns of The General Election* (Carson City: Secretary of State, 1974, 1970, 1966, 1962), with 1978 data supplied by William D. Swackhamer, Secretary of State.

The governor has considerable appointive power, however. He selects the heads of departments and divisions, other than those headed by the elective officials, and chooses the members of over a hundred boards and commissions. He also fills vacancies in elected state offices, including the Board of Regents of the University of Nevada System, the State Board of Education, and Nevada's congressional seats. A 1976 amendment to the constitution has somewhat limited the governor's power to fill judicial vacancies, as he now must choose from three nominations made by the Commission on Judicial Selection. Unlike the president, the governor does not have to secure senate confirmation of major appointees; he is required, however, to inform the legislature when he makes an appointment.

The governor is a member of several important boards and commissions. One of these is the Board of Pardons Commissioners, which also includes the justices of the supreme court and the attorney general. In 1960, upon the recommendation of the supreme court justices that they should not participate in the exercise of the pardon power inasmuch as it is supposed to be a check on the judiciary, the legislature placed a constitutional amendment on the ballot designed to grant the sole pardoning

8

power to the governor. (The president of the United States has the exclusive power to grant pardons to individuals who have been convicted of federal offenses.) However, Nevada voters decisively defeated the amendment. The governor does, in effect, have a veto over any pardon or commutation granted by the board, for he must be on the majority side for such a decision to be effective.[6] The governor also has certain duties connected with supervision of the state prison. The governor, the secretary of state, and the attorney general make up the Board of State Prison Commissioners and the Board of Examiners. The latter board reviews all claims against the state, excluding salaries, and no claim "shall be passed upon by the Legislature without having been considered and acted upon by said Board of Examiners."[7]

In addition to his constitutionally-mandated executive duties, the governor, like the president, is the ceremonial chief of state. He is asked to be present and to speak at all kinds of public and private "openings" and meetings throughout the state. When the governor and lieutenant governor are of the same party, the latter is often asked to share some of these time-consuming ceremonial burdens. If the lieutenant governor has higher political ambitions, he is usually delighted to have such opportunities for exposure. Table 6.2 shows the major agencies through which the governor acts and indicates the other elected officials who share in administrative duties.

TABLE 6.2

THE EXECUTIVE BRANCH

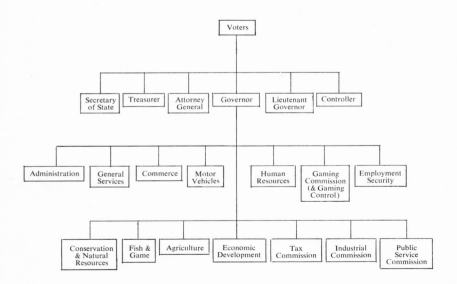

Chief Legislator

Like the president, the governor has the constitutional power to recommend legislation and the duty to deliver what is called a "state of the state" message to the legislature each session. Nevada governors use the "state of the state" address to set forth the outlines of the major programs they wish to have enacted. Thus, Nevada chief executives have followed the development of the modern presidency and have become the chief legislators as well.

Usually the most important proposal the governor presents to the legislature is the executive budget. The budget director, an appointee of the governor, and his staff hold hearings with the representatives of the various divisions, departments, and agencies on their respective biennial requests during the fall of the even-numbered years. The governor is heavily involved in the process, and agencies often appeal to him if the preliminary budget office figures are considered too low. The budget director takes orders from the governor and the latter often changes the budget director's recommendations after consulting with political advisers.

The executive budget is very influential in the deliberations and decisions of the legislative money committees. Although the legislative fiscal analysts provide an important check on the executive, the members of the appropriations committees have only the time and manpower during a four-month legislative session to investigate closely the budget requests of a few of the major agencies and departments. During the eight years of the O'Callaghan administration in the 1970s, the legislature rarely departed from the governor's budget.

The governor of Nevada, like the president of the United States, possesses the veto power; but neither has the authority to veto parts of a measure, the "item veto." Both executives must accept all of a bill or reject all of a bill. Nevada is among the minority of states not granting to the governor the power to veto items in appropriation bills; in 1976 governors in forty-three states had that power. No action is in progress to secure this power for the executive in Nevada.

Although, like the president of the United States, the Nevada governor must sign or veto a bill as a whole, he has one advantage over the president in respect to the construction of bills presented for his signature: each bill is required to "embrace but one subject."[8] Thus, the governor is not faced with "riders"—nongermane additions to a bill. The president is sometimes obliged to sign a bill even though it has an objectionable "rider" attached to it; this is particularly true when the bill to which the "rider" has been added is an appropriation bill.

To pass a bill over the governor's veto requires a two-thirds vote of the *elected* membership of both houses of the Nevada legislature. The national average for overriding a governor's veto is 1 percent. Nevada's governors have been more rudely treated—12 percent of their vetoes have been overridden by the legislature.[9] When the legislature is in session, the governor has five days to consider his action on a measure presented for his signature; if he fails to act, the bill becomes law without his approval. When the legislature has adjourned, the governor has ten days to reach a decision on a bill; again, if he takes no action, the bill becomes a law after the ten days (Sundays excepted) have elapsed. If the governor decides to veto a bill *after* the legislature has adjourned, he files the bill and his objections to it with the secretary of state, who brings the veoted bill before the next session of the legislature. The president of the United States has the "pocket veto" available to him. The Nevada governor does not. The "pocket veto" permits the president to disregard any bill presented to him after the Congress adjourns; if he fails to act, the bill is dead. Since the Nevada governor does not have the "pocket veto," if he fails to act after the legislature has gone home, the bill automatically becomes a law.

The governor is empowered to call special sessions of the legislature in extraordinary circumstances; in such special sessions no legislative business may be transacted except matters placed before the session by the governor. In the latter respect, the governor's power exceeds that of the president, who does not have the constitutional power to restrict the agenda during special sessions.

Protector of the State's Interests

In addition to his constitutionally-mandated roles, the governor of Nevada is expected to provide leadership in protecting the state's natural resources, in supervising the regulation of the state's largest industry—gaming, and in providing a favorable political climate for economic development. He is also expected to be the spokesman for the state's interest vis-a-vis federal authorities.

The regulation of gaming deserves special attention because of its importance to the economic health of the state. Although other attractions bring tourists to Nevada, most of them come because of gambling. It is imperative that tourists have confidence in the honesty of the games. It is also imperative that casinos report their income accurately for tax purposes. Thus, Nevada is deeply engaged in policing an industry that, with the exception of New Jersey and states which allow betting on horse racing, is illegal elsewhere.

Gambling has a long history in Nevada, as it does in most frontier states. The first territorial legislature banned gambling in 1861, but little attention was paid to the law. The second session of the territorial legislature (1862) considered a bill to license gambling. Andrew J. Marsh, reporter of the territorial legislative proceedings, said that the gambling bill was rejected "without a word of comment. There is one iniquitous profession squelched, and no time lost over it."[10] In 1865, after Nevada had become a state, the legislature passed an antigambling law. This law was repealed in 1867, but Governor H. G. Blasdel vetoed the repeal. Again, in 1869, the legislature repealed the law, and again Governor Blasdel issued a veto, but this time the legislature had enough power to override the veto by the necessary two-thirds vote in each house. So from 1869 to 1909 gambling was legal in Nevada. In 1909 various women's groups and religious organizations succeeded in getting another antigambling bill passed. Once more the law was widely ignored, and the seamy consequences of widespread lawbreaking were apparent, particularly bribery of local officials by gambling proprietors.

Extensive and notorious taking of graft money was thought by many legislators to have become an evil more serious than gambling itself. So the 1931 legislature decided to bring gambling out in the open, where it could be taxed, licensed, and policed. The bill was introduced by Republican assemblyman Phil M. Tobin of Humboldt County, after the Democratic leadership had passed the word to their members to have nothing to do with so controversial a measure. The legalized gambling bill was referred to the committee on public morals composed of four Republicans and one Democrat. Many citizens appeared before the committee to protest the bill. The Nevada Federation of Women's Clubs was opposed; their spokesman objected to legalized gambling on moral and economic grounds and predicted an era of greater lawlessness and racketeering because gambling was not a legitimate business and would place a stigma upon the state. Opposition came from the Mormon church, the Methodist church, and the Women's Christian Temperance Union, which viewed gambling as a parasitic business preying upon society; the opponents felt that if gambling were legalized, the state, county, and city governments would become copartners in undermining society.

But economic necessity and the fact that gambling flourished in defiance of the law overcame the opposition, and the bill was passed thirteen to three in the senate and twenty-four to eleven in the assembly, with Republicans strongly supporting the measure and Democrats about evenly divided.

Although Nevada legalized gambling in 1931, the state did not enter the regulatory picture until 1945. The only control in the early years was exercised by local licensing officials when they were determining whether or not to grant a gambling license to a particular applicant. In 1945, the legislature granted responsibility for issuing gambling licenses to the Tax Commission; the commission was not empowered to authorize background checks of applicants until four years later. Jerome Skolnick, a University of California law professor who did an investigative study of gaming control in Nevada in the mid-seventies, claimed that failure to set up a separate gambling control agency prior to 1955 set the scene for most of the later problems with organized crime. Skolnick charged that the state did not attempt to "clean house," but "grandfathered in" the gamblers already doing business, including many who had connections with organized crime in other states.[11]

The three-member State Gaming Control Board was established in 1955 and provided with an investigative staff; four years later the legislature established the five-member State Gaming Commission. The members of both the board and commission are appointed by the governor for four-year staggered terms. The board is a nonpolitical professional body; one member must have had five years of responsible experience in administration; one must be a certified public accountant with five years of increasingly responsible experience in general accounting and with a comprehensive knowledge of corporate finance; and one must have had training and experience in investigation, law enforcement, law, or gaming. Board members are removable only for misconduct in office.

The Gaming Control Board oversees and administers the work of an agency which has three divisions: investigations, enforcement, and audit; the 1979 legislature set the number of authorized agents at forty, forty-nine, and seventy-one, for the respective divisions. These figures represent a substantial increase in the number of agents, following criticism that the board's budget had not kept pace with the phenomenal expansion of gaming in the seventies. However, Nevada still had fewer agents in 1980 to police its hundreds of gaming operations than had the state of New Jersey with its handful of hotel-casinos.

The primary responsibility of the board is to investigate license applicants and recommend that the Gaming Commission grant or deny the licenses. The board members also inspect the books and records of all licensees and make sure that all laws and regulations are being observed. The board files complaints against violators with the commission, which, following a public hearing, determines whether the licensee may continue in business and if so, on what terms. The board also collects state taxes from gaming licensees.

The commission is a bipartisan lay body composed of business and professional leaders; its members are subject to removal by the governor for malfeasance or for neglect of duty; they may be removed by the governor without cause upon concurrence of a majority of the Legislative Commission. In addition to considering recommendations from the board as noted above, the Gaming Commission is responsible for the adoption of policies pertaining to gaming.

Another body connected with gambling is the Gaming Policy Committee. The governor is chairman, and the membership is composed of one member from the Gaming Commission, one from the Control Board, two representing the gaming industry, and two representing the public. This committee is authorized to discuss matters of gaming policy. Its recommendations are advisory only and do not bind the Gaming Commission or the Control Board.

A significant change made by the legislature in 1969 provided for corporate gambling in the state under authority of a law passed in 1967. Whether corporations should be allowed to own and trade stock in gambling was, and is, disputed. Proponents of corporate ownership of Nevada casinos argued that the revenue was needed; that the image of the state would improve because the taint of hoodlum control of casinos would be removed; and that approval of the Securities and Exchange Commission was further assurance of the caliber of corporate ownership. Former Governor Paul Laxalt, the legislature, and many legitimate gamblers were deeply concerned because television and national newspapers and magazines were exposing hoodlum interests in Nevada casinos, and there was a strong possibility of action by the federal government. It was anticipated that corporate gambling would diminish the hidden interests in the industry and thereby remove the threat of national intervention.

Opponents of corporate gambling entertained many fears: develpment of monopolies; lessened local control; hidden, undesirable ownership of gambling stocks, particularly because the long-standing requirement that every stockholder in a gambling operation must be licensed by the state would be reversed; and the difficulty of discovering subsidiaries of conglomerates attracted to investment in gambling. The ban on ownership of casinos or on investment in them by persons with gambling connections outside Nevada was modified in 1973 to allow Nevada gambling licensees to hold interests in gaming operations outside the state as permitted under carefully restricted provisions (NRS 3.060).

Another control device is the "Black Book," a list of underworld figures "of notorious or unsavory reputation" who are forbidden to be in any Nevada casino. Any gambling establishment catering to a person in the "Black Book" could lose its license. Nevada's right to forbid undesirables from entering casinos was upheld in federal court.[12] When additional names are added to the "Black Book," persons about to be listed have an opportunity to argue against being included, a protection that was not available when the first list was compiled.

The federal departments of Justice and Internal Revenue have occasionally raised questions concerning the accuracy of income tax reporting by some casinos. They have alleged that casino profits have been taken out—"skimmed"—before receipts were officially counted for tax purposes and that such money was channeled into the underworld. Such a charge was made in a 1979 federal grand jury indictment in Detroit based on F.B.I. wiretaps that allegedly uncovered hidden ownership in some Las Vegas casinos by Kansas City racketeering elements. The disclosures led to demands from the Gaming Commission and the Control Board that the casinos with the hidden ownership be sold and that the 1981 legislature pass legislation permitting selective wiretaps by state authorities. Sale of the casinos was completed by early 1980, and Governor List and the regulatory officials announced their determination to keep mobster elements out of casino ownership, thus forestalling further federal intervention. The governor, the legislature, and the regulatory officials face the problem of determining where the line whould be drawn between the gaming industry's fear of overregulation and the amount of supervision needed to ensure public trust both within and outside the state.

Other Elected Executive Officials

In addition to the governor and the lieutenant governor, there are four elected officials in the executive branch: the attorney general, the controller, the secretary of state, and treasurer. The other offices have the same qualifications as the governor, i.e., age twenty-five, a qualified elector, and two years a resident of the state. There are no other requirements; curiously missing is the stipulation that the attorney general be an attorney. The salaries of these officials are set by the legislature; in 1980 the attorney general received $40,500 and was prohibited from engaging in the private practice of law. The lieutenant governor received $8,000 for his minimal responsibilities; in addition, he receives daily compensation while presiding over the senate during a legislative session or serving as acting governor. The secretary of state received $32,500 in 1980 and the treasurer and controller, $31,500.

The main duties of the officers whose posts were created by the constitution are as follows:

Secretary of State—maintains the archives, attests all official acts of the governor, supplies written information on any subject relating to his office when requested to do so by the governor, supervises the printing of official acts and journals, manages the photocopy room, and makes a biennial report to the governor. The secretary maintains records of corporations licensed to do business in the state and serves as a local "securities and exchange commission" to insure that Nevada-based corporations are making sound offerings and not defrauding the public. The 1975 legislature increased his duties by assigning to him the appointment and commissioning of notaries public and supervision over the registration of lobbyists.

Treasurer—receives and keeps state money, supplies the controller with receipts for money received, disburses money upon warrants drawn by the controller, makes an annual report to the governor, and acts as the state's disbursing officer for the federal government.

The Governor's Mansion, Carson City. (Courtesy of Adrian Atwater.)

Controller—provides an annual report to the governor of the condition of state revenues and the amount expended in the past year, audits all claims against the state, draws all warrants upon the treasury and keeps an account of them, serves as the state's fiscal officer for compliance with federal revenue and income tax measures, and maintains an account with each county and with the federal government.

Attorney General—serves as legal adviser on all state matters arising in the executive department, prosecutes or defends state cases in the Nevada Supreme Court, supplies written opinions at the request of other state executive officers or state institutions, exercises supervisory power over district attorneys, and provides the governor with a biennial report.

The Convention and the Executive

The *Debates* do not reveal that the drafters of the constitution had great difficulty in describing the powers of the executive branch. Only one substantive disagreement occurred and that was a not very dramatic difference of opinion over whether to include a surveyor general as a constitutional officer. Some delegates thought that such an officer would not have enough to do and that establishing this office would be just one more example of creating a sinecure into which an overpaid incompetent would settle. The decision was made to include the office; an amendment to the constitution, effective in 1954, reversed this decision and eliminated the post of surveyor general. In the only important matter respecting the executive branch, the delegates, without counterargument, changed the governor's term of office, which had been two years in the first constitution, to four years.

CHAPTER 7

THE JUDICIAL BRANCH

THE UNITED STATES made a unique contribution to government in developing the theory and practice of judicial review. Specifically spurned by Switzerland but followed by Australia and some other countries, this controversial dogma elevates the courts to a position of potential supremacy over the executive and legislative branches. When, in a case before a court, an individual claims injury under a law or an executive act and challenges that law or act as being unconstitutional, and when the application of the law is pivotal to the determination of the case, courts in countries practicing judicial review will rule on whether or not the challenged law is constitutional. The United States Supreme Court has found more than one hundred federal laws to be unconstitutional.

Another aspect of judicial review, one that usually creates fewer antagonisms than the supremacy of the courts over the national legislature and the national executive, consists of the courts' power to make determinations when an act of a state government is challenged as an infringement of a power vested by the Constitution in the national government, or when an act of the national government is challenged as an infringement of a power reserved by the Constitution to the states. This aspect ordinarily arouses fewer objections because it is evident that in the division of power characteristic of federalism some agency must have the authority to decide whether a disputed power belongs rightfully to a state or to the nation. The United States Supreme Court has found more than seven hundred state laws unconstitutional and, therefore, void.

Judicial review is not described in the Constitution; it became part of the fabric of government through John Marshall's decision in *Marbury v. Madison.* [1] Marshall held that an act of Congress that had enlarged the Supreme Court's original jurisdiction was beyond the power of Congress and hence void and unenforceable by the courts. From this famous decision grew the doctrine that it is the province of the judiciary to determine whether contested acts are harmonious with the Constitution, a doctrine as firmly established today as is any part of the written Constitution.

First Justices, Supreme Court of Nevada, 1864: H. O. Beatty; James F. Lewis, Chief Justice; and C. M. Brosnan. (Courtesy of Nevada Historical Society.)

Most of the parliamentary democracies, Great Britain being the best example, vest supremacy in the elected legislative body. In these countries, laws passed by the parliament are not subject to invalidation for being "unconstitutional"; improper or overzealous enforcement of a law may be challenged, but the law itself is not subject to judicial disallowance.

Both federal and state courts in the United States exercise the power of judicial review. The Nevada courts, when an act of the legislature or an act of the governor is challenged as unconstitutional, decide whether the protested action is proper or not; if the act is found to be outside lawful authority, the court will declare the law unconstitutional and so not enforceable. Thus, in Nevada as in the national government, the judiciary is in a position to restrain the actions of the other two branches.

Basis of Nevada Law

Along with other states, Nevada courts are bound by the supremacy clause of Article VI of the United States Constitution, which reads: "This Constitution, and the laws of the United States which shall be made in pursuance therof; and all treaties made, or which shall be made, under the authority of the United States, shall be the supreme law of the land; and the judges in every state shall be bound thereby, any thing in the constitution or laws of any state to the contrary, notwithstanding."[2]

Nevada law is based on the common law, buttressed and modified by statutes, which are laws passed by a legislative body. Nevada's statute law is compiled under subject headings in the *Nevada Revised Statutes*. Common law is judge-made, with origins going back to at least twelfth-century English practice. This law is found in court decisions and is grounded in precedent, which means that a judge will usually apply the rule from past cases when the facts in a case he is hearing are similar. In the event of a conflict between common law and statute law, the latter is controlling.

The Nevada Court System

For the most part, the federal and state court systems in the United States operate separately, with appeal from a state court to a federal court being possible when a federal question or constitutional right is involved. Well over ninety percent of court cases in the nation start and end in state courts because the overwhelming majority of criminal violations and civil suits involve state or local laws.

The Nevada court system consists of a supreme court, district courts, and justice and municipal courts, with the latter two having limited jurisdiction. As of 1979, twenty-seven states had an appellate court system intermediary between the trial courts and the highest court in the state. Nevada's relatively small population made such an intermediate court seem unnecessary until the population growth of the 1960s and 1970s. The large increase in criminal appeals to the Nevada Supreme Court in the 1960s resulted in the inclusion of a criminal court of appeals in an onmibus judicial reform amendment to the constitution proposed by the 1969 and 1971 legislatures. The amendment was defeated by the voters in 1972. The 1977 and 1979 legislatures reaffirmed support for establishment of a criminal court of appeals; a separate amendment establishing such a court was placed on the 1980 general election ballot.

The Nevada Supreme Court

All states have a court of last resort; such courts are variously called Supreme Court of Errors, Supreme Judicial Court, Supreme Court of Appeals, Court of Appeals, or more commonly, as in Nevada, Supreme Court. Most of the business of the highest court of the states is appellate; that is, the case has been tried in a lower court and has come before the supreme court for review. Unlike the United States Supreme Court, the Nevada Supreme Court must hear all cases appealed to it. The constitution also gives the state's highest court original jurisdiction to grant certain writs, a power it shares with the district courts.[3] As is the case with all appellate courts, the Nevada Supreme Court does not use a jury in either appeals or original cases.

Nevada's highest court is composed of five justices elected for six-year terms on a nonpartisan ballot. Until the number of justices was increased by the 1967 legislature, the court had been composed of three members. An amendment was not necessary to increase the size of the supreme court. The constitution provided that the number could be enlarged to five if a majority of the elected membership of the legislature voted to do so; the 1967 legislature exercised this option and increased the size of the court. Although increasing the size of the supreme court did not lessen the amount of time each justice must devote to hearing and analyzing cases, the total work load was decreased to some extent because the researching and writing of the court opinions are now distributed among five instead of three members. In view of the increase in the number of cases filed with the supreme court from 208 in calendar year 1968 to 1019 in 1978, even a modest decrease in the load is important. Because of the large increase in cases in recent years, the legislature proposed, and the people approved in 1976, a constitutional amendment authorizing the legislature to increase the number of justices and to provide for such an enlarged court to hear cases in panels of three justices in places other than Carson City. In the late 1970s, the court began to meet periodically in Las Vegas, thus saving travel expenses for a considerable number of plaintiffs, defendants, and lawyers.

The office of chief justice is rotated and is held by the senior justice for the final two years of his tenure. During the more than one hundred years of a three-man court, this was ordinarily accomplished without difficulty.

The Nevada Supreme Court, 1978: From left to right, back row, John Mowbray, Gordon Thompson; front row, E. M. Gunderson, Cameron M. Batjer, and Noel Manoukian.

Since 1967, however, two justices have held the same seniority in commission most of the time; in such cases, the chief justiceship is decided by lot. Should a vacancy occur on the Nevada Supreme Court during a term of office, the governor is authorized by the constitution to appoint a replacement (until the next general election) from a list of nominees supplied by a judicial selection commission. This commission, established by a constitutional amendment in 1976, is composed of the chief justice or an associate justice designated by him, three attorneys appointed by the board of governors of the State Bar of Nevada, and three non-lawyers appointed by the governor. In recent years most justices have attained their positions by appointment. It is noteworthy that the 1980 election for a seat on the Nevada Supreme Court caused by the retirement of Justice Gordon Thompson was only the second such election since 1950 in which an incumbent was not involved. Four of the five members of the 1980 court had originally been appointed by the governor to fill vacancies created by the expansion of the court or caused by retirements in mid-term and had then run successfully for re-election thereafter.

Although the constitution specifies that justices shall receive a salary and that the amount fixed shall be neither increased nor diminished during the term for which a justice has been elected, it leaves the determination of the salary to the legislature. Members of the supreme court receive annual salaries of $47,250. In addition to the requirements set down in the constitution, the legislature has added these stipulations: a justice must be at least twenty-five years old, a qualified elector, a licensed attorney admitted to practice in Nevada, and a two-year resident of the state.[4] Retirement provisions for justices were also arranged by the legislature; a justice may retire on two-thirds salary at age sixty after twenty years of service or on one-third salary at age sixty after twelve years of service.

Practices vary among the states on lengths of terms, qualifications, and salaries for the jurists of the highest court. In 1979 seventeen states, including Nevada, provided six-year terms for justices of the supreme court; no states had less than six-year terms; Rhode Island followed the federal patten of life terms; and Massachusetts and New Hampshire had a mandatory retirement age of seventy, with no set term. Annual salaries ranged from $29,000 in Maine to $62,935 in California.[5]

The Nevada Supreme Court, like all final courts, is called upon to make many decisions that affect the entire political process and reach far beyond disposing of the claims of the immediate parties in a given case. Certain examples will illustrate both the extensive impact of supreme court rulings and the role of the court in the political system.

It will be recalled that a lieutenant governor is entitled to act as chief executive only when the governor is effectively absent from the state, not just away on a short trip, and then only in case of urgent need. This important "fact" of the Nevada political system is not to be found in the constitution or in an act of the legislature, but in a decision, *Sawyer v. District Court* (1966), in which the Nevada Supreme Court interpreted the meaning of the constitutional provision that the powers and duties of the executive devolve upon the lieutenant governor in the absence of the governor. The ruling that the absence must be effective and the need for action crucial applies to any future situation and plainly modifies the relationship of the governor and the lieutenant governor.

The Nevada high court also has power and responsibility in government finance. In *State ex rel. Nevada Building Authority v. Hancock* (1970), the court invalidated a legislative plan to finance capital improvements, holding that it violated the constitutional debt limit. It has spoken on the limit of legislative involvement in university affairs in the *King* (1948) and *Richardson* (1954) cases. It has rejected judicial involvement in land use decisions, in the absence of arbitrary regulations (*Eagle Thrifty v. Hunter Lake P.T.A.* 1968), by holding that the function of zoning is vested in legislative bodies.

In these and many other cases the Nevada Supreme Court, in interpreting the state constitution, determines intergovernment relations, limits of executive action, and limits of legislative action. When federal constitutional issues are concerned, the Nevada Supreme Court follows the requirement of the state's constitution that national Supreme Court decisions are controlling. Thus, in the case of *Bean v. State* (1965), the Nevada Supreme Court, having affirmed Bean's conviction and death penalty, later remanded the case for a separate penalty hearing. This action created certain loud outcries and some demands for impeachment of the justices. But the United States Supreme Court had ruled that a jury from which persons with doubts about their ability to apply the death penalty had been excluded was a hanging jury, stacked against the accused. So the Nevada court was obliged to follow the federal ruling. In general, the Nevada Supreme Court has not made significant rulings in the field of criminal law because it is obliged to adhere to national interpretations.

Nevada District Courts

Nevada is divided into nine judicial districts. The distict court is the trial court in which most cases begin and terminate. District courts are essentially courts of original jurisdiction, although cases do reach them on appeal from municipal and justice courts. Such cases are finally disposed of by the district court to which the appeal is brought; no further appeal to the state supreme court is possible.

Three of the nine districts have been assigned two or more judges by the legislature: District 1 (Carson City and Storey), District 2 (Washoe), and District 8 (Clark). In the multi-judge districts, the judges sit singly in separate departments and exercise concurrent jurisdiction. Each judge makes his own determinations in cases before him, without official consultation with other judges in his district. The other six districts are presently (1980) served by single judges and are composed as follows: District 3 (Churchill, Eureka, and Lander counties); District 4 (Elko County); District 5 (Mineral, Esmeralda, and Nye counties); District 6 (Pershing and Humboldt counties); District 7 (White Pine and Lincoln counties); and District 9 (Douglas and Lyon counties).

The legislature has the constitutional power to increase or decrease the number of judicial districts and judges and in recent sessions has invariably added to the number of judges. In July 1975, the first black jurist in Nevada's history, Addeliar D. Guy, was appointed to the district court in Las Vegas. A new position had been created when the 1975 legislature increased District 8 from ten to eleven judges. The 1977 legislature added yet another judge for Clark County and a second judge for District 1. The 1979 legislature created two new judgeships for District 2, bringing the total to nine, to help relieve the burgeoning court dockets in Reno. However, the filling of the last two positions was hamstrung by a constitutional provision that states that "no such change" (apparently referring to increasing or diminishing the number of district judges) "shall take effect, except in case of a vacancy, or the expiration of the term of an incumbent of the office."[6] Prior to the establishment of the commission on judicial selection in 1976, a judge could temporarily resign to create a vacancy with the assurance from the governor that he would be reappointed. Now a judge cannot be certain that the commission will include his name on the list of three nominees from which the governor must make his selection; consequently, the two new Washoe County judgeships were still unfilled in 1980.

District judges are elected for six-year terms and run on a nonpartisan ballot. Their salaries are set by the legislature, with the annual pay being $43,000 in 1981. They are entitled to the same retirement benefits as justices of the supreme court and must have the same qualifications except for residence; district court judges need meet only the minimum residence requirement necessary for eligibility to vote.

Vacancies in district judgeships during a term are filled in the same manner as are vacancies on the Nevada Supreme Court. However, an *ad hoc* commission on judicial selection is established for each vacancy, with two residents of the judicial district involved (one being an attorney and the other a non-lawyer) added to the regular commission.

Other Nevada Courts

In Nevada there are two courts of limited jurisdiction: justice courts and municipal courts. Justice courts originated in England, to provide courts in every community to settle minor difficulties without requiring petty cases to be carried to the county seat. These courts have existed in the United States since the colonial period, but they are being eliminated in some states, particularly in urban areas. In a state such as Nevada with a vast amount of acreage and sparse population in the rural areas, justices of the peace serve an important purpose: people don't have to travel great distances to the county seat to appear before a judge to settle minor traffic violations or misdemeanor cases. Justices of the peace are elected by the voters in a township, which is a subdivision of a county. In 1980 there were fifty-four townships in the state, with Clark County having eleven and Washoe County five. Each township has one justice court, except for Las Vegas with five courts and Reno with two.

A justice of the peace in Nevada is elected for a four-year term, and the only requirement for the office is that a candidate be a qualifed elector. The county commissioners fix the compensation for the office, providing for either salary, fees, or a combination of both. Prior to 1979, the jurisdiction of justice courts extended only to civil actions in which the matter in dispute did not exceed $300, preliminary hearings in felony criminal cases, and trials of misdemeanor cases. A 1978 constitutional amendment removed the $300 limitation in civil cases and gave the legislature the power to set the maximum amount. The 1979 legislature raised the limit to $750. With the exception of the comparatively few cases taken to the county grand jury, felony cases have a preliminary hearing in justice court to determine that a crime has taken place and that the accused *could be* the one who committed it.

The incorporated cities and towns in Nevada may establish municipal courts, with the term of office and salary set either by charter or city ordinance. These courts hear only misdemeanors, with the great majority of the cases involving minor traffic violations such as speeding within the city limits.

A gross description of the structure and function of a court system tells nothing about the quality of justice available, the caliber of the jurists who staff the courts, or the tormenting problems of cost and delay that characterize the judicial process. Judges and citizens in Nevada and many other states have spent long hours studying ways to speed the hearing of cases, to reduce costs so that justice can be made available to all, and to insure the highest quality on the bench. The success of their efforts is measured, as are all aspects of the political process, by how much attention citizens pay to the way the courts function and by how willing they are to work for a good judicial system.

One method of improving the courts is to stimulate judges to keep up to date; the National Judicial College serves this function. It became permanently established at the University of Nevada in Reno in 1965 through the support of a Fleischmann Foundation grant. It conducts seminars for judges on techniques of trial procedures, on court administration, and on other matters relating to continuing education for judges of state courts of general jurisdiction. The college has a library of 50,000 volumes and an extensive periodical collection. More than 10,000 judges and other court officials from among the fifty states have participated in the intensive seminars conducted by a staff of experienced trial judges. Educational values contributed by the college extend beyond the judiciary, because university students of constitutional law and related subjects are permitted to use the law library.

Election of Judges

All federal judges are appointed by the president and confirmed by the Senate; they have life appointments and may be removed against their will only upon conviction under impeachment. Election of judges is the procedure in many states; hence, a state judge may lose his office at the ballot box. Nevada, in company with eighteen other states, elects rather than appoints the state judiciary (1979). In the states that do not provide for selection of the judiciary by the voters, judges are appointed by the governor or elected by the legislature. Most commonly, judges are appointed by the governor from a list of nominees, usually three, prepared by a commission; these judges run for continuation in office at a later election.

The question of whether judges should be elected or appointed is frequently argued. Some people prefer election of judges, because that method widens the involvement of the electorate in the governing process. Most judges, bar associations, and students of the court system, however, favor appointment, because it produces a high-quality bench and eliminates the fear that judicial independence could be threatened by a judge's need to win an election. Certainly the "judicial temperament" and the qualities that make a man a popular candidate can coexist. But it is important that "judicial temperament" be paramount: a jurist must be able, when necessary, to make a widely unpopular decision without jeopardizing his future on the bench.

The Missouri Plan combines voter approval of the judiciary with appointment. Under this plan, judges are appointed by the governor from a list of candidates prepared by a commission of judges, lawyers, and laymen. Following a stipulated period of time during which the appointee serves on the bench, his name is placed on the ballot without an opposing candidate. The voter is asked to approve or disapprove the continuance of the judge in his office. Modifications of the Missouri Plan, in some instances providing for legislative rather than executive selection of the bench, were in effect, in 1979, in fifteen states.

Evidence indicates that such a system retains high-caliber judges and still furnishes involvement of the citizens in the judicial process. Perhaps the Missouri Plan's greatest contribution to judicial excellence is that it spares the judge the experience of conducting an election campaign in which, occasionally, his crowd-pleasing rather than his judicial ability is at issue. Although students of politics increasingly recognize that courts and judges are part of the political process, it appears desirable to limit the accountability of judges to electoral success in order to protect them from external pressure and to insure the independence of the judiciary from retaliation for unpopular decisions.

Pressure to change to some form of the Missouri Plan is mounting in the states that elect judges. The Nevada Legislature authorized the Legislative Council Bureau to study the judicial system and bring recommendations for improving it to the 1969 session. The preliminary report of the subcommittee that undertook the study strongly favored adoption of the Missouri Plan. A citizens' conference on the judiciary was held in Nevada in July 1968 to study the present system and analyze trends in other states; Nevada was the fourteenth state to involve citizens in discussions on selection and retention of judges. The result of these activities was the judiciary amendment that was voted down in 1972; it included some features of the Missouri Plan—specifically, initial appointment of supreme court justices, followed by voter approval.

Persons concerned that the voters' free choice may be reduced if the bench becomes appointive might be surprised to learn that the majority of "elected" judges first attained office by appointment. Because of deaths, resignations, or expansion of the court system, state governors have commonly had many judicial appointments to make. Since such appointments are rarely subject to legislative confirmation and since an incumbent judge running for election is not often opposed and has the usual advantage of the incumbent, the electorate has little to do with the selection of judges. Therefore, the Missouri Plan, with its arrangement for informed initial selection of jurists followed by voter confirmation at established intervals, appears to provide in theory and in practice for a qualified bench and for giving the voters an appropriate voice in determining the continuance of judges in office.

Removal of Judges and Other Elected Officials

There are four methods by which a Nevada Supreme Court justice or district judge may be removed from office *during* a term: recall, impeachment, legislative removal, and removal by the Commission on Judicial Discipline. The number of methods contrasts sharply with the federal system, wherein a judge may be removed only through the impeachment process.[7]

All elected judges in Nevada are subject to removal during their terms through the recall process, which is discussed in Chapter 3.[8] Recall is the only device which can be used to remove a justice of the peace during his term.

Another way to seek removal of an unsatisfactory public official is by impeachment. Provisions for impeachment in the United States Constitution, upon which most states have based their own impeachment provisions, are that the House of Representatives prefers charges[9] against an official, the Senate tries the official, and, to convict, two-thirds of the senators present must vote him guilty. Conviction causes the removal of the official and may be extended to disqualify him from ever again holding a federal office. The framers of the United States Constitution obviously did not wish impeachment to be used lightly or for political retaliation. Only twelve times has a federal officer been impeached, and only four times has the impeachment resulted in a conviction. In July 1974 former president Richard Nixon had three articles of impeachment voted against him by the House Judiciary Committee. His resignation a few weeks later halted the impeachment process.

Nevada is one of forty-nine states that provide for impeachment of state officials and their removal from office upon conviction; Oregon is the lone exception. The Nevada Constitution specifically excludes justices of the peace from being subject to impeachment, perhaps because of the minimal requirements for the office. As in the federal example, impeachment is rarely used at the state level; in all the fifty states, only thirteen governors have been impeached, of whom six were convicted and removed from office.[10] The requirements in the Nevada Constitution[11] for impeachment and conviction are like the federal requirements, with two slight differences. (1) Impeachment charges in Nevada must be brought by a majority of the *elected* members of the assembly, while only a majority of those *present* in the House of Representatives is required at the national level. (2) Conviction in Nevada requires the concurrence of two-thirds of the *elected* members of the Senate, while at the national level two-thirds of the senators *present* suffice to convict.

Another device not included in federal practice is found in Nevada: provision for removal of judges by the legislature. For "reasonable cause," the justices of the supreme court and judges of district courts may be removed from office upon a two-thirds vote of the elected membership of both houses of the legislature. The purpose of this device was to provide a procedure to be used in case of an emergency, such as in a situation where a judge had clearly become mentally incompetent but refused to resign.

In an earlier chapter, the unusual dissatisfaction of Nevadans with the judiciary at the time of the drafting of the constitution was discussed. This dissatisfaction was one reason why the drafters provided for legislative removal of judges for causes that "may or may not be sufficient grounds for impeachment. . . ."[12] Some of the delegates at the constitutional convention were aware that there could be defective judges who were not indictable under the impeachment section, which requires a charge of misdemeanor or malfeasance in office. George A. Nourse (Washoe) made this point very clear. He said:

> . . . there are so many cases where valid reasons may exist for the removal of an officer, although there may not be sufficient cause for impeachment, that I think there should be a provision of this kind. A stupid judge is as bad as a dishonest one, and so is a judge whose habits are such as to disgrace, not only the bench, but the community in which he lives; and yet you cannot get at such a judge without a provision of this kind, unless he commits some wrongful act in the discharge of his duties. There are innumerable cases of men whose incompetency, or something worse, unfits them for the bench, and prevents their doing any good upon it, and yet who cannot be impeached.[13]

James A. Banks (Humboldt) was, however, more afraid that the independence of judges would be lost if they could be removed by the legislature than he was that possibly defective judges would be continued on the bench. He asserted: "There will be no such thing as judicial independence, but on the contrary there will be inaugurated a state of things . . . but little removed from pure Red Republican Democracy—little less than anarchy."[14]

The possibility of expelling judges, whether by recall or be legislative removal, is conceivably a threat to judicial independence. President Taft, who later became chief justice of the United States, was so offended by the idea that a judge could be subject to removal by the voters that he vetoed the admission of Arizona to the Union because its constitution provided for recall of judges. This veto illustrates an important aspect of federal-state relations. Arizona deleted the clause that had offended the president, was admitted to the Union, and then restored the clause providing for recall of judges! This restoration was entirely legal. In 1911 the Supreme Court had enunciated the doctrine that new states were on an equal footing with existing states and not subject to any special requirements different from those applying to all states.[15] Once a state is part of the Union, it has the same rights as any other state—including the right to recall state judges.

The fourth method of removal of judges in Nevada was added by constitutional amendment in 1976 and was based on the California plan for retirement, censure, and removal of judges. The Nevada Commission on Judicial Discipline is composed of two jurists appointed by the supreme court, two attorneys appointed by the board of governors of the state bar, and three non-lawyers appointed by the governor. The commission elects its chairman from among the three lay members. The commission is empowered to make determinations concerning the removal of supreme court justices and district judges for inability to perform or neglect of judicial duties. (An attempt by the 1977 legislature to add jurisdiction over municipal judges to the commission's powers was struck down by a court decision in 1978; the decision is likely to be appealed, however.)

A jurist may appeal the action of the commission to the Nevada Supreme Court. This amendment, although it seems to make judges extraordinarily vulnerable to attempts to remove them, is designed rather to permit a judge to rectify a fault, or possibly to retire, without making his failings unnecessarily public through the cumbersome procedures of impeachment or legislative removal.

The Court System in the Constitutional Convention

The first argument in the convention concerning the judiciary arose over a motion by E. F. Dunne (Humboldt), whose opposition to the constitution was expressed several times at the convention, that a memorial be drafted to Congress requesting a change in the judicial system "in the event of the non-adoption of the Constitution."[16] Dunne explained that everyone recognized a great need for altering the judiciary arrangements of the territory. Because he believed that the constitution would be defeated, he wanted steps taken to start judicial reform.

Opponents of Dunne's resolution argued that it would actually lead to the defeat of the new constitution. Charles E. DeLong (Storey) said:

> I know that many are going to vote for the Constitution in order that we may be released from the present judiciary system; but if we pass a resolution like this, many will say there is no use of adopting the Constitution in order to secure that end, because we can trust it to Congress.[17]

Others who opposed the resolution believed that the purpose of its introduction was to defeat the constitution; all the speakers, however, referred to dissatisfaction with the existing judicial system. The resolution was not adopted.

Following several brief discussions on jurisdiction of the courts, the first substantive argument dealing with the judicial branch concerned the question of whether there should be three or five supreme court justices. James A. Banks (Humboldt), replying to the argument that it would be harder to use improper influence on five men than on three, averred that small bodies are actually less easy to corrupt. He contended that when responsibility is less divided, the public eye can be fixed more steadily on a small group. He also doubted that five qualified jurists could be found, "for if we have five, in all probability there will be one or two blockheads among them, while if the selection is confined to three, there will be a greater probability of our securing not only a pure but an able Supreme judiciary."[18]

DeLong (Storey), reminding his colleagues that one reason for the defeat of the first constitution had been the expense involved in state government, urged the solution ultimately adopted: a three-member supreme court and a provision that the legislature could increase the number to five.

The first, and defeated, constitution had provided for county courts; the draft of the second constitution contained the same provision. These courts would have stood between the justice courts and the district courts and would have had appellate jurisdiction in cases arising in justice court. At the time of the second convention only Storey County had a large enough population to justify establishing a county court; none of the other counties had any need for one. The central dispute in the convention was whether or not one county should have a special, and different, judicial arrangement. The argument that the Nevada judicial pattern should be uniform throughout the state prevailed and no county courts were established.

Throughout the debates on the judicial department there were lengthy and well-informed discussions on jurisdiction of the courts, separation of powers, and the problem of court costs for the poor litigant. Occasional comments were made on the popular belief in the corruptibility of judges, but the delegates were cautious and temperate in their own expressions on this matter and indicated that the charges were unproved.

Chapter 5 ended with a quotation from the convention showing an irreverent attitude toward legislators; the legal profession was not immune from such shafts. Lloyd Frizell (Storey), himself an attorney, observed during a debate on the judiciary: "I read law once myself, and have been admitted to the bar in two States, but I do not think I would ever make a good lawyer, because I am too honest. [Laughter.]"[19]

CHAPTER 8

TAXATION AND INTERGOVERNMENT RELATIONS

TODAY, THE UNITED STATES GOVERNMENT relies mainly upon individual and corporate income taxes to produce its revenue. Nearly three-fourths of the national government's income is derived from these two sources. The largest revenue producers for most of the fifty state governments are sales, individual income, licenses, and corporation net income taxes; the real-property tax usually is levied by county governments. Both the national and state governments tax gasoline, tobacco, and liquor; forty-one states join the national government in levying a personal income tax and forty-six have a corporation income tax. In recent years, increased taxation on tobacco and liquor has been popular with legislators, for such taxation has the advantage of supposedly discouraging people from using products considered detrimental to their health while also providing funds for state services.

Population and State Revenues

Nevada's population has grown erratically from approximately 7,000 people in 1860 to more than 700,000 in 1980. A prodigious increase occurred between 1860 and 1880, followed by a steep decline as the resources of the Comstock dwindled and the treasure seekers left the state. Another abrupt increase was recorded in the first years of the twentieth century, when the wealth of the Tonopah and Goldfield mines brought thousands of people into the state; when the mines ran out, population dropped again. Since the legalization of gambling in 1931, and particularly since the development of big casinos featuring well-known entertainers after World War II, the state's population growth has been uninterrupted. New migrants have been attracted by job opportunities in gambling and the services related to it. People fleeing from metropolitan areas beset with problems of pollution and crime have also moved to Nevada, as have those attracted by favorable taxing arrangements—no state income or inheritance taxes.

TABLE 8.1

NEVADA'S POPULATION BY DECADES

Year	Population	Percentage Difference
1860	6,857	....
1870	42,491	519.67
1880	62,266	46.54
1890	47,355	—23.95
1900	42,335	—10.60
1910	81,875	93.40
1920	77,407	—5.46
1930	91,058	17.64
1940	110,247	21.07
1950	160,083	45.20
1960	285,278	78.21
1970	488,738	71.32
1980 (est.)	702,000	43.64

SOURCE: Compiled by E. Muriel Bennett from data contained in U.S. Department of Commerce, Bureau of the Census, PC (1)–A30 Nevada, 1971, p. 7, and *Nevada State Journal,* February 24, 1980, p. 1.

As Table 8.1 shows, growth in population has been a major characteristic of this state in the post-World War II period. Nevada overtook Vermont and Wyoming in the 1960s; it will pass Delaware and probably both Dakotas in the 1980 census, and at its present rate of growth Nevada's population may surpass that of Montana, Idaho, and New Hampshire by 1990. The Nevada population explosion of the 1960s and 1970s took place mainly in the urban areas; by the end of the seventies, it was estimated that Clark and Washoe counties contained about eighty-two percent of the state's population. At the same time five Nevada counties—Esmeralda, Lincoln, Nye, Pershing, and White Pine—were losing residents in the 1970s. However, increased mining activity sparked by skyrocketing prices for gold and silver and plans of the Carter administration to expend billions of dollars in the construction of MX missile sites in the desert areas of central Nevada in the 1980s presaged a large increase in the population of many rural counties.

Political issues arise from rapid population growth, whether it be in the urban or rural areas. Mounting pressures for expenditures for schools, welfare, roads, and so on become troublesome for the legislature, especially in the face of demands in the late seventies for reductions in taxes.

Have tax revenues kept pace with population growth, and what is the outlook for revenues in the 1980s? The state's general fund revenues increased dramatically in the 1968–1978 decade; a recent study performed by Andrew P. Grose, director of research for the Legislative Counsel Bureau, has determined that all but 37 percent of the 217 percent increase in the revenues can be accounted for by inflation and the increase of the population over the same ten-year period.[1] The energy crisis threatens to slow the explosive growth of the gaming industry and tourism which occurred in the 1970s. However, the 14.7 percent increase in state revenue in calendar year 1979 from the tax on casino gross winnings of $2.12 billion is an indication that Nevada's principal industry is still healthy and will continue to be a major source of revenue.

Gambling Taxes

By the 1970s, gambling taxes had become the largest source of revenue for the state general fund. In the 1977–78 fiscal year, gambling taxes accounted for 43.7 percent of general fund revenue, with the bulk of the money coming from the state tax on the *gross* gambling income of the casinos. When net profits of the casinos fell during the 1974–75 recession because of increased expenditures to attract tourists, the state's revenues actually increased because of the gross-income criterion. The tax on gambling tables is split equally among the seventeen counties and is a very important source of income for the smaller-population counties.

Nevada benefitted in the 1970s by congressional legislation that returned a large percentage of proceeds from the federal slot machine tax to the state. Due to the efforts of a handful of state legislators and the support of Governor O'Callaghan and the Nevada congressional delegation, Congress in 1971 stipulated that 80 percent of the slot machine tax should be returned to the state's treasury, earmarked for education. The 1977 legislature, at the behest of athletic boosters on the two university campuses, petitioned Congress to increase the rebate to 95 percent; the next year Congress went even farther and decided to phase out the annual federal tax of $250 per slot machine entirely. The 1979 Nevada Legislature then passed a measure providing a state slot machine tax to replace the federal tax when the latter is eliminated.

Until 1978 Nevada was unique among the states in allowing most forms of casino gambling. However, New Jersey broke that monopoly, and other states are considering the legalization of gambling as a ''painless'' means of producing revenue during a time when the voters are in rebellion against high taxes. Actually, taxes on horse race betting, which is legal in thirty-two states, produced more revenue for the states of New York and California during the 1976–77 fiscal year than state gaming taxes did for Nevada.[2] Of course, gambling taxes provide a greater proportion of state revenue in Nevada than in any other state.

Although fourteen other states have established state-operated lotteries in recent years, the Nevada Constitution prohibits lotteries and the sale of lottery tickets. An attempt to amend the constitution by initiative to establish a private lottery was defeated by the voters in 1968. The amendment was vigorously opposed by then-Governor Paul Laxalt, other public officials, and various business and civic groups who feared that private operation would jeopardize the whole meticulously ordered structure of state controlled gambling. They were particularly concerned that a lottery managed by a private association might violate interstate commerce laws and so call down extensive federal activity in Nevada's primary industry. The voters rejected the proposition unambiguously; more than 75 percent of those voting voted no. Two lottery bills were introduced in the 1975 legislative session. One would have established a state operated lottery similar to those already functioning in thirteen states; the other would have authorized charities to conduct lotteries. Neither received serious consideration.

Voter rejection of private lotteries and legislative indifference to state operated lotteries, except to counterbalance privately operated ones, mark the death of lotteries in Nevada. They have been rejected partly because government officials and most of the voters believe that lottery operations might arouse antagonism in neighboring states and unsettle gambling arrangements in general, and partly because they doubt that lotteries would generate any appreciable revenue.

The Sales Tax

The sales tax is the largest single source of tax revenue for the overwhelming number of states; in fact, in 1977 the tax was responsible for over half of all the state tax revenues in the nation.[3] However, in Nevada the 2 percent tax accounted for only 38.7 percent of the general fund revenues in the 1977–78 fiscal year.

Nevada did not impose a sales tax until 1955, when the legislature felt compelled to do so because of the critical need for additional revenue to support the public schools and the university. The 2 percent general sales and use tax was placed on the ballot by a referendum petition in 1956 and was upheld by the voters by a better than two-to-one majority. The state constitution provides that a law approved in a referendum cannot be changed except by vote of the people. Thus, when the 1963 legislature felt the need to increase the tax from 2 to 3 percent to provide more funds for the public schools, the proposal had to go to the voters, who turned down the increase decisively. Faced with this verdict of the people, Senator Carl Dodge of Fallon introduced in the 1967 legislative session a 1 percent "school-support" tax which would be collected at the same time as the 2 percent sales tax, with the proviso that the 1 percent would be returned to the county of origin and earmarked for the support of the public schools.[4] Opponents of the tax argued that it was a subterfuge to get around the constitutional restriction on the legislature, but the Nevada Supreme Court ruled in a two-to-one vote that the tax provided revenues for the schools and not for the general fund as did the original sales tax.[5]

The "school-support" tax opened the door for the 1969 legislature to pass a county-option half-cent tax, with the proceeds to be used by city and county governments. Voters approved of legislative recommendations to remove the sales tax from prescription drugs and food in 1970 and 1978, respectively. However, the sales tax on food will be restored if the voters approve the constitutional amendment initiative to reduce property taxes in the 1980 election.

In most counties in Nevada, the sales tax amounts to 3½ percent (taking into account the 1 percent "school-support" and the ½ percent county taxes). This percentage is exceeded by twenty-eight states which have the sales tax, with Connecticut's 7 percent being the highest in the country.

The State Highway Fund

Most fiscal experts agree that the tax on motor vehicle fuel, earmarked in Nevada and most states for the construction and upkeep of highways and streets, is the fairest of all taxes, because the people using the roads are paying for them. However, as the national freeway program was being completed in the late 1970s and early 1980s, Nevada and other states were faced with shortages of highway funds to maintain their roads and highways because of three major factors: less federal money, inflationary construction costs, and the fact that people were paying less fuel taxes because of fuel conservation. One of the reasons why the motor vehicle fuel revenue did not keep pace with inflation is that the tax is levied on gallons sold rather than on cost; otherwise, the skyrocketing increases in gasoline prices might have increased the revenue by a sufficient amount to keep up with inflation. Given the circumstances, it appears that either the state tax on motor vehicle fuel will have to be increased in the near future or else revenue from the state general fund will have to be used to supplement the highway fund.

Counties and cities also have the responsibility of keeping certain roads and streets in repair. Although Governor List opposed an increase in the state motor vehicle fuel tax in 1979, he did go along with the legislature's approval of an optional 2 cents addition to the local tax on gasoline for motor vehicles, with such an increase dependent upon proposal by the board of county commissioners and approval by the voters.

Other State Taxes

In addition to the revenue from the gaming and sales taxes, receipts from the casino entertainment, liquor, and insurance premium taxes go into the state general fund. In recent years many legislators have favored a constitutional amendment to allow the levying of an estate tax which would take advantage of a federal tax credit which is allowed states which have their own tax: no additional taxes on an estate would be collected. Opponents of the amendment fear that some wealthy individuals who plan to retire in Nevada because the state does not have an estate tax would go elsewhere, not realizing that the state tax would not enlarge the size of the total tax on the estate. A proposed constitutional amendment was passed by the 1975 legislature but failed in the 1977 session. The 1979 legislature resurrected and passed the amendment; if approved again by the 1981 legislature it will go on the ballot in the 1982 election.

Nevada imposes a cigarette tax; its proceeds are distributed monthly to the counties on the basis of the latest federal census figures. In the two large-population counties, the county's revenue is split among the incorporated cities on the basis of their respective populations in the census. All fifty states levy such a tax, with only ten states assessing a lower tax than Nevada's ten cents a pack.

In four significant areas of taxation, Nevada differs from an over-whelming number of states. The majority of states, forty-one, tax personal income; Nevada does not, even though for many years Nevada has had one of the highest per capita incomes in the United States. One of the reasons the Nevada Legislature is not likely to impose an income tax is because it would fall almost entirely on residents of the state; therefore, an increase in gaming taxes is more likely because they are largely paid from money collected from tourists. Nevada is also one of only four states that does not levy a corporate income tax. Nor does the state have an inheritance tax, which is levied on a person who inherits property, or an estate tax, which is levied on the net amount of the deceased's property. As pointed out above, Nevada is alone in not imposing estate or inheritance taxes; the Nevada Constitution expressly prohibits such taxes.

The Property Tax

Throughout most of Nevada's history, the property tax was the main source of revenue to the state's general fund. However, the legalization of gambling in 1931 and the passage of the sales tax in 1955 enabled the state legislature to relinquish all but a small portion of the property tax to local governmental units; the state's share of the tax was totally eliminated by the 1979 legislature. The property tax was established in the original constitution; in 1936 the people approved an amendment that limits the tax to "five cents on one dollar of assessed valuation." Then in 1963, the legislature mandated that property be assessed in Nevada at 35 percent of real market value and be reassessed at least every five years. The increase in the property tax during the 1968–1978 period did not keep pace with inflation and population growth,[6] perhaps because many of the county assessors did not have the manpower to make reassessments in timely enough fashion to keep up with the explosive growth in property values during the decade.

In 1978 the voters approved a constitutional amendment placed on the ballot via the initiative process which, if approved a second time in the 1980 general election, would roll back property values to the 1975–76 assessments for tax purposes and limit the property tax to one percent of market value. Most legislators were concerned about the equity of another provision of the initiative that would assess all property sold after

1975–76 at 35 percent of the sales price. Thus, homes in the same neighborhood with the same initial cost would be assessed at different values when sales occurred.

In order to counter the appeal of the proposed constitutional amendment, the 1979 legislature enacted a tax-reduction package that included a limit on the total property tax of 3.64 cents on each dollar of assessed valuation and the elimination of the tax on all household goods and furniture in single-family dwellings. This tax reduction, along with the aforementioned elimination of the sales tax on food, will "self-destruct" if the constitutional amendment is approved.

State Debt Limit

Congress has the power to set the debt limit for the national government; the Nevada Legislature does not have this type of financial flexibility. It is authorized to contract public debts but is severely limited by the constitutional stipulation that the debt may not exceed 1 percent of the assessed valuation of the state.[7] According to the constitution, determination of the state's assessed valuation is made by compiling the reports of each of the county assessors. The limitation to 1 percent has made some state operations very difficult and has made others impossible. An effort was made in 1960 to secure voter approval of an amendment that would increase the debt limit to 2 percent, but the effort failed: 73 percent of those voting on the amendment opposed it. Again, in 1968, voter approval was sought on an amendment to increase the debt limit, this time to 3 percent. Once more the voters rejected the increase, but by a smaller margin, 54 percent; the better showing in the 1968 election was the result of efforts by then-Governor Laxalt and other officials and business leaders to convince the public that necessary capital improvements depended upon passage of the measure. An amendment to raise the debt limit to 3 percent appeared once again on the 1974 ballot. This time the governor, Mike O'Callaghan, opposed the measure. Other public leaders were not active in explaining the need for the increase or in urging passage of the amendment. It lost by a wide margin. Seventy percent of those voting voted no.

Normally, capital construction for state buildings, including higher education facilities, is funded by the selling of bonds which are retired over a twenty-year period. The debt limit would have sharply curtailed construction of needed buildings during the rapid population growth of the 1970s if it had not been for the large state surpluses that accumulated during each biennial budget period. The legislature tended to use most of the surpluses for "one-shot" capital construction projects rather than for increases in ongoing operating expenses that would be likely to continue at the higher levels in future budgets. The state saved a considerable

10

amount of interest costs by such "pay-as-you-go" financing, although some financial experts pointed out that the high inflation of the period would have meant retirement of the bonds with devalued dollars.

Relation Between Federal and State Constitutions

All fifty states manage their own territories under the authority of their respective state constitutions, but there is a "higher law" in every state— the United States Constitution. That document is supreme and no state constitution or state law may contravene it. The supremacy of the national Constitution and of acts of Congress made under its authority is stated directly and unequivocally in the document itself. Conflicts between the national and a state government do not arise, then, over the propriety of the national government's right to finality in the sphere of its competence. Rather, they arise over the question of whether a particular act *is* within the competence of the national government or is, instead, reserved to the states by the Constitution.

Disputes over jurisdiction occur in all federal systems; they are not peculiar to United States federalism. The national Constitution grants certain powers to the central government and prohibits the exercise of certain powers by the nation, by the states, or by both; the remaining powers are "reserved" to the states. It is obvious that neither the federal Constitution nor any state constitution can describe the total and precise range of each government's authority. There are bound to be areas in which powers overlap and areas in which the power of either government to act is unclear. So disputes will inevitably arise between the nation and the states. It follows that there must be an authority superior to both nation and states to settle disagreements over which government is entitled to exercise a given power. This authority need not be a court.

The nature of this peculiarly federal problem can be observed in the conflict in recent years between the national government and some of the state governments over civil rights, defendants' rights, and legislative apportionment. Serious friction has arisen over federal efforts to secure desegregation of schools and other public facilities, to require state courts to supply legal counsel and other protections to the accused, and to determine the basis upon which state legislatures must be apportioned. Some of the states have insisted that these matters are solely within their own jurisdiction and that federal action is an illegal intrusion into concerns reserved by the United States Constitution to each state.

A conspicuous instance of federal-state conflict is the refusal of some states to comply with a Supreme Court decision[8] that it is unconstitutional to segregate children in public schools on the basis of color. Although the Court recognized that educational policy is basically within the control of the states, it found that the overriding consideration in the matter of school admission policy is the requirement of the Fourteenth Amendment that no state may deprive any person of the equal protection of the laws. The Court held that separating children into different schools because of their color was a denial of equal protection and was, therefore, unconstitutional. The equal protection clause was also the main basis upon which federal action was justified in state criminal procedures and in apportionment.

Most people do not question the Supreme Court's position as ultimate determiner of the meaning of the Constitution, whether they agree with a particular Court decision or not. They accept, for example, the national government's efforts to secure admission of black Americans to public schools on an equal basis with white Americans as *legally* correct, even though some of them may deplore the political or social consequences of school desegregation. Good citizens are entirely free to disagree with a Court decision, as they have done throughout our history, and are entirely free to seek reversal of a decision to which they object. But the right of the Court to interpret the Constitution is as firmly established by precedent as is the right to the public to protest a particular Court decision and to try to have it reversed.

Nevada and the Federal Constitution

The Nevada Constitution is unusual in specifically stating the primacy of the national government in its sphere of competence and in specifically stating that the federal Supreme Court is the interpreter of the intent and application of the national Constitution. Nevada's Declaration of Rights states:

> But the paramount allegiance of every citizen is due to the Federal Government, in the exercise of all its constitutional powers, as the same have been, or may be, defined by the Supreme Court of the United States, and no power exists in the people of this or any other state of the Federal Union to dissolve their connection therewith, or perform any act tending to impair, subvert, or resist the supreme authority of the Government of the United States.[9]

This statement, reflecting great devotion to the nation, is a reminder that Nevada's admission to the Union occurred during the Civil War.

The Nevada Constitution not only says that a citizen's paramount allegiance is to the national government but also declares that the limits of the national government's power to act are rightfully determined by the Supreme Court. The Nevada Constitution recognizes that the federal Constitution is not a self-interpreting document and requires that when the Supreme Court has decided that a contested power is properly within the jurisdiction of the national government, its ruling must be obeyed. So it is unlikely that a conflict could ever develop between Nevada and the national government comparable to the conflict that has developed in some southern states. Nevadans could hardly claim that, in determining where a disputed power lies, the Supreme Court had exceeded its authority, since their own constitution says that the Court defines the constitutional power of the national government.

Jurisdictional disputes between Nevada and the national government have normally not been of great consequence. However, in the 1970s problems developed between Nevada ranchers, backed by the Nevada congressional delegation, and the Bureau of Land Management, which administers the federal land that amounts to about 87 percent of the state's total acreage. The 1979 Nevada Legislature went so far as to lay claim to most of the federal land for the state, on the basis that most of the eastern states have little federal land and that the western states should be able to claim similar treatment under the "equal footing" doctrine. However, the federal government rested its case for control of the land on the fact that one of Congress's conditions for admitting Nevada to the Union stipulated that the state constitution contain a disclaimer to any right over unappropriated public lands in the territory. The "irrevocable" ordinance which precedes the Nevada Constitution states that such public lands "shall be and remain at the sole and entire disposition of the United States."

The use of the federal land in Nevada became controversial in another matter in late 1979 and 1980 when the Air Force, with the backing of President Carter, unveiled its plans to construct a multi-billion dollar racetrack system for the MX missile in central Nevada. At first, Governor List and most Nevadans who were surveyed supported the project, primarily because of the purported economic benefits for the eastern and central areas of the state. However, when the environmental and socioeconomic implications were developed, the governor, other political leaders, and many citizens began to be critical of the proposal. Damage to the environment, the "boom and bust" economic impact, and water problems were cited by critics, along with the contention that the missile system would become a prime target in the event of a nuclear war. However, the Air Force and the administration held the trump card in the dispute: the area in question was federal land; furthermore, the 1955 legislature had enacted legislation giving consent to the United States to acquire any land in the state for defense purposes, upon the authorization of Congress.[10] Thus, the only recourse for Nevadans opposed to the MX-missile project was an appeal to Congress to refuse to appropriate the funds for construction.

Cooperative Relations Between Federal and State Governments

An area of federal-state relationship more enduringly significant than the "conflict of laws" sketched above is that of cooperative action between the nation and the fifty states. This cooperative action is various and extensive; grants-in-aid programs, such as aid to dependent children and aid to the blind, are typical activities for which the national government provides money to the states. Grants are usually made on a matching-fund basis, the national government stipulating the amount it will provide and the amount Nevada, or any state cooperating with the national government on a project, must provide to be eligible for federal assistance. The national government also establishes standards by which the joint funds must be disbursed to insure fairness and to insure that the money will be used to achieve Congress's purpose; to receive federal funds, then, the states must comply with the federal rules for distribution.

Grants are made available by Congress to support activities that Congress believes will benefit the people and that some of the states would not or could not undertake without federal prodding or assistance.

Federal funds are also available for projects not related to aiding the indigent or unfortunate. Federal-state activities in highway construction, farm programs, and prevention of water pollution are examples of such jointly sponsored projects.

In 1972, the Nixon administration developed a system called "revenue sharing" by which funds were distributed to state and local governments on a noncategorical basis, meaning that the money was granted without federal supervision of how or where it could be spent.

Although intergovernment activity has been criticized, particularly by people who fear that the federal government is encroaching upon areas reserved to the states, federal aid appears to be an established fact of political life. Efforts to reverse the states' dependence upon federal funds and to stimulate the states to assume greater financial responsibility for their own programs have not succeeded. Some of the reasons are: states do not want to raise their own taxes for the various programs; some states do not have enough taxable revenue to continue the programs unaided; some state politicians, although distrusting federal involvement in their states, do not move to discontinue federal aid because they fear the political consequences of abandoning certain programs more than they fear the alleged invasions of states' rights. Thus, Nevada participates in a number of intergovernment programs, such as aid to the blind, to dependent children, and to the chronically ill; civil defense; highway construction; employment security; and social security.

Local Units of Government

The four tiers of government in which nearly all citizens are involved—national, state, county, and city—to say nothing of the many special boards and districts that affect citizens' attitudes toward government—are baffling in their complexity and the overlapping of their functions. Even so, it is important to observe the formal structure of county and municipal government and to note the basic lines along which responsibility is delegated to these units. The Nevada Legislature, in obedience to its constitutional responsibilities, has established the organizational pattern within which cities and counties must operate and has granted sufficient power, presumably, to the two local entities of government for them to carry out their assigned tasks. Thus, the cities and counties of Nevada are subdivisions of the state, possessing powers derived from the state. In general, these powers are subject to withdrawal or modification by the legislature. Cities and counties, then, do not bear the same relationship to the state as the state does to the national government, since a state's powers do not derive from grants by the national government and are not subject to revocation or to direct modification by the national government.

The Nevada Legislature has the authority to create new counties; it last used this power in 1919 when it divided Humboldt County to create Pershing County. An amendment to the state constitution, approved in 1940, restricts the legislature's otherwise complete control over county boundaries by stipulating that no county can be abolished without the approval of the majority of the county's voters.[11] It would probably be very difficult to combine one of the small counties with a larger one because of this constitutional provision, despite the views of some scholars that several of Nevada's counties have too few people to form the financial base for efficient operation of a county.[12] (For example, Esmeralda, Eureka, and Storey counties contain fewer than a thousand people each.) In addition to the strong historical sentiment against doing away with the county identity, there are probably enough relatives and friends of county office holders in each of the sparsely-populated counties to vote down any move to abolish the county. Another factor in the present ability of the small-population counties to fund the salaries of county officials and to maintain county buildings can be attributed to the equal division of the gambling table tax revenue among the seventeen counties.

All sixteen counties and the one city-county in Nevada have a similar basic organizational structure, namely multimember boards that combine executive and legislative functions. The Carson City-Ormsby County merger in 1968 formed the first city-county unit in the state. Carson City is managed by a five-member board of supervisors, Clark County by a seven-member board of commissioners, and Washoe and Douglas counties by five-member boards. The remaining counties are governed by three-member boards. All commissioners serve four-year terms; salaries are established by the legislature. Vacancies on the county boards are filled by the governor. Terms and salaries of other county officials—district attorneys, sheriffs, clerks, assessors, treasurers, recorders—are also fixed by the legislature. Counties are empowered to employ a manager, and the trend in populous counties throughout the United States has been to do so; Carson City, Churchill, Clark, Elko, Mineral, and Washoe have managers. Major responsibilities of county governments are to provide judicial, public health, and certain welfare services. The primary source of revenue for counties is the real-property tax.

Cities also derive their power directly from the legislature. The legislative grants of power to cities in Nevada are broader than they are to counties: cities exercise general governmental power within their own boundaries, whereas counties have only the powers specifically granted to them. The trend in city government is toward "home rule." Home rule permits the city freedom of decision in major areas and frees it from having to go repeatedly to the state legislature for approval of measures. Boulder City has a home rule charter; the other cities in Nevada are organized under general or special charters. A general charter, as the title suggests, is a standard form of city government drawn up by the legislature that permits creation of a municipal government under its terms; Ely and Winnemucca are examples of cities organized under the general charter. A special charter—again the title suggests its nature—is usually drafted by a city to reflect its particular requirements, requirements that for various reasons could not be satisfied under the general charter. The special charter must be approved, of course, by the legislature. Elko, Las Vegas, and Reno are governed by special charters, as are the majority of Nevada cities. Most are run by the mayor-council form of government. The larger cities employ a city manager for the regular day-to-day operation of government; the manager is responsible to the city council.

There are two methods whereby a city charter may be amended. The common approach is amendment by the legislature, which may so act at any time. Normally a proposal for amendment by the legislature is made by the city council. The other method of changing the charter may be accomplished without reference to the legislature. If a petition is signed by registered voters of the city equal in number to 15 percent or more of voters who cast ballots in the last preceding general municipal election, a proposed amendment is placed on the ballot at the next general municipal election.[13]

An innovative realignment of Clark County's government was passed by the 1975 legislature. It provided for consolidating the government functions of Las Vegas with those of certain adjacent areas. The plan was devised (1) to effect savings in taxes by eliminating overlapping services, (2) to provide for coordinated planning, and (3) to increase government accountability to the voters. However, the Nevada Supreme Court ruled that the consolidation plan violated the constitution because it was special legislation not applying uniformly throughout the state.[14]

Educational Governance

Although the administration of the public schools and higher education in Nevada is not part of the executive branch, the funding of education is one of the principal concerns of the governor and the money committees of the Nevada Legislature. In the 1977–78 fiscal year, approximately 55 percent of the expenditures from the state general fund was used for the support of education.

The 1955 Nevada Legislature consolidated the public school districts into seventeen districts, with the boundaries being coterminous with county boundaries. Nevada thus acted well in advance of the majority of states in achieving consolidation reform. The seventeen district school boards have considerable autonomy over the operation of the schools in their areas. Each district superintendent is selected by and serves at the pleasure of the elected school board. On the state level, the nine-member State Board of Education is elected from three geographical areas, with five from Clark County, two from Washoe, and two from the remainder of the state. The state superintendent of public instruction was an elective position for most of the state's history; in 1956 a constitutional amendment made the office appointive by the state board.

The nine-member board of regents of the University of Nevada System controls all public higher education in Nevada. Regents are elected for six-year terms from the same geographical areas as are members of the State Board of Education, with apportionment also being the same. The first woman regent, Edna C. Baker, was elected in 1916; the first Chinese-American regent, Lilly Fong, was elected in 1974 and re-elected in 1978; and the first black regent, Brenda Mason, was elected in 1974. The regents set policy and oversee the operation of the two university campuses in Las Vegas and Reno; the community colleges, of which there were four in 1980 (Northern Nevada, Clark County, Western Nevada, and Truckee Meadows); and the Desert Research Institute, located just north of the Reno campus. The board selects a system chancellor and presidents of the various campuses, all of whom serve at its pleasure.

Since 1959, Nevada has been a member of the Western Interstate Commission for Higher Education, which operates a professional student exchange program. Under the WICHE program, the state of Nevada presently pays fees to cooperating professional schools in other western states in dentistry, law, optometry, physical therapy, and veterinary medicine as partial tuition payment for a set number of Nevada residents. The number of students who receive assistance in each field is recommended to the governor by Nevada's three WICHE commissioners, with the governor in turn making a recommendation to the legislature for funding.

Supporters of the establishment of a medical school in Nevada have been successful whereas the backers of a law school have not. In 1966, the university board of regents, with the strong urging of two members who were physicians, recommended that a two-year medical school be established on the Reno campus. The regents argued that not enough Nevada students were being admitted to medical school under the WICHE program; with a two-year program of its own, positions for the last two years could be arranged either through WICHE schools or by bilateral contracts with medical schools in other parts of the nation. Strong opposition to the proposed medical school surfaced in the 1967 session of the legislature because of the long-range budget implications; it appeared that a resolution supporting establishment of the school would be defeated. At a critical time in the legislative consideration, word was received from an aide of Howard Hughes, who was ensconced in the penthouse of the Desert Inn in Las Vegas at the time, that the multimillionaire recluse was willing to make a gift of $6 million to the medical school, payable over a period of twenty years. The offer turned the tide, changing enough votes to assure legislative approval of the resolution; the assembly passage was by unrecorded voice vote and the senate divided along regional lines with all Clark County senators opposing the resolution.[15] The vote in the 1969 legislative session granting initial appropriations for the health sciences program was also regional; only one senator broke ranks with the other twenty-three Clark County legislators and supported the funding.[16] The board of regents requested that the 1977 legislature expand the program to four years. The medical school faculty and supporters among the state's physicians were very effective in their lobbying efforts, and the resolution passed with almost no opposition. Indeed, the resolution had thirty-nine co-sponsors in the assembly!

Students and faculty at the University of Nevada, Las Vegas, spearheaded a drive to establish a law school on their campus in the early 1970s. The 1973 legislature asked the board of regents to set up an ad hoc board to study the issue and report to the 1975 session. Although some members of the study board favored establishment of a law school on the Reno campus because of the presence there of the National Judicial College (see chapter 7) and its excellent law library, it was obvious that a majority of the study group, the regents, and the legislature would not support having both the medical school and a law school on the Reno campus. Therefore, the study board, noting that a law school is one of the least expensive of the professional schools and that the majority of the population resided in the Las Vegas area, recommended that a school be established at UNLV. Governor O'Callaghan did not include the law school in his executive budget, perhaps at least partially because the board of governors of the state bar association opposed the law school, citing the large number of attorneys already practicing in the state. The legislature finally provided a compromise of sorts by not funding the law school but agreeing to provide partial tuition support for eighteen new law students each year through the WICHE exchange program. The basic reason for the success of the much more costly medical school proposal and the defeat of the law school seemed to be the difference in attitudes of the respective professional associations in Nevada.

The state's first community college was established in Elko in 1967 through the efforts of local people and the vigorous support of then-Governor Paul Laxalt. It appeared at first that the community college system would not get off the ground, for the special session of the legislature in 1968 refused to make an appropriation for the college at Elko. However, once again Howard Hughes came to the rescue by donating $250,000, half of it earmarked for a feasibility study of possible sites for other community colleges and the other half going to the Elko college. A question was raised about the governing board for community colleges. A 1968 opinion by then-Attorney General Robert List held that the state constitution required that any tax-supported institution offering college-level courses must be under control of the University of Nevada Board of Regents. Thus, despite the complaints of those favoring a separate board for the community colleges, Nevada has just one governing board for higher education.

The Clark County and Western Nevada community colleges were established in the early 1970s, with the latter having campuses in Carson City and Reno. In 1979, the Reno campus became the separate Truckee Meadows Community College.

Financing Education

Since the "school-support" tax was enacted by the Nevada Legislature in 1967, financing of public education has been on a sound footing.[17] A legislative special session to "bail out" school districts financially has not been necessary since 1966.

Although the state's prosperous economy in the 1970s made possible increases in state support for public education in order to cope with inflation, the outlook for the 1980s is not so favorable. The 1979 legislature imposed spending "caps" on local governments and school districts; increases in the future will be allowed only on the bases of increased enrollment and 80 percent of the inflation which has occurred.[18] A comparative statistic of great concern to many educators in the state discloses that Nevada had the highest pupil-teacher ratio of any state in the nation in 1976.[19]

During the 1975–77 biennium, the legislature appropriated about 22 percent of the state general fund expenditures for the support of the operating budget of the University of Nevada System and the WICHE student exchange program.[20] The average expenditure per full-time student placed Nevada *forty-fifth* among the fifty states.[21] This comparatively low rating in spending for higher education, which does not take into account capital expenditures, is even more striking when it is considered that Nevada ranked *fourth* among states in per capita income in 1977.[22]

Conclusion

Nevada is one of the fastest-growing states in the nation and there is evidence that its growth rate will remain high. Making policies to manage this rapid growth is the central governmental problem for the state. New residents, although they are generally viewed as a great asset, bring with them the need for more classrooms, more parking spaces in already congested downtown areas, more water, and more frequent street repair—in general, the need for more services. There arises the crucial question of how to pay for these needed services. The will and the capacity to find solutions to this problem in Nevada, as in all the states, determine whether we have "good" government. They determine how well satisfied the majority of citizens are with what their government does. And they determine how well the citizens will accept the taxes they must pay to enable their government to function. Direct participation by the citizens in their government enlarges their sense of community responsibility for education, public health, and myriad other matters.

As in all democratic systems, the final decisions in Nevada are made by the people. The extent to which the citizens understand government, discuss government, and participate in government is the true test of free government and the best measure of its capacity to endure.

APPENDIX

CONSTITUTION OF THE STATE OF NEVADA

(As amended to June 1980)

PRELIMINARY ACTION

[Preamble]

WHEREAS, The act of Congress approved March twenty-first, A.D. eighteen hundred and sixty-four, "To enable the people of the Territory of Nevada to form a constitution and state government, and for the admission of such state into the Union on an equal footing with the original states," requires that the members of the convention for framing said constitution shall, after organization, on behalf of the people of said territory, adopt the constitution of the United States; therefore be it

[Untited States constitution adopted]

Resolved, That the members of this convention, elected by the authority of the aforesaid enabling act of Congress, assembled in Carson City, the capital of said Territory of Nevada, and immediately subsequent to its organization, do adopt, on behalf of the people of said territory, the constitution of the United States.

ORDINANCE

[Ordinance made irrevocable]

In obedience to the requirements of an act of the Congress of the United States, approved March twenty-first, A.D. eighteen hundred and sixty-four, to enable the people of Nevada to form a constitution and state government, this convention, elected and convened in obedience to said enabling act, do ordain as follows, and this ordinance shall be irrevocable, without the consent of the United States and the people of the State of Nevada:

[Slavery prohibited]

First. That there shall be in this state neither slavery nor involuntary servitude, otherwise than in the punishment for crimes, whereof the party shall have been duly convicted.

[Freedom of worship secured]

Second. That perfect toleration of religious sentiment shall be secured, and no inhabitant of said state shall ever be molested, in person or property, on account of his or her mode of religious worship.

[Right to public land disclaimed]

Third. That the people inhabiting said territory do agree and declare, that they forever disclaim all right and title to the unappropriated public lands lying within said territory, and that the same shall be and remain at the sole and entire disposition of the United States; and that lands belonging to citizens of the United States, residing without the said state, shall never be taxed higher than the land belonging to the residents thereof; and that no taxes shall be imposed by said state on lands or property therein belonging to, or which may hereafter be purchased by, the United States, unless otherwise provided by the Congress of the United States.

The Ordinance was amended in 1956 by addition of the final phrase "unless otherwise provided . . ."; these words were added to permit Nevada to tax certain federal property if congressional action provided for such taxation.

Preamble

[Constitution proclaimed]

We, the people of the State of Nevada, grateful to Almighty God for our freedom, in order to secure its blessings, insure domestic tranquility, and form a more perfect government, do establish this

CONSTITUTION

ARTICLE I

DECLARATION OF RIGHTS

[Declaration of rights]

SECTION 1. All men are, by nature, free and equal, and have certain inalienable rights, among which are those of enjoying and defending life and liberty; acquiring, possessing and protecting property, and pursuing and obtaining safety and happiness.

[Paramount allegiance; right of secession denied]

SEC. 2. All political power is inherent in the people. Government is instituted for the protection, security and benefit of the people; and they have the right to alter or reform the same whenever the public good may require it. But the paramount allegiance of every citizen is due to the federal government, in the exercise of all its constitutional powers, as the same have been, or may be, defined by the supreme court of the United States, and no power exists in the people of this or any other state of the federal union to dissolve their connection therewith, or perform any act tending to impair, subvert, or resist the supreme authority of the government of the United States. The constitution of the United States confers full power on the federal government to maintain and perpetuate its existence, and whensoever any portion of the states, or people thereof, attempt to secede from the federal union, or forcibly resist the execution of its laws, the federal government may, by warrant of the constitution, employ armed force in compelling obedience to its authority.

[Trial by jury secured]

SEC. 3.   The right of trial by jury shall be secured to all, and remain inviolate forever; but a jury trial may be waived by the parties in all civil cases, in the manner to be prescribed by law; and in civil cases, if three-fourths of the jurors agree upon a verdict, it shall stand and have the same force and effect as a verdict by the whole jury; *provided,* the legislature, by a law passed by a two-thirds vote of all the members elected to each branch thereof, may require a unanimous verdict, notwithstanding this provision.

[Freedom of worship secured]

SEC. 4.   The free exercise and enjoyment of religious profession and worship, without discrimination or preference, shall forever be allowed in this state; and no person shall be rendered incompetent to be a witness on account of his opinions on matters of his religious belief; but the liberty of conscience hereby secured shall not be so construed as to excuse acts of licentiousness, or justify practices inconsistent with the peace or safety of this state.

[Habeas corpus suspended, when]

SEC. 5.   The privilege of the writ of *habeas corpus* shall not be suspended, unless when, in cases of rebellion or invasion, the public safety may require its suspension.

[Bail, fines, and punishments limited]

SEC. 6.   Excessive bail shall not be required, nor excessive fines imposed; nor shall cruel or unusual punishments be inflicted; nor shall witnesses be unreasonably detained.

SEC. 7.   All persons shall be bailable by sufficient sureties, unless for capital offenses when the proof is evident or the presumption great.

[Presentment, indictment, and information; double jeopardy; due process]

SEC. 8.   No person shall be tried for a capital or other infamous crime (except in cases of impeachment, and in cases of the militia when in actual service, and the land and naval forces in time of war or which this state may keep, with the consent of Congress, in time of peace, and in cases of petit larceny, under the regulation of the legislature) except on presentment or indictment of the grand jury, or upon information duly filed by a district attorney, or attorney-general of the state, and in any trial, in any court whatever, the party accused shall be allowed to appear and defend in person, and with counsel, as in civil actions. No person shall be subject to be twice put in jeopardy for the same offense; nor shall he be compelled, in any criminal case, to be witness against himself, nor be deprived of life, liberty, or property, without due process of law; nor shall private property be taken for public use without just compensation having been first made, or secured, except in cases of war, riot, fire, or great public peril, in which case compensation shall be afterward made.

[Freedom of speech and press]

SEC. 9.   Every citizen may freely speak, write and publish his sentiments on all subjects, being responsible for the abuse of that right; and no law shall be passed to restrain or abridge the liberty of speech or of the press. In all criminal prosecutions and civil actions for libels the truth may be given in evidence to the jury, and if it shall appear to the jury that the matter charged as libelous is true, and was published with good motives, and for justifiable ends, the party shall be acquitted or exonerated.

[Right of assembly and petition]

SEC. 10.   The people shall have the right freely to assemble together to consult for the common good, to instruct their representatives, and to petition the legislature for redress of grievances.

[Military establisment limited]

SEC. 11.   The military shall be subordinate to the civil power. No standing army shall be maintained by this state in time of peace, and in time of war no appropriation for a standing army shall be for a longer time than two years.

[Soldiers quartered, how]

SEC. 12.   No soldier shall, in time of peace, be quartered in any house without the consent of the owner, nor in time of war, except in the manner to be prescribed by law.

[Representation]

SEC. 13.   Representation shall be apportioned according to population.

[Debtor's property exempt from execution]

SEC. 14.   The privilege of the debtor to enjoy the necessary comforts of life shall be recognized by wholesome laws, exempting a reasonable amount of property from seizure or sale for payment of any debts or liabilities hereafter contracted; and there shall be no imprisonment for debt, except in cases of fraud, libel, or slander, and no person shall be imprisoned for a militia fine in time of peace.

[Certain prohibitions]

SEC. 15.   No bill of attainder, *ex post facto* law, or law impairing the obligation of contracts, shall ever be passed.

[Property rights of foreigners]

SEC. 16.   *(repealed)*

[Slavery prohibited]

SEC. 17.   Neither slavery nor involuntary servitude, unless for the punishment of crimes, shall ever be tolerated in this state.

[Search and seizure regulated]

SEC. 18.   The right of the people to be secure in their persons, houses, papers, and effects against unreasonable seizures and searches, shall not be violated; and no warrant shall issue but on probable cause, supported by oath or affirmation particularly describing the place or places to be searched, and the person or persons, and thing or things to be seized.

[Treason defined]

SEC. 19.   Treason against the state shall consist only in levying war against it, adhering to its enemies, or giving them aid and comfort. And no person shall be convicted of treason, unless on the testimony of two witnesses to the same overt act, or on confession in open court.

SEC. 20.   This enumeration of rights shall not be construed to impair or deny others retained by the people.

Section 8 was amended in 1912 to add after ". . . indictment of the grand jury," the words: "or upon information duly filed by a district attorney, or attorney general of the state. . . ."

The original Section 16, which provided that foreigners who were bona fide *residents of Nevada should have the same rights in property as native-born citizens, was repealed in 1924.*

ARTICLE II

RIGHT OF SUFFRAGE

[How and by whom the franchise may be enjoyed]

SECTION 1.   All citizens of the United States (not laboring under the disabilities named in this constitution) of the age of eighteen years and upwards, who shall have actually, and not constructively, resided in this state six months, and in the district or county thirty days next preceding any election, shall be entitled to vote for all officers that now or hereafter may be elected by the people, and upon all questions submitted to the electors at such election; *provided,* that no person who has been or may be convicted of treason or felony in any state or territory of the United States, unless restored to civil rights, and no idiot or insane person shall be entitled to the privilege of an elector. There shall be no denial of the elective franchise at any election on account of sex. The legislature may provide by law the conditions under which a citizen of the United States who does not have the status of an elector in another state and who does not meet the residence requirements of this section may vote in this state for President and Vice President of the United States.

[Residence defined]

SEC. 2.　For the purpose of voting, no person shall be deemed to have gained or lost a residence solely by reason of his presence or absence while employed in the service of the United States, nor while engaged in the navigation of the waters of the United States or of the high seas; nor while a student of any institution of learning; nor while kept at any charitable institution or medical facility at public expense; nor while confined in any public prison.

[Armed Forces personnel]

SEC. 3.　*(repealed)*

[Civil process suspended]

SEC. 4.　During the day on which any general election shall be held in this state, no qualified elector shall be arrested by virtue of any civil process.

[Elections by Ballot]

SEC. 5.　All elections by the people shall be by ballot, and all elections by the legislature, or by either branch thereof, shall be *"viva voce."*

[Elections registered]

SEC. 6.　Provision shall be made by law for the registration of the names of the electors within the counties of which they may be residents, and for the ascertainment, by proper proofs, of the persons who shall be entitled to the right of suffrage, as hereby established, to preserve the purity of elections, and to regulate the manner of holding and making returns of the same; and the legislature shall have power to prescribe by law any other or further rules or oaths as may be deemed necessary as a test of electoral qualifications.

[Poll tax provided for; obsolete]

SEC. 7.　The legislature shall provide by law for the payment of an annual poll tax, of not less than two nor exceeding four dollars, from each male person resident in the state between the ages of twenty-one and sixty years (uncivilized American Indians excepted), to be expended for the maintenance and betterment of the public roads.

[Who may vote on constitution]

SEC. 8.　All persons qualified by law to vote for representatives to the general assembly of the Territory of Nevada, on the twenty-first day of

March A.D. eighteen hundred and sixty-four, and all other persons who may be lawful voters in said territory on the first Wednesday of September next following, shall be entitled to vote directly upon the question of adopting or rejecting this constitution.

[Recall of public officers; procedure]

SEC. 9.   Every public officer in the State of Nevada is subject, as herein provided, to recall from office by the registered voters of the state, or of the county, district, or municipality, from which he was elected. For this purpose a number of registered voters not less than twenty-five percent (25%) of the number who actually voted in the state or in the county, district, or municipality electing said officer, at the preceding general election, shall file their petition in the manner herein provided, demanding his recall by the people; they shall set forth in said petition, in not exceeding two hundred (200) words, the reasons why said recall is demanded. If he shall offer his resignation it shall be accepted and take effect on the day it is offered, and the vacancy thereby caused shall be filled in the manner provided by law. If he shall not resign within five (5) days after the petition is filed, a special election shall be ordered to be held within twenty (20) days after the issuance of the call therefore, in the state or county, district, or municipality electing said officer, to determine whether the people will recall said officer. On the ballot at said election shall be printed verbatim as set forth in the recall petition, the reasons for demanding the recall of said officer, and in not more than two hundred (200) words, the officer's justification of his course in office. He shall continue to perform the duties of his office until the result of said election shall be finally declared. Other candidates for the office may be nominated to be voted for at said special election. The candidate who shall receive the highest number of votes at said special election shall be deemed elected for the remainder of the term, whether it be the person against whom the recall petition was filed, or another. The recall petition shall be filed with the officer with whom the petition for nomination to such office shall be filed, and the same officer shall order the special election when it is required. No such petition shall be circulated or filed against any officer until he has actually held his office six (6) months, save and except that it may be filed against a senator or assemblyman in the legislature at any time after ten (10) days from the beginning of the first session after his election. After one such petition and special election, no further recall petition shall be filed against the same officer during the term for which he was elected, unless such further petitioners shall pay into the public treasury from which the expenses of said special election have been paid, the whole amount paid out of said public treasury as expenses for the preceding special election. Such additional legislation as may aid the operation of this section shall be provided by law.

Section 1 was amended in 1880, in 1914, and in 1970; the first change eliminated the earlier restriction of voting to white *males and the second extended the right to vote to women. Women citizens in Nevada were thus entitled to vote six years before the Nineteenth Amendment to the United States Constitution was passed. A second amendment, also passed in 1914, deleted the denial of voting to those who had voluntarily fought against the Union or held office under the Confederacy. The 1970 amendment added the last sentence of the section, which permits new residents of Nevada who have not met the state's voting requirements but who are ineligible to vote in their former state to vote in Nevada for president and vice-president. Voters rejected an amendment in 1976 to change the residency requirement from six months to thirty days; the constitution will continue to read "six months," but because of a United States Supreme Court ruling new residents can actually register after thirty days in the state.*

Section 2 was modified in 1972 by the addition of the word "solely" in line two and by substituting "institution" for "seminary" and "charitable institution or medical facility" for "almshouse or other asylum."

Section 3 was eliminated entirely in 1972. It had preserved the voting rights of military personnel who were residents when they entered military service and had provided for recording their ballots in the county of their residence.

Section 7 was amended in 1910. The amendment eliminated the original clause, which authorized the legislature to make payment of the poll tax a condition for voting, and added the clause that the poll tax is to be used for maintaining and bettering public roads. The Twenty-fourth Amendment to the United States Constitution (1964) forbids collection of a poll tax as a prerequiste for voting in a primary or general election for president, vice-president or members of Congress. In 1966 the voters approved a constitutional amendment deleting Section 7.

Section 9 was not in the original constitution; it was added in 1912. An amendment adopted in 1970 stiffened the recall requirements with the stipulation that 25 percent of the number of those voting in the preceding general election must sign the recall petition. The earlier requirement had been that 25 percent of those voting for a supreme court justice must sign the petition; the former requirement was easier to meet because many voters did not bother to cast a ballot for justice, and so the total for that office was usually considerably lower than the total of voters who went to the polls.

ARTICLE III

DISTRIBUTION OF POWERS

[Powers of government]

SECTION 1. The powers of the government of the State of Nevada shall be divided into three separate departments—the legislative, the executive, and the judicial; and no person charged with the exercise of powers properly belonging to one of these departments shall exercise any functions appertaining to either of the others, except in the cases herein expressly directed or permitted.

ARTICLE IV

LEGISLATIVE DEPARTMENT

[Legislative authority vested]

SECTION 1. The legislative authority of this state shall be vested in a senate and assembly, which shall be designated "The Legislature of the State of Nevada," and the sessions of such legislature shall be held at the seat of government of the state.

[To convene, when]

SEC. 2. The sessions of the legislature shall be biennial, and shall commence on the 3rd Monday of January next ensuing the election of members of the Assembly, unless the Governor of the State shall, in the interim, convene the legislature by proclamation.

[Assemblymen chosen]

SEC. 3. The members of the assembly shall be chosen biennially by the qualified electors of their respective districts, on the Tuesday next after the first Monday in November, and their term of office shall be two years from the day next after their election.

[Senators chosen]

SEC. 4. Senators shall be chosen at the same time and places as members of the assembly, by the qualified electors of their respective districts, and their term of office shall be four years from the day next after their election.

[Who eligible]

SEC. 5. Senators and members of the assembly shall be duly qualified electors in the respective counties and districts which they represent, and the number of senators shall not be less than one-third nor more than one-half of that of the members of the assembly. It shall be the mandatory duty of the legislature at its first session after the taking of the decennial census of the United States in the year 1950, and after each subsequent decennial census, to fix by law the number of senators and assemblymen, and apportion them among the several counties of the state, or among legislative districts which may be established by law, according to the number of inhabitants in them, respectively.

[Powers of each]

SEC. 6.   Each house shall judge of the qualifications, elections, and returns of its own members, choose its own officers (except the president of the senate), determine the rules of its proceedings, and may punish its members for disorderly conduct, and, with the concurrence of two-thirds of all the members elected, expel a member.

SEC. 7.   Either house, during the session, may punish, by imprisonment, any person, not a member, who shall have been guilty of disrespect to the house by disorderly or contemptuous behavior in its presence; but such imprisonment shall not extend beyond the final adjournment of the session.

[Members not to be beneficiaries]

SEC. 8.   No senator or member of assembly shall, during the term for which he shall have been elected, nor for one year thereafter, be appointed to any civil office of profit under this state which shall have been created, or the emoluments of which shall have been increased, during such term, except such office as may be filled by elections by the people.

[Persons not eligible, when]

SEC. 9.   No person holding any lucrative office under the government of the United States, or any other power, shall be eligible to any civil office of profit under this state; *provided,* that postmasters whose compensation does not exceed five hundred dollars per annum, or commissioners of deeds, shall not be deemed as holding a lucrative office.

[Disqualified from office holding]

SEC. 10.   Any person who shall be convicted of the embezzlement or defalcation of the public funds of this state, or who may be convicted of having given or offered a bribe to procure his election or appointment to office, or received a bribe to aid in the procurement of office for any other person, shall be disqualified from holding any office of profit or trust in this state. And the legislature shall, as soon as practicable, provide by law for the punishment of such defalcation, bribery, or embezzlement as a felony.

[Members exempt from civil process during session of legislature]

SEC. 11.   Members of the legislature shall be privileged from arrest on civil process during the session of the legislature, and for fifteen days next before the commencement of each session.

[Vacancies, how filled]

SEC. 12.   In case of the death or resignation of any member of the legislature, either senator or assemblyman, the county commissioners of the county from which such member was elected shall appoint a person of the same political party as the party which elected such senator or assemblyman to fill such vacancy; *provided,* that this section shall apply only in cases where no biennial election or any regular election at which county officers are to be elected takes place between the time of such death or resignation and the next succeeding session of the legislature.

[Rules relating to legislative procedure]

SEC. 13.   A majority of all the members elected to each house shall constitute a quorum to transact business, but a smaller number may adjourn, from day to day, and may compel the attendance of absent members in such manner and under such penalties as each house may prescribe.

SEC. 14.   Each house shall keep a journal of its own proceedings, which shall be published, and the yeas and nays of the members of either house, on any question, shall at the desire of any three members present, be entered on the journal.

SEC. 15.   The doors of each house shall be kept open during its session, except the senate while sitting in executive session, and neither shall, without the consent of the other, adjourn for more than three days, nor to any other place than that in which they may be holding their sessions.

SEC. 16.   Any bill may originate in either house of the legislature, and all bills passed by one may be amended in the other.

SEC. 17.   Each law enacted by the legislature shall embrace but one subject, and matter properly connected therewith, which subject shall be briefly expressed in the title; and no law shall be revised or amended by reference to its title only; but, in such case, the act as revised, or section as amended, shall be reenacted and published at length.

SEC. 18.   Every bill, except a bill placed on a consent calendar adopted as provided in this section, shall be read by sections on three several days in each house, unless, in case of emergency, two-thirds of the house where such bill may be pending shall deem it expedient to dispense with this rule; but the reading of a bill by sections, on its final passage, shall in no case be dispensed with, and the vote on the final passage of every bill or joint resolution shall be taken by yeas and nays, to be entered on the journals of each house; and a majority of all the members elected to each house shall be necessary to pass every bill or joint resolution, and all bills or joint resolutions so passed shall be signed by the presiding officers of the respective houses, and by the secretary of the senate and clerk of the assembly. Each house may provide by rule for the creation of a consent calendar and establish the procedure for the passage of uncontested bills.

[Public moneys, how disbursed]

SEC. 19. No moneys shall be drawn from the treasury but in consequence of appropriations made by law.

[Legislative powers restricted]

SEC. 20. The legislature shall not pass local or special laws in any of the following enumerated cases, that is to say: Regulating the jurisdiction and duties of justices of the peace and of constables, and fixing their compensation; for the punishment of crimes and misdemeanors; regulating the practice of courts of justice; providing for changing the venue in civil and criminal cases; granting divorces; changing the names of persons; vacating roads, town-plots, streets, alleys and public squares; summoning and empaneling grand and petit juries, and providing for their compensation; regulating county and township business; regulating the election of county and township officers; for the assessment and collection of taxes for state, county, and township purposes; providing for opening and conducting elections of state, county, or township officers, and designating the places of voting; providing for the sale of real estate belonging to minors or other persons laboring under legal disabilities; giving effect to invalid deeds, wills, or other instruments; refunding money paid into the state treasury, or into the treasury of any county; releasing the indebtedness, liability or obligation of any corporation, association, or person to the state, or to any county, town or city of this state; but nothing in this section shall be construed to deny or restrict the power of the legislature to establish and regulate the compensation and fees of county officers, to authorize and empower the boards of county commissioners of the various counties of the state to establish and regulate the compensation and fees of township officers in their respective counties, to establish and regulate the rates of freight, passage, toll, and charges of railroads, tollroads, ditch, flume, and tunnel companies incorporated under the laws of this state or doing business therein.

[Laws general and uniform]

SEC. 21. In all cases enumerated in the preceding section, and in all other cases where a general law can be made applicable, all laws shall be general and of uniform operation throughout the state.

[Suit may be brought against the state]

SEC. 22. Provision may be made by general law for bringing suit against the state as to all liabilities originating after the adoption of this constitution.

[Enacting clause]

SEC. 23. The enacting clause of every law shall be as follows: "The people of the State of Nevada, represented in Senate and Assembly, do enact as follows," and no law shall be enacted except by bill.

[Lottery prohibited]

SEC. 24   No lottery shall be authorized by this state, nor shall the sale of lottery tickets be allowed.

[County government]

SEC. 25.   The legislature shall establish a system of county and township government, which shall be uniform throughout the state.

SEC. 26.   The legislature shall provide by law for the election of a board of county commissioners in each county, and such county commissioners shall, jointly and individually, perform such duties as may be prescribed by law.

[Who may be excused from juries]

SEC. 27.   Laws shall be made to exclude from serving on juries all persons not qualified electors of this state, and all persons who shall have been convicted of bribery, perjury, forgery, larceny, or other high crimes, unless restored to civil rights; and laws shall be passed regulating elections, and prohibiting, under adequate penalties, all undue influence thereon from power, bribery, tumult, or other improper practice.

[Compensation fixed by law]

SEC. 28.   No money shall be drawn from the state treasury as salary or compensation to any officer or employee of the legislature, or either branch thereof, except in cases where such salary or compensation has been fixed by a law in force prior to the election or appointment of such officer or employee, and the salary or compensation so fixed shall neither be increased nor diminished so as to apply to any officer or employee of the legislature, or either branch thereof, at such session; *provided,* that this restriction shall not apply to the first session of the legislature.

[Homestead exempt from forced sale]

SEC. 30.   A homestead, as provided by law, shall be exempt from forced sale under any process of law, and shall not be alienated without the joint consent of husband and wife, when the relation exists; but no property shall be exempt from sale for taxes or for the payment of obligations contracted for the purchase of said premises, or for the erection of improvements thereon; *provided,* the provisions of this section shall not apply to any process of law obtained by virtue of a lien given by the consent of both husband and wife, and laws shall be enacted providing for the recording of such homestead within the county in which the same shall be situated.

[Property of married persons]

SEC. 31.   All property, both real and personal, of a married person owned or claimed by such person before marriage, and that acquired afterward by gift, devise or descent, shall be the separate property of such person. The legislature shall more clearly define the rights of married persons in relation to their separate property and other property.

[Power of legislature over county officers]

SEC. 32.   The legislature shall have power to increase, diminish, consolidate, or abolish the following county officers: County clerks, county recorders, auditors, sheriffs, district attorneys, and public administrators. The legislature shall provide for their election by the people, and fix by law their duties and compensation. County clerks shall be ex officio clerks of the courts of record and of the boards of county commissioners in and for their respective counties.

[Compensation of legislators]

SEC. 33.   The members of the legislature shall receive for their services, a compensation to be fixed by law and paid out of the public treasury, for not to exceed 60 days during any regular session of the legislature and not to exceed 20 days during any special session convened by the governor; but no increase of such compensation shall take effect during the term for which the members of either house shall have been elected provided, that an appropriation may be made for the payment of such actual expenses as members of the legislature may incur for postage, express charges, newspapers and stationery not exceeding the sum of sixty dollars for any general or special session to each member; and furthermore provided, that the speaker of the assembly, and lieutenant governor, as president of the senate, shall each, during the time of their actual attendance as such presiding officers receive an additional allowance of two dollars per diem.

[Election of United States senators; obsolete]

SEC. 34.   In all elections for United States senators, such elections shall be held in joint convention of both houses of the legislature. It shall be the duty of the legislature which convenes next preceding the expiration of the term of such senator, to elect his successor. If a vacancy in such senatorial representation from any cause occur, it shall be the duty of the legislature then in session, or at the succeeding session thereof, to supply such vacancy. If the legislature shall, at any time, as herein provided, fail to unite in a joint convention within twenty days after the commencement of the session of the legislature for the election [of] such senator, it shall be the duty of the governor, by proclamation, to convene the two houses of the legislature in joint convention within not less than five days, nor exceeding ten days, from the publication of his proclamation, and the joint convention when so assembled shall proceed to elect the senator as herein provided.

[Governor's action on bills; veto]

SEC. 35. Every bill which may have passed the legislature shall, before it becomes a law, be presented to the governor. If he approve it, he shall sign it; but if not, he shall return it with his objections, to the house in which it originated, which house shall cause such objections to be entered upon its journal, and proceed to reconsider it. If, after such reconsideration, it again pass both houses, by yeas and nays, by a vote of two-thirds of the members elected to each house, it shall become a law, notwithstanding the governor's objections. If any bill shall not be returned within five days after it shall have been presented to him (Sunday excepted), exclusive of the day on which he received it, the same shall be a law in like manner as if he had signed it, unless the legislature, by its final adjournment, prevent such return, in which case it shall be a law, unless the governor, within ten days next after the adjournment (Sunday excepted) shall file such bill, with his objections thereto, in the office of the secretary of state, who shall lay the same before the legislature at its next session, in like manner as if it had been returned by the governor; and if the same shall receive the vote of two-thirds of the members elected to each branch of the legislature, upon a vote taken by yeas and nays, to be entered upon the journals of each house, it shall become a law.

[County not to be abolished without consent of voters]

SEC. 36. The legislature shall not abolish any county unless the qualified voters of the county affected shall at a general or special election first approve such proposed abolishment by a majority of all the voters voting at such election. The legislature shall provide by law the method of initiating and conducting such election.

[Emergency continuity of government]

SEC. 37(A) The legislature, in order to insure continuity of state and local governmental operations in periods of emergency resulting from disasters caused by enemy attack, shall have the power and the immediate duty to provide for immediate and temporary succession to the powers and duties of public offices, of whatever nature and whether filled by election or appointment, the incumbents of which may become unavailable for carrying on the powers and duties of such offices, and to adopt such other measures as may be necessary and proper for insuring the continuity of governmental operations, including changes in quorum requirements in the legislature and the relocation of the seat of government. In the exercise of the powers hereby conferred, the legislature shall conform to the requirements of this constitution except to the extent that in the judgment of the legislature so to do would be impracticable or would admit of undue delay.

SEC. 37(B) Notwithstanding the general provisions of sections 20, 25, 26, and 36 of this article, the legislature may by law consolidate into one municipal government, with one set of officers, the city designated as the seat of government of this state and the county in which such city is situated. Such consolidated municipality shall be considered as a county for the purpose of representation in the legislature, shall have all the powers conferred upon counties by this constitution or by general law, and shall have such other powers as may be conferred by its charter. Notwithstanding the general provisions of section 1 of article 10 the legislature may create two or more separate taxing districts within such consolidated municipality.

Section 2 has been amended three times. The first time was in 1889 and merely changed the opening day of the legislature from the first to the third Monday in January. The second time was in 1958, when the voters approved changing from biennial to annual sessions of the legislature; in 1960 the voters reversed themselves, revoked their approval of annual sessions, and returned the legislature to biennial sessions.

Section 5 was amended in 1950, at which time the last sentence was added. A second amendment, adopted in 1970, added the reference to senators as well as assemblymen being elected on a population basis.

Section 12 in the original constitution read: "When vacancies occur in either House, the Governor shall issue writs of election to fill such vacancy." the section was amended in 1922 and 1944 to its present wording.

Section 18 was amended in 1976 to include provision for a consent calendar.

Section 19 was changed in 1954 to eliminate the former requirement that receipts and expenditures of public money must be published with the laws at each regular session of the legislature.

Section 20 was amended in 1889, in 1922, and in 1926, by adding to the section as originally written the words "and fixing their compensation" following the word "constables," and by adding all the material beginning with "giving effect to invalid deeds . . ." and continuing to the end of the section.

Section 29 was repealed in 1958. It had provided that the first regular session of the legislature could continue for ninety days, and that subsequent regular sessions could not exceed sixty days, nor special sessions twenty days.

Section 31 was amended in 1978 in order to change the application from the property of a wife to the property of married persons.

Section 32 was amended in 1889. All of this section was changed except the part beginning "and fix by law their . . ." and continuing to the end of the section. The original wording would not have permitted the consolidation of offices in the less populous counties. In

1972 the section was amended again to remove county surveyors and superintendents of schools from the list of officers controlled by the legislature.

Section 33 was amended in 1958. The amendment limits the number of days for which legislators may receive compensation to sixty for a regular session and twenty for a special session. An effort to extend the salary period to 100 days was defeated in 1976.

Section 34 was made obsolete by the Seventeenth Amendment of the United States Constituion, which established direct election of senators.

Section 36 was added in 1940.

Section 37, designated as (A) above, was added in 1964.

Section 37, designated as (B) above, was added in 1968. It permits the consolidation of Ormsby County and Carson City, the first city-county merger in Nevada history. By error, the 1968 amendment was passed in the 1965 and 1967 sessions of the legislature and appeared on the 1968 ballot as amending ". . . Article 4 of the Constitution by the addition of a new section to be designated Section 37." Since there already was a section 37, adopted in 1964, it is unclear what the legal designation of the 1968 amendment is or ought to be. Until the matter is officially determined, it seeming unlikely that any constitution should bear the weight of two section 37s, this book will refer to the 1964 amendment as (A), and the 1968 amendment as (B).

ARTICLE V

EXECUTIVE DEPARTMENT

[Executive power vested]

SECTION 1.   The supreme executive power of the state shall be vested in a chief magistrate, who shall be governor of the State of Nevada.

[Governor elected]

SEC. 2.   The governor shall be elected by the qualified electors at the time and places of voting for members of the legislature, and shall hold his office for four years from the time of his installation, and until his successor shall be qualified.

[Who eligible to office for governor]

SEC. 3.   No person shall be eligible to the office of governor who is not a qualified elector, and who, at the time of such election, has not attained the age of twenty-five years, and who shall not have been a citizen resident of this state for two years next preceding the election; nor shall any person be elected to the office of governor more than twice; and no person who has held the office of governor, or acted as governor for more than two years of a term to which some other person was elected governor shall be elected to the office of governor more than once.

[Disposition of election returns]

SEC. 4.   The returns of every election for United States senator and member of Congress, district and state officers, and for and against any questions submitted to the electors of the State of Nevada, voted for at the general election, shall be sealed up and transmitted to the seat of government, directed to the secretary of state, and the chief justice of the supreme court, and the associate justices, or a majority thereof, shall meet at the office of the secretary of state, on a day to be fixed by law, and open and canvass the election returns for United States senator and member of Congress, district and state officers, and for and against any questions submitted to the electors of the State of Nevada, and forthwith declare the result and publish the names of the persons elected and the results of the vote cast upon any question submitted to the electors of the State of Nevada. The persons having the highest number of votes for the respective offices shall be declared elected, but in case any two or more have an equal and the highest number of votes for the same office, the legislature shall, by joint vote of both houses, elect one of said persons to fill said office.

[Military authority of governor]

SEC. 5.   The governor shall be commander-in-chief of the military forces of the state, except when they shall be called into the service of the United States.

[Duties of governor]

SEC. 6.   He shall transact all executive business with the officers of the government, civil and military, and may require information in writing from the officers of the executive department upon any subject relating to the duties of their respective offices.

SEC. 7.   He shall see that the laws are faithfully executed.

[May fill vacancies]

SEC. 8.   When any office shall, from any cause, become vacant, and no mode is provided by the constitution and laws for filling such vacancy, the governor shall have the power to fill such vacancy by granting a commission which shall expire at the next election and qualification of the person elected to such office.

[May convene legislature]

SEC. 9.   The governor may, on extraordinary occasions, convene the legislature by proclamation, and shall state to both houses, when organized, the purpose for which they have been convened, and the legislature shall transact no legislative business except that for which they were especially convened, or such other legislative business as the governor may call to the attention of the legislature while in session.

[Message to legislature]

SEC. 10.   He shall communicate by message to the legislature at every regular session the condition of the state, and recommend such measures as he may deem expedient.

[May adjourn legislature]

SEC. 11.   In case of a disagreement between the two houses, with respect to the time of adjournment, the governor shall have power to adjourn the legislature to such time as he may think proper; *provided,* it be not beyond the time fixed for the meeting of the next legislature.

[Certain persons ineligible.]

SEC. 12.   No person shall while holding any office under the United States government hold the office of governor, except as herein expressly provided.

[Duties of governor as to fines and forfeitures]

SEC. 13.   The governor shall have the power to suspend the collection of fines and forfeitures, and grant reprieves for a period not exceeding sixty days dating from the time of conviction, for all offenses, except in cases of impeachment. Upon conviction for treason, he shall have power to suspend the execution of the sentence until the case shall be reported to the legislature at its next meeting, when the legislature shall either pardon, direct the execution of the sentence, or grant a further reprieve. And if the legislature should fail or refuse to make final disposition of such case, the sentence shall be enforced at such time and place as the governor by his order may direct. The governor shall communicate to the legislature, at the beginning of every session, every case of fine or forfeiture remitted, or reprieve, pardon, or commutation granted, stating the name of the convict, the crime of which he was convicted, the sentence, its date, and the date of the remission, commutation, pardon, or reprieve.

[Personnel of the board of pardons]

SEC. 14.   The governor, justices of the supreme court, and attorney general, or a major part of them, of whom the governor shall be one, may, upon such conditions and with such limitations and restrictions as they may think proper, remit fines and forfeitures, commute punishments, and grant pardons, after convictions, in all cases, except treason and impeachments, subject to such regulations as may be provided by law relative to the manner of applying for pardons. The legislature is authorized to pass laws conferring upon the district courts authority to suspend the execution of sentences, fix the conditions for, and to grant probation, and within the minimum and maximum periods authorized by law, fix the sentence to be served by the person convicted of crime in said courts.

[Seal of state]

SEC. 15. There shall be a seal of this state, which shall be kept by the governor, and used by him officially, and shall be called "The Great Seal of the State of Nevada."

[Grants in name of state]

SEC. 16. All grants and commissions shall be in the name and by the authority of the State of Nevada, sealed with the great seal of the state, signed by the governor and countersigned by the secretary of state.

[Election and duties of lieutenant-governor]

SEC. 17. A lieutenant-governor shall be elected at the same time and places, and in the same manner as the governor, and his term of office and his eligibility shall also be the same. He shall be president of the senate, but shall only have a casting vote therein. If, during a vacancy of the office of governor, the lieutenant-governor shall be impeached, displaced, resign, die, or become incapable of performing the duties of the office, or be absent from the state, the president pro tempore of the senate shall act as governor until the vacancy be filled or the disability cease.

[Lieutenant-governor to succeed governor]

SEC. 18. In case of the impeachment of the governor, or his removal from office, death, inability to discharge the duties of the said office, resignation or absence from the state, the powers and duties of the office shall devolve upon the lieutenant-governor for the residue of the term, or until the disability shall cease. But when the governor shall, with the consent of the legislature, be out of the state in time of war, and at the head of any military force thereof, he shall continue commander-in-chief of the military forces of the state.

[State officers, terms of office]

SEC. 19. A secretary of state, a treasurer, a controller, and an attorney-general, shall be elected at the same time and places, and in the same manner as the governor. The term of office of each shall be the same as is prescribed for the governor. Any elector shall be eligible to either of said offices.

[Duties of secretary of state]

SEC. 20. The secretary of state shall keep a true record of the official acts of the legislative and executive departments of the government, and shall, when required, lay the same, and all matters relative thereto, before either branch of the legislature.

[Personnel of board of state prison commissioners and board of examiners]

SEC. 21. The governor, secretary of state, and attorney-general shall constitute a board of state prison commissioners, which board shall have supervision of all matters connected with the state prison as may be provided by law. They shall also constitute a board of examiners, with power to examine all claims against the state (except salaries or compensation of officers fixed by law), and perform such other duties as may be prescribed by law. And no claim against the state (except salaries or compensation of officers fixed by law) shall be passed upon by the legislature without having been considered and acted upon by said board of examiners.

[Duties of state officers]

SEC. 22. The secretary of state, state treasurer, state controller, attorney-general, and superintendent of public instruction shall perform such other duties as may be prescribed by law.

Section 3 was amended in 1970 to restrict the tenure of the governor to two terms; this amendment is similar to the restriction on presidential terms established by the Twenty-second Amendment to the United States Constitution.

Section 4 was amended in 1940. The changes were made to include federal offices and questions submitted to the voters; the section originally had referred only to the canvass of the election returns for state offices.

Section 14 was changed in 1950 by the addition of the last sentence.

Section 19 was amended in 1954 by eliminating the surveyor general from the list of elected state officers.

Section 22 originally had included the surveyor general also, and this section was amended with Section 19.

ARTICLE VI

JUDICIAL DEPARTMENT

[Judicial power vested]

SECTION 1. The judicial power of this state shall be vested in a court system, comprising a supreme court, district courts, and justices of the peace. The legislature may also establish, as part of the system, courts, for municipal purposes only, in incorporated cities and towns.

[Supreme Court, how constituted]

SEC. 2. 1. The supreme court consists of the chief justice and two or more associate justices, as may be provided by law. In increasing or diminishing the number of associate justices, the legislature shall provide for the arrangement of their terms so that an equal number of terms, as nearly as may be, expire every 2 years.

2. The legislature may provide by law:

(a) If the court consists of more than five justices, for the hearing and decision of cases by panels of no fewer than three justices, the resolution by the full court of any conflicts between decisions so rendered, and the kinds of cases which must be heard by the full court.

12

(b) For the places of holding court by panels of justices, if established, and by the full court.

[Election of justices of supreme court; terms; chief justice]

SEC. 3.   The justices of the supreme court shall be elected by the qualified electors of the state at the general election, and shall hold office for the term of six years from and including the first Monday of January next succeeding their election; *provided,* that there shall be elected, at the first election under this constitution, three justices of the supreme court, who shall hold office from and including the first Monday of December, A.D. eighteen hundred and sixty-four, and continue in office thereafter, two, four, and six years, respectively, from and including the first Monday of January next succeeding their election. They shall meet as soon as practicable after their election and qualification, and at their first meeting shall determine, by lot, the term of office each shall fill, and the justice drawing the shortest term shall be chief justice, and after the expiration of his term, the one having the next shortest term shall be chief justice, after which the senior justice in commission shall be chief justice, and in case the commission of any two or more of said justices shall bear the same date, they shall determine by lot who shall be chief justice.

[Jurisdiction and powers of]

SEC. 4.   The supreme court shall have appellate jurisdiction in all civil cases arising in district courts, and also on questions of law alone in all criminal cases in which the offense charged is within the original jurisdiction of the district courts. The court shall also have power to issue writs of *mandamus, certiorairi,* prohibition, *quo warranto,* and *habeas corpus* and also all writs necessary or proper to the complete exercise of its appellate jurisdiction. Each of the justices shall have power to issue writs of *habeas corpus* to any part of the state, upon petition by, or on behalf of, any person held in actual custody, and may make such writs returnable, before himself or the supreme court, or before any district court in the state or before any judge of said courts.

In case of the disability or disqualification, for any cause, of the chief justice or one of the associate justices of the supreme court, or any two of them, the governor is authorized and empowered to designate any district judge or judges to sit in the place or places of such disqualified or disabled justice or justices, and said judge or judges so designated shall receive their actual expense of travel and otherwise while sitting in said supreme court.

[Judicial districts; election of district judges]

SEC. 5.   The state is hereby divided into nine judicial districts, of which the county of Storey shall constitute the first; the county of Ormsby the second; the county of Lyon the third; the county of Washoe the fourth; the counties of Nye and Churchill the fifth; the county of Humboldt the sixth; the county of Lander the seventh; the county of Douglas the eighth; and the county of Esmeralda the ninth. The county of Roop shall be attached to the county of Washoe for judicial purposes, until otherwise provided by law. The legislature may, however, provide by law for an alteration in the boundaries or divisions of the districts herein prescribed, and also for increasing or diminishing the number of the judicial districts and judges therein. But no such change shall take effect, except in case of a vacancy, or the expiration of the term of an incumbent of the office. At the first general election under this constitution, there shall be elected in each of the respective districts (except as in this section hereafter otherwise provided) one district judge, who shall hold office from and including the first Monday of December, A.D. eighteen hundred and sixty-four, and until the first Monday of January, in the year eighteen hundred and sixty-seven. After the said first election, there shall be elected at the general election which immediately precedes the expiration of the term of his predecessor, one district judge in each of the respective judicial districts (except in the first district as in this section hereinafter provided). The district judges shall be elected by the qualified electors of their respective districts, and shall hold office for the term of six years (excepting those elected at said first election) from and including the first Monday of January next succeeding their election and qualification; *provided,* that the first judicial district shall be entitled to, and shall have three district judges, who shall possess coextensive and concurrent jurisdiction, and who shall be elected at the same times, in the same manner, and shall hold office for the like terms as herein prescribed in relation to the judges in other judicial districts. Any one of said judges may preside on the empaneling of grand juries, and the presentment and trial on indictments, under such rules and regulations as may be prescribed by law.

[Jurisdiction of district courts]

SEC. 6. The district courts in the several judicial districts of this state shall have original jurisdiction in all cases excluded by law from the original jurisdiction of justices' courts. They shall also have final appellate jurisdiction in cases arising in justices courts and such other inferior tribunals as may be established by law. The district courts and the judges thereof shall have power to issue writs of *mandamus,* injunction, *quo warranto, certiorari,* and all other writs proper and necessary to the complete exercise of their jurisdiction; and also shall have power to issue writs of *habeas corpus* on petition by, or in behalf of, any person held in actual custody in their respective districts.

[Times of holding court fixed]

SEC. 7. The times of holding the supreme court and district courts shall be as fixed by law. The terms of the supreme court shall be held at the seat of government unless the legislature otherwise provides by law, except that the supreme court may hear oral argument at other places in the state. The terms of the district court shall be held at the county seats of their respective counties; *provided,* that in case any county shall be hereafter divided into two or more districts, the legislature may by law designate the places of holding courts in such districts.

[Jurisdiction of justices courts]

SEC. 8.   The legislature shall determine the number of justices of the peace to be elected in each city and township of the state, and shall fix, by law, their qualifications, their terms of office and the limits of their civil and criminal jurisdiction, according to the amount in controversy, the nature of the case, the penalty provided, or any combination of these.

The provisions of this section affecting the number, qualifications, terms of office and jurisdiction of Justices of the Peace become effective on the first Monday of January, 1979.

The legislature shall also prescribe by law the manner and determine the cases in which appeals may be taken from justices and other courts. The supreme court, the district courts, and such other courts as the legislature shall designate, shall be courts of record.

[Possible municipal courts]

SEC. 9.   Provision shall be made by law prescribing the powers, duties, and responsibilities of any municipal court that may be established in pursuance of section one of this article; and also fixing by law the jurisdiction of said court, so as not to conflict with that of the several courts of record.

SEC. 10.   No judicial officer, except justices of the peace and city recorders, shall receive to his own use any fees or perquisites of office.

[Eligibility of office limited]

SEC. 11.   The justices of the supreme court and the district judges shall be ineligible to any office, other than a judicial office, during the term for which they shall have been elected or appointed; and all elections or appointments of any such judges by the people, legislature, or otherwise, during said period, to any office other than judicial, shall be void.

[Matters of practice]

SEC. 12.   Judges shall not charge juries in respect to matters of fact, but may state the testimony and declare the law.

SEC. 13.   The style of all process shall be "The State of Nevada," and all prosecutions shall be conducted in the name and by the authority of the same.

SEC. 14.   There shall be but one form of civil action, and law and equity may be administered in the same action.

[Compensation of judicial officers]

SEC. 15. The justices of the supreme court and district judges shall each receive for their services a compensation to be fixed by law and paid in the manner provided by law, which shall not be increased or diminished during the term for which they shall have been elected, unless a vacancy occurs, in which case the successor of the former incumbent shall receive only such salary as may be provided by law at the time of his election or appointment; and provision shall be made by law for setting apart from each year's revenue a sufficient amount of money to pay such compensation.

[Relating to court fees]

SEC. 16. The legislature at its first session, and from time to time thereafter, shall provide by law that upon the institution of each civil action and other proceedings, and also upon the perfecting of an appeal in any civil action or proceeding in the several courts of record in this state, a special court fee or tax shall be advanced to the clerks of said courts, respectively, by the party or parties bringing such action or proceeding, or taking such appeal; and the money so paid in shall be accounted for by such clerks, and applied towards the payment of the compensation of the judges of said courts, as shall be directed by law.

[Leaves of absence of judicial officers limited]

SEC. 17. The legislature shall have no power to grant leave of absence to a judicial officer, and any such officer who shall absent himself from the state for more than ninety consecutive days shall be deemed to have vacated his office.

SEC. 18. No judicial officer shall be superseded, nor shall the organization of the several courts of the Territory of Nevada be changed until the election and qualification of the several officers provided for in this article.

SEC. 19. 1. The chief justice is the administrative head of the court system. Subject to such rules as the supreme court may adopt, the chief justice may:

(a) Apportion the work of the supreme court among justices;

(b) Assign district judges to assist in other judicial districts or to specialized functions which may be established by law;

(c) Recall to active service any retired justice or judge of the court system who consents to such recall and who has not been removed or retired for cause or defeated for retention in office and may assign him to appropriate temporary duty within the court system.

2. In the absence or temporary disability of the chief justice, the associate justice senior in commission shall act as chief justice.

SEC. 20. 1. When a vacancy occurs before the expiration of any term of office in the supreme court or among the district judges, the governor shall appoint a justice or judge from among three nominees selected for such individual vacancy by the commission on judicial selection.

2.   The term of office of any justice or judge so appointed expires on the first Monday of January following the next general election.

3.   Each nomination for the supreme court shall be made by the permanent commission, composed of:

(a) The chief justice or an associate justice designated by him;

(b) Three members of the State Bar of Nevada, a public corporation created by statute, appointed by its board of governors; and

(c) Three persons, not members of the legal profession, appointed by the governor.

4.   Each nomination for the district court shall be made by a temporary commission composed of:

(a) The permanent commission;

(b) A member of the State Bar of Nevada resident in the judicial district in which the vacancy occurs, appointed by the board of governors of the State Bar of Nevada; and

(c) A resident of such judicial district, not a member of the legal profession, appointed by the governor.

5.   If at any time the State Bar of Nevada ceases to exist as a public corporation or ceases to include all attorneys admitted to practice before the courts of this state, the legislature shall provide by law, or if it fails to do so the court shall provide by rule, for the appointment of attorneys at law to the positions designated in this section to be occupied by members of the State Bar of Nevada.

6.   The term of office of each appointive member of the permanent commission, except the first members, is 4 years. Each appointing authority shall appoint one of the members first appointed for a term of 2 years. If a vacancy occurs, the appointing authority shall fill the vacancy for the unexpired term. The additional members of a temporary commission shall be appointed when a vacancy occurs, and their terms shall expire when the nominations for such vacancy have been transmitted to the governor.

7.   An appointing authority shall not appoint to the permanent commission more than:

(a) One resident of any county;

(b) Two members of the same political party.

No member of the permanent commission may be a member of a commission on judicial discipline.

8.   After the expiration of 30 days from the date on which the commission on judicial selection has delivered to him its list of nominees for any vacancy, if the governor has not made the appointment required by this section, he shall make no other appointment to any public office until he has appointed a justice or judge from the list submitted. If a commission

on judicial selection is established by another section of this constitution to nominate persons to fill vacancies on the supreme court, such commission shall serve as the permanent commission established by subsection 3 of this section.

SEC. 21. 1. A justice of the supreme court or a district judge may, in addition to the provision of article 7 for impeachment, be censured, retired, or removed by the commission on judicial discipline. A justice or judge may appeal from the action of the commission to the supreme court, which may reverse such action or take any alternative action provided in this subsection.

2. The commission is composed of:

(a) Two justices or judges appointed by the supreme court;

(b) Two members of the State Bar of Nevada, a public corporation created by statute, appointed by its board of governors; and

(c) Three persons, not members of the legal profession, appointed by the governor. The commission shall elect a chairman from among its three lay members.

3. If at any time the State Bar of Nevada ceases to exist as a public corporation or ceases to include all attorneys admitted to practice before the courts of this state, the legislature shall provide by law, or if it fails to do so the court shall provide by rule, for the appointment of attorneys at law to the positions designated in this section to be occupied by members of the State Bar of Nevada.

4. The term of office of each appointive member of the commission, except the first members, is 4 years. Each appointing authority shall appoint one of the members first appointed for a term of 2 years. If a vacancy occurs, the appointing authority shall fill the vacancy for the unexpired term. An appointing authority shall not appoint more than one resident of any county. The governor shall not appoint more than two members of the same political party. No member may be a member of a commission on judicial selection.

5. The supreme court shall make appropriate rules for:

(a) The confidentiality of all proceedings before the commission, except a decision to censure, retire, or remove a justice or judge;

(b) The grounds of censure;

(c) The conduct of investigations and hearings.

6. No justice or judge may by virtue of this section be:

(a) Removed except for willful misconduct, willful or persistent failure to perform the duties of his office, or habitual intemperance; or

(b) Retired except for advanced age which interferes with the proper performance of his judicial duties, or for mental or physical disability which prevents the proper performance of his judicial duties and which is likely to be permanent in nature.

7. Any person may bring to the attention of the commission any matter relating to the fitness of a justice or judge. The commission shall, after preliminary investigation, dismiss the matter or order a hearing to be held before it. If a hearing is ordered, a statement of the matter shall be served upon the justice or judge against whom the proceeding is brought. The commission in its discretion may suspend a justice or judge from the exercise of his office pending the determination of the proceedings before the commission. Any justice or judge whose removal is sought is liable to indictment and punishment according to law. A justice or judge retired for disability in accordance with this section is entitled thereafter to receive such compensation as the legislature may provide.

8. If a proceeding is brought against a justice of the supreme court, no justice may sit on the commission for that proceeding. If a proceeding is brought against a district judge, no judge from the same judicial district may sit on the commission for that proceeding. If an appeal is taken from an action of the commission to the supreme court, any justice who sat on the commission for that proceeding is disqualified from participating in the consideration or decision of the appeal. When any member of the commission is disqualified by this subsection, the supreme court shall appoint a substitute from among the eligible judges.

9. The commission may:

(a) Designate for each hearing an attorney or attorneys at law to act as counsel to conduct the proceeding;

(b) Summon witnesses to appear and testify under oath and compel the production of books, papers, documents, and records;

(c) Grant immunity from prosecution or punishment when the commission deems it necessary and proper in order to compel the giving of testimony under oath and the production of books, papers, documents, and records; and

(d) Exercise such further powers as the legislature may from time to time confer upon it.

Section 1 was amended in 1976 to provide for a court system.

Section 2 was entirely revised in 1976.

Section 4 has been amended three times. In 1920 the sentence was added designating the governor to fill a vacancy on the court, and the description of criminal jurisdiction was changed. The 1976 amendment added the last paragraph, and in 1978 the reference to the district courts' jurisdiction in cases involving property valued in excess of three hundred dollars was removed.

Section 5, amended in 1976, raised district judges' terms from four to six years.

Section 6 was amended in 1978 to remove reference to the district courts' jurisdiction in cases involving property valued in excess of three hundred dollars.

Section 7 was amended in 1976, adding the provision for court sittings outside Carson City.

Section 8 was amended in 1978 to give the legislature the authority to determine the qualifications, terms of office, and the limits of civil and criminal jurisdiction of justices' courts.

Section 11 was amended in 1950 by the addition of the words "or appointed."

Section 15 was amended in 1968 to repeal requirements for quarterly payment of judges and for payment of district judges from county treasuries.

Sections 19, 20, and 21 were added in their entirety in 1976.

ARTICLE VII

IMPEACHMENT AND REMOVAL FROM OFFICE

[Powers of impeachment conferred]

SECTION 1.   The assembly shall have the sole power of impeaching. The concurrence of a majority of all the members elected shall be necessary to an impeachment. All impeachments shall be tried by the senate, and, when sitting for that purpose, the senators shall be upon oath or affirmation to do justice according to law and evidence. The chief justice of the supreme court shall preside over the senate while sitting to try the governor or lieutenant-governor upon impeachment. No person shall be convicted without the concurrence of two-thirds of the senators elected.

[Who may be impeached]

SEC. 2.   The governor and the other state and judicial officers, except justices of the peace, shall be liable to impeachment for misdemeanor or malfeasance in office; but judgment in such case shall not extend further than removal from office, and disqualification to hold any office of honor, profit, or trust, under this state. The party, whether convicted or acquitted, shall, nevertheless, be liable to indictment, trial, judgment, and punishment according to law.

[Judicial officers, how impeached]

SEC. 3.   For any reasonable cause, to be entered on the journals of each house, which may or may not be sufficient grounds for impeachment, the chief justice and associate justices of the supreme court and judges of the district courts shall be removed from office on the vote of two-thirds of the members elected to each branch of the legislature, and the justice or judge complained of shall be served with a copy of the complaint against him, and shall have an opportunity of being heard in person, or by counsel, in his defense; *provided,* that no member of either branch of the legislature shall be eligible to fill the vacancy occasioned by such removal.

SEC. 4.   Provision shall be made by law for the removal from office of any civil officer other than those in this article previously specified, for malfeasance or nonfeasance in the performance of his duties.

ARTICLE VIII

MUNICIPAL AND OTHER CORPORATIONS

[Special acts concerning corporations]

SECTION 1.   The legislature shall pass no special act in any manner relating to corporate powers except for municipal purposes; but corporations may be formed under general laws, and all such laws may, from time to time, be altered or repealed.

[Property of corporations taxed]

SEC. 2.   All real property and possessory rights to the same, as well as personal property in this state, belonging to corporations now existing or hereafter created, shall be subject to taxation the same as property of individuals; *provided,* that the property of corporations formed for municipal, charitable, religious, or educational purposes may be exempted by law.

SEC. 3.   Dues from corporations shall be secured by such means as may be prescribed by law; *provided,* that corporators in corporations formed under the laws of this state shall not be individually liable for the debts or liabilities of such corporation.

SEC. 4.   Corporations created by or under the laws of the Territory of Nevada shall be subject to the provisions of such laws until the legislature shall pass laws regulating the same, in pursuance of the provisions of this constitution.

SEC. 5.   Corporations may sue and be sued in all courts, in like manner as individuals.

[Certain paper money interdicted]

SEC. 6.   No bank-notes or paper of any kind shall ever be permitted to circulate as money in this state, except the federal currency and the notes of banks authorized under the laws of Congress.

[Compensation for rights of way]

SEC. 7.   No right of way shall be appropriated to the use of any corporation until full compensation be first made or secured therefor.

[Credit of cities and towns limited]

SEC. 8.   The legislature shall provide for the organization of cities and towns by general laws, and shall restrict their power of taxation, assessment, borrowing money, contracting debts and loaning their credit, except for procuring supplies of water; *provided, however,* that the legislature may, by general laws, in the manner and to the extent therein provided, permit and authorize the electors of any city or town to frame, adopt and amend a charter for its own government, or to amend any existing charter of such city or town.

[State forbidden to speculate]

SEC. 9.   The state shall not donate or loan money or its credit, subscribe to or be interested in the stock of any company, association, or corporation, except corporations formed for educational or charitable purposes.

[Limitation of county indebtedness]

SEC. 10.   No county, city, town, or other municipal corporation shall become a stockholder in any joint-stock company, corporation, or association whatever, or loan its credit in aid of any such company, corporation, or association, except railroad corporations, companies, or associations.

Section 8 was amended in 1924 by the addition of all the materials beginning "provided, however . . ."; this change permits cities a degree of "home rule."

ARTICLE IX

FINANCE AND STATE DEBT

[Fiscal year]

SECTION 1.   The fiscal year shall commence on the first day of July of each year.

[State tax]

SEC. 2.   The legislature shall provide by law for an annual tax sufficient to defray the estimated expenses of the state for each fiscal year; and whenever the expenses of any year shall exceed the income, the legislature shall provide for levying a tax sufficient, with other sources of income, to pay the deficiency, as well as the estimated expenses of such ensuing years or two years. Any moneys paid for the purpose of providing compensation for industrial accidents and occupational diseases, and for administrative expenses incidental thereto, and for the purpose of funding and administering a public employees' retirement system, shall be segregated in proper accounts in the state treasury, and such moneys shall never be used for any other purposes, and they are hereby declared to be trust funds for the uses and purposes herein specified.

[Limitation of state debt; exception]

SEC. 3.   The state may contract public debts; but such debts shall never, in the aggregate, exclusive of interest, exceed the sum of one percent of the assessed valuation of the state, as shown by the reports of the county assessors to the state controller, except for the purpose of defraying extraordinary expenses, as hereinafter mentioned. Every such debt shall be authorized by law for some purpose or purposes, to be distinctly specified therein; and every such law shall provide for levying an annual tax sufficient to pay the interest semiannually, and the principal within twenty years from the passage of such law, and shall specially appropriate the proceeds of said taxes to the payment of said principal and interest; and such appropriation shall not be repealed nor the taxes postponed or diminished until the principal and interest of said debts shall have been wholly paid. Every contract of indebtedness entered into or assumed by or on behalf of the state, when all its debts and liabilities amount to said sum before mentioned, shall be void and of no effect, except in cases of money borrowed to repel invasion, suppress insurrection, defend the state in time of war, or, if hostilities be threatened, provide for the public defense.

The state, notwithstanding the foregoing limitations, may, pursuant to authority of the legislature, make and enter into any and all contracts necessary, expedient or advisable for the protection and preservation of any of its property or natural resources, or for the purposes of obtaining the benefits thereof, however, arising and whether arising by or through any undertaking or project of the United States or by or through any treaty or compact between the states, or otherwise. The legislature may from time to time make such appropriations as may be necessary to carry out the obligations of the state under such contracts, and shall levy such tax as may be necessary to pay the same or carry them into effect.

[State assumption of debts of political subdivisions]

SEC. 4.   The state shall never assume the debts of any county, town, city, or other corporation whatever, unless such debts have been created to repel invasion, suppress insurrection, or to provide for the public defense.

[Disposition of fees]

SEC. 5.   The proceeds from the imposition of any license or registration fee and other charge with respect to the operation of any motor vehicle upon any public highway in this state and the proceeds from the imposition of any excise tax on gasoline or other motor vehicle fuel shall, except costs of administration, be used exclusively for the construction, maintenance, and repair of the public highways of this state.

The provisions of this section do not apply to the proceeds of any tax imposed upon motor vehicles by the legislature in lieu of an ad valorem property tax.

Section 1 was amended in 1930 to change the beginning of the fiscal year from January 1 to July 1.

Section 2 was changed in 1956 by the addition of the last sentence and was changed again in 1974 by adding the state employees' retirement system to the list of segregated funds.

Section 3 was amended in 1916 and in 1934. The section had originally limited the debt to $300,000; this limitation was changed to 1 percent of assessed valuation in 1916. The other change was the addition of the last paragraph in 1934. Attempts to raise the debt limit in 1960, 1968, and 1974 were defeated.

Section 5 was added in 1940, except for the last sentence. An amendment enacted in 1962 added the final sentence.

ARTICLE X

TAXATION

[Taxation]

SECTION 1. The legislature shall provide by law for a uniform and equal rate of assessment and taxation, and shall prescribe such regulations as shall secure a just valuation for taxation of all property, real, personal and possessory, except mines and mining claims, when not patented, the proceeds alone of which shall be assessed and taxed, and when patented, each patented mine shall be assessed at not less than five hundred dollars ($500), except when one hundred dollars ($100) in labor has been actually performed on such patented mine during the year, in addition to the tax upon the net proceeds; shares of stock (except shares of stock in banking corporations), bonds, mortgages, notes, bank deposits, book accounts and credits, and securities and choses in action of like character are deemed to represent interest in property already assessed and taxed, either in Nevada or elsewhere, and shall be exempt. Notwithstanding the provisions of this section, the legislature may constitute agriculture and open-space real property having a greater value for another use than that for which it is being used, as a separate class for taxation purposes and may provide a separate uniform plan for appraisal and valuation of such property for assessment purposes. If such plan is provided, the legislature shall also provide for retroactive assessment for a period of not less than seven years when agricultural and open-space real property is converted to a higher use conforming to the use for which other nearby property is used. Personal property which is moving in interstate commerce through or over the territory of the State of Nevada, or which was consigned to a warehouse, public or private, within the State of Nevada from outside the State of Nevada for storage in transit to a final destination outside the State of Nevada, whether specified when transportation begins or afterward, shall be deemed to have acquired no situs in Nevada for purposes of taxation and shall be exempt from taxation. Such property shall not be deprived of such exemption because while in the warehouse the property is assembled, bound, joined, processed, disassembled, divided, cut, broken in bulk, relabeled or repackaged. The legislature may exempt motor vehicles from the provisions of the tax required by this section, and in lieu thereof, if such exemption is granted, shall provide for a uniform and equal rate of assessment and taxation of motor vehicles, which rate shall not exceed five cents on one dollar of assessed valuation. The legislature shall provide by law for a progressive reduction in the tax upon business inventories by 20 percent in each year following the adoption of this provision, and after the expiration of the fourth year such inventories are exempt from taxation. The legislature may exempt other personal property, including livestock. No inheritance or estate tax shall ever be levied, and there shall also be excepted such property as may be exempted by law for municipal, educational, literary, scientific or other charitable purposes.

[Total tax levy limited]

SEC. 2.   The total tax levy for all public purposes, including levies for bonds, within the state, or any subdivision thereof, shall not exceed five cents on one dollar of assessed valuation.

> *Section 1 was amended in 1902, 1906, 1942, 1960, 1962, 1974, and 1978. The 1902 and 1906 amendments concerned the references to patented mines and all the material beginning "and when patented. . . ." The 1942 addition prohibited inheritance and estate taxes, and the "free port" clause, which exempts from taxation goods that are stored in Nevada awaiting further shipment outside the state, was added in 1960. The 1974 amendment permits assessment of agricultural and open-space property at a low rate but provides for recapture of taxes if the property is sold for another use, for example, condominiums or casinos. The 1978 amendment provides for the phasing out of the business inventories tax and gives the legislature the authority to exempt other personal property from taxation.*
>
> *Section 2 was added in its entirety in 1936.*

ARTICLE XI

EDUCATION

[Education encouraged]

SECTION 1.   The legislature shall encourage by all suitable means the promotion of intellectual, literary, scientific, mining, mechanical, agricultural, and moral improvements, and also provide for a superintendent of public instruction and by law prescribe the manner of appointment, term of office and the duties thereof.

[Public schools fostered]

SEC. 2.   The legislature shall provide for a uniform system of common schools, by which a school shall be established and maintained in each school district at least six months in every year, and any school district which shall allow instruction of a sectarian character therein may be deprived of its proportion of the interest of the public school fund during such neglect or infraction, and the legislature may pass such laws as will tend to secure a general attendance of the children in each school district upon said public schools.

[Lands, funds dedicated to support of public education]

SEC. 3.   All lands, including the sixteenth and thirty-sixth sections in any township donated for the benefit of public schools in the act of the thirty-eighth Congress to enable the people of Nevada Territory to form a state government, the thirty thousand acres of public lands granted by an act of Congress, approved July second, A. D. eighteen hundred and sixty-two, for each senator and representative in Congress, and all proceeds of lands that have been or may hereafter be granted or appropriated by the United States to this state, and also the five hundred thousand acres of land granted to the new states under the act of Congress distributing the proceeds of the public lands among the several states of the Union, approved A. D. eighteen hundred and forty-one; *provided,* that Congress make provision for or authorize such diversion to be made for the purpose herein contained; all estates that may escheat to the state; all of such per centum as may be granted by Congress on the sale of lands; all fines collected under the penal laws of the states; all property given or bequeathed to the state for educational purposes, and all proceeds derived from any or all of said sources shall be and the same are hereby solemnly pledged for educational purposes, and shall not be transferred to any other funds for other uses; and the interest thereon shall, from time to time, be apportioned among the several counties as the legislature may provide by law; and the legislature shall provide for the sale of floating land warrants to cover the aforesaid lands, and for the investment of all proceeds derived from any of the above-mentioned sources, in United States bonds, or the bonds of this state, or the bonds of other states of the Union, or the bonds of any county in the State of Nevada, or in loans at a rate of interest of not less than six per cent per annum, secured by mortgage on agricultural lands in this state of not less than three times the value of the amount loaned, exclusive of perishable improvements, of unexceptional title and free from all encumbrances, said loans to be under such further restrictions and regulations as may be provided by law; *provided,* that the interest only of the aforesaid proceeds shall be used for educational purposes, and any surplus interest shall be added to the principal sum; *and provided further,* that such portion of said interest as may be necessary may be appropriated for the support of the state university.

[State university]

SEC. 4.   The legislature shall provide for the establishment of a state university, which shall embrace departments for agriculture, mechanic arts and mining, to be controlled by a board of regents, whose duties shall be prescribed by law.

[Normal school]

SEC. 5.   The legislature shall have power to establish normal schools, and such different grades of schools, from the primary department to the university, as in their discretion they may deem necessary, and all professors in said university, or teachers in said schools, of whatever grade, shall be required to take and subscribe to the oath as prescribed in article XV of this constitution. No professor or teacher who fails to comply with the provisions of any law framed in accordance with the provisions of this section shall be entitled to receive any portion of the public moneys set apart for school purposes.

[Educational appropriation]

SEC. 6.   In addition to other means provided for the support and maintenance of said university and common schools, the legislature shall provide for their support and maintenance by direct legislative appropriation from the general fund, upon the presentation of budgets in the manner required by law.

[Board of regents constituted]

SEC. 7.   The governor, secretary of state, and superintendent of public instruction shall, for the first four years and until their successors are elected and qualified, constitute a board of regents, to control and manage the affairs of the university and the funds of the same, under such regulations as may be provided by law. But the legislature shall at its regular session next preceding the expiration of the term of office of said board of regents, provide for the election of a new board of regents, and define their duties.

[Providing for organization of university]

SEC. 8.   The board of regents shall, from the interest accruing from the first funds which come under their control, immediately organize and maintain the said mining department in such manner as to make it most effective and useful; *provided,* that all the proceeds of the public lands donated by act of Congress approved July second, A. D. eighteen hundred and sixty-two, for a college for the benefit of agriculture, the mechanic arts, and including military tactics, shall be invested by the said board of regents in a separate fund, to be appropriated exclusively for the benefit of the first-named departments to the university, as set forth in section four above; and the legislature shall provide that if, through neglect or any other contingency, any portion of the fund so set apart shall be lost or misappropriated, the State of Nevada shall replace said amount so lost or misappropriated in said fund, so that the principal of said fund shall remain forever undiminished.

[Sectarian instruction forbidden]

Sec. 9.   No sectarian instruction shall be imparted or tolerated in any school or university that may be established under this constitution.

[Public funds not to be used for sectarian purposes]

Sec. 10.   No public funds of any kind or character whatever, state, county, or municipal, shall be used for sectarian purposes.

Section 1 was amended in 1956 to provide for the appointment of the superintendent of public instruction; the original provision was for election of this official.

Section 2 was amended in 1938 by the elimination of these words: "neglecting to establish and maintain such a school, or"; this phrase originally followed the words, "and any school district."

Section 3 was changed in 1889, in 1912, and again in 1916. The constitution had originally required that the interest be apportioned among the counties in proportion to the number of persons in each county between the ages of six and eighteen; this requirement was changed by amendment to permit apportionment among the counties "as the legislature may provide by law"; the other change was the addition of all the material following ". . . or the bonds of this state" and continuing through ". . . as may be provided by law."

Section 6 was amended in 1889, 1938, and 1954. The original reqirement of this section was that the legislature should have a special tax of one-half mill on the dollar on all taxable property for support of education.

Section 10 was added in its entirety in 1880.

ARTICLE XII

MILITIA

[State militia]

Section 1.   The legislature shall provide by law for organizing and disciplining the militia of this state, for the effectual encouragement of volunteer corps, and the safekeeping of the public arms.

[Power of governor]

Sec. 2.   The governor shall have power to call out the militia to execute the laws of the state, or to suppress insurrection or repel invasion.

ARTICLE XIII

PUBLIC INSTITUTIONS

[Benevolent institutions fostered]

Section 1.   Institutions for the benefit of the insane, blind and deaf and dumb, and such other benevolent institutions as the public good may

13

require, shall be fostered and supported by the state, subject to such regulations as may be prescribed by law.

[State prison]

SEC. 2.   A state prison shall be established and maintained in such manner as may be prescribed by law; and provision may be made by law for the establishment and maintenance of a house of refuge for juvenile offenders.

Section 3 was repealed in 1937; it had described county aid to the indigent and was no longer significant because of federal-state action in such matters.

ARTICLE XIV

BOUNDARY

[Boundaries of state]

SECTION 1.   The boundary of the State of Nevada shall be as follows: Commencing at a point formed by the intersection of the thirty-eighth degree of longitude west from Washington with the thirty-seventh degree of north latitude; thence due west along said thirty-seventh degree of north latitude to the eastern boundary line of the State of California; thence in a northwesterly direction along the said eastern boundary line of the State of California to the forty-third degree of longitude west from Washington; thence north along said forty-third degree of west longitude and said eastern boundary line of the State of California to the forty-second degree of north latitude; thence due east along the said forty-second degree of north latitute to a point formed by its intersection with the aforesaid thirty-eighth degree of longitude west from Washington; thence due south down said thirty-eighth degree of west longitude to the place of beginning. And whensoever Congress shall authorize the addition to the Territory or State of Nevada of any portion of the territory on the easterly border of the foregoing defined limits, not exceeding in extent one degree of longitude, the same shall thereupon be embraced within and become a part of this state. *And furthermore provided,* that all such territory lying west of and adjoining the boundary line herein prescribed, which the State of California may relinquish to the Territory or State of Nevada, shall thereupon be embraced within and constitute a part of this state.

ARTICLE XV

MISCELLANEOUS PROVISIONS

[Seat of government]

SECTION 1.   The seat of government shall be at Carson City, but no appropriation for the erection or purchase of capitol buildings shall be made during the next three years.

[Official oath]

SEC. 2.   Members of the legislature, and all officers, executive, judicial and ministerial, shall, before they enter upon the duties of their respective offices, take and subscribe to the following oath:

"I,--, do solemnly swear (or affirm) that I will support, protect and defend the constitution and government of the United States, and the constitution and government of the State of Nevada, against all enemies, whether domestic or foreign, and that I will bear true faith, and allegiance and loyalty to the same, any ordinance, resolution or law of any state notwithstanding, and that I will well and faithfully perform all the duties of the office of--, on which I am about to enter; (if an oath) so help me God; (if an affirmation) under the pains and penalties of perjury."

[Eligibility for office]

SEC. 3.   No person shall be eligible to any office who is not a qualified elector under this constitution.

[Perpetuities]

SEC. 4.   No perpetuities shall be allowed except for eleemosynary purposes.

[General election]

SEC. 5.   The general election shall be held on the Tuesday next after the first Monday of November.

[Legislature limited]

SEC. 6.   The aggregate number of members of both branches of the legislature shall never exceed seventy-five.

[Offices of county officers]

SEC. 7.   All county officers shall hold their offices at the county-seat of their respective counties.

[Publication of statutes and reports]

SEC. 8.   The legislature shall provide for the speedy publication of all statute laws of a general nature, and such decisions of the supreme court as it may deem expedient and all laws and judicial decisions shall be free for publication by any person; *provided,* that no judgment of the supreme court shall take effect and be operative until the opinion of the court in such case shall be filed with the clerk of said court.

[Salaries may be increased or diminished]

SEC. 9.   The legislature may, at any time, provide by law for increasing or diminishing the salaries or compensation of any of the officers whose salaries or compensation is fixed in this constitution; *provided,* no such change of salary or compensation shall apply to any officer during the term for which he may have been elected.

[Election, appointment of officers]

SEC. 10.   All officers whose election or appointment is not otherwise provided for shall be chosen or appointed as may be prescribed by law.

[Tenure of office limited]

SEC. 11.   The tenure of any office not herein provided for may be declared by law, or, when not so declared, such office shall be held during the pleasure of the authority making the appointment, but the legislature shall not create any office the tenure of which shall be longer than four (4) years, except as herein otherwise provided in this constitution. In the case of any officer or employee of any municipality governed under a legally adopted charter, the provisions of such charter with reference to the tenure of office or the dismissal from office of any such officer or employee shall control.

[Office at capital]

SEC. 12.   The governor, secretary of state, state treasurer, state controller, and clerk of the supreme court shall keep their respective offices at the seat of government.

[Census taken, when]

SEC. 13.   The enumeration of the inhabitants of this state shall be taken under the direction of the legislature, if deemed necessary, in A. D. eighteen hundred and sixty-five, A. D. eighteen hundred and sixty-seven, A. D. eighteen hundred and seventy-five, and every ten years thereafter; and these enumerations, together with the census that may be taken under the direction of the Congress of the United States in A. D. eighteen hundred and seventy, and every subsequent ten years, shall serve as the basis of representation in both houses of the legislature.

[Plurality a choice]

SEC. 14.   A plurality of votes given at an election by the people shall constitute a choice, where not otherwise provided by this constitution.

SEC. 15.   The legislature shall provide by law for a state merit system governing the employment of employees in the executive branch of state government.

Section 2 was amended in 1914 to eliminate from the oath of office the references to dueling, which had required the new official to swear that he had not participated, and would not participate in any capacity, in a duel.

Section 3 was amended in 1889 and 1912; in 1978 the provisions regarding ineligibility for office for those persons involved in dueling were removed, leaving only the first sentence in the section.

Section 11 was changed in 1946 by the addition of the last sentence, which permits city charters to describe tenure of city officials.

Section 15 was added in its entirety in 1970.

ARTICLE XVI

AMENDMENTS

[Constitution amended, how]

SECTION 1.   1. Any amendment or amendments to this constitution may be proposed in the senate or assembly; and if the same shall be agreed to by a majority of all the members elected to each of the two houses, such proposed amendment or amendments shall be entered on their respective journals, with the yeas and nays taken thereon, and referred to the legislature then next to be chosen, and shall be published for three months next preceding the time of making such choice. And if, in the legislature next chosen as aforesaid, such proposed amendment or amendments shall be agreed to by a majority of all the members elected to each house, then it shall be the duty of the legislature to submit such proposed amendment or amendments to the people in such manner and at such time as the legislature shall prescribe; and if the people shall approve and ratify such amendment or amendments by a majority of the electors qualified to vote for members of the legislature voting thereon, such amendment or amendments shall, unless precluded by subsection 2, become a part of the constitution.

2.   If two or more amendments which affect the same section of the constitution are ratified by the people at the same election:

(a) If all can be given effect without contradiction in substance, each shall become a part of the constitution.

(b) If one or more contradict in substance the other or others, that amendment which received the largest favorable vote, and any other amendment or amendments compatible with it, shall become a part of the constitution.

3.   If after the proposal of an amendment, another amendment is ratified which affects the same section of the constitution but is compatible with the proposed amendment, the next legislature if it agrees to the proposed amendment shall submit such proposal to the people as a further amendment to the amended section. If, after the proposal of an amendment, another amendment is ratified which contradicts in substance the proposed amendment, such proposed amendment shall not be submitted to the people.

[Revision of constitution; convention]

SEC. 2.   If at any time the legislature, by a vote of two-thirds of the members elected to each house, shall determine that it is necessary to cause a revision of this entire constitution, they shall recommend to the electors, at the next election for members of the legislature, a vote for or against a convention, and if it shall appear that a majority of the electors voting at such election shall have voted in favor of calling a convention, the legislature shall, at its next session, provide by law for calling a convention to be holden within six months after the passage of such law; and such convention shall consist of a number of members not less than that of both branches of the legislature. In determining what is a majority of the electors voting at such election, reference shall be had to the highest number of votes cast at such election for the candidates for any office or on any question.

In 1972 subsections 2 and 3 were added in their entirety.

ARTICLE XVII

SCHEDULE

[Acts of territory made valid]

SECTION 1.   That no inconvenience may arise by reason of a change from a territorial to a permanent state government, it is declared that all rights, actions, prosecutions, judgments, claims, and contracts, as well of individuals as of bodies corporate, including counties, towns, and cities, shall continue as if no change had taken place; and all process which may issue under the authority of the Territory of Nevada, previous to its admission into the Union as one of the United States, shall be as valid as if issued in the name of the State of Nevada.

[Territorial laws effective]

SEC. 2.   All laws of the Territory of Nevada, in force at the time of the admission of this state, not repugnant to this constitution, shall remain in force until they expire by their own limitations, or be altered or repealed by the legislature.

[Fines and penalties: territory to state]

SEC. 3.   All fines, penalties and forfeitures accruing to the Territory of Nevada, or to the people of the United States in the Territory of Nevada, shall inure to the State of Nevada.

[Prosecutions and civil actions]

SEC. 4   All recognizances heretofore taken, or which may be taken before the change from a territorial to a state government, shall remain valid, and shall pass to and may be prosecuted in the name of the state, and all bonds executed to the governor of the territory, or to any other officer or court in his or their official capacity, or to the people of the United States in the Territory of Nevada, shall pass to the governor, or other officer, or court, and his or their successors in office, for the uses therein respectively expressed, and may be sued on, and recovery had accordingly; and all property real, personal, or mixed, and all judgments, bonds, specialties, choses in action, claims and debts of whatsoever description, and all records and public archives of the Territory of

Nevada shall issue to and vest in the State of Nevada, and may be sued for and recovered in the same manner and to the same extent by the State of Nevada, as the same could have been by the Territory of Nevada. All criminal prosecutions and penal actions, which may have arisen, or which may arise before the change from a territorial to a state government, and which shall then be pending, shall be prosecuted to judgment and execution in the name of the state. All offenses committed against the laws of the Territory of Nevada, before the change from a territorial to a state government, and which shall not be prosecuted before such change, may be prosecuted in the name and by the authority of the State of Nevada with like effect as though such change had not taken place; and all penalties incurred shall remain the same as if this constitution had not been adopted. All actions at law and suits in equity, and other legal proceedings, which may be pending in any of the courts of the Territory of Nevada at the time of the change from a territorial to a state government, may be continued and transferred to and determined by any court of the state which shall have jurisdiction of the subject-matter thereof. All actions at law and suits in equity, and all other legal proceedings, which may be pending in any of the courts of the Territory of Nevada at the time of the change from a territorial to a state government, shall be continued and transferred to, and may be prosecuted to judgment and execution in any court of the state, which shall have jurisdiction of the subject-matter thereof; and all books, papers and records relating to the same shall be transferred in like manner to such court.

[Salaries of state officers]

SEC. 5.   For the first term of office succeeding the formation of a state government, the salary of the governor shall be four thousand dollars per annum; the salary of the secretary of state shall be three thousand six hundred dollars per annum; the salary of the state controller shall be three thousand six hundred dollars per annum; the salary of the state treasurer shall be three thousand six hundred dollars per annum; the salary of the surveyor-general shall be one thousand dollars per annum; the salary of the attorney-general shall be two thousand five hundred dollars per annum; the salary of the superintendent of public instruction shall be two thousand dollars per annum; the salary of each judge of the supreme court shall be seven thousand dollars per annum. The salaries of the foregoing offices shall be paid quarterly, out of the state treasury. The pay of state senators and members of the assembly shall be eight dollars per day, for each day of actual service, and forty cents per mile for mileage going to and returning from the place of meeting. No officer mentioned in this section shall receive any fee or perquisites to his own use for the performance of any duty connected with his office, or for the performance of any additional duty imposed upon him by law.

[Apportionment of legislators]

SEC. 6. Until otherwise provided by law, the apportionment of senators and assemblymen in the different counties shall be as follows, to wit: Storey County, four senators and twelve assemblymen; Douglas County, one senator and two assemblymen; Esmeralda County, two senators and four assemblymen; Humboldt County, two senators and three assemblymen; Lander County, two senators and four assemblymen; Lyon County, one senator and three assemblymen; Lyon and Churchill counties, one senator jointly; Churchill County, one assemblyman; Nye County, one senator and one assemblyman; Ormsby County, two senators and three assemblymen; Washoe and Roop counties, two senators and three assemblymen.

[Territorial debt assumed by state]

SEC. 7 All debts and liabilities of the Territory of Nevada, lawfully incurred, and which remain unpaid at the time of the admission of this state into the Union, shall be assumed by and become the debt of the State of Nevada; *provided,* that the assumption of such indebtedness shall not prevent the state from contracting the additional indebtedness, as provided in section three of Article IX of this constitution.

[Terms of officers]

SEC. 8. The term of state officers (except judicial) elected at the first election under this constitution, shall continue until the Tuesday after the first Monday of January, A. D. eighteen hundred and sixty-seven, and until the election and qualification of their successors.

SEC. 9. The senators to be elected at the first election under this constitution shall draw lots, so that the term of one-half of the number, as nearly as may be, shall expire on the day succeeding the general election in A. D. eighteen hundred and sixty-six, and the term of the other half shall expire on the day succeeding the general election in A. D. eighteen hundred and sixty-eight; *provided,* that in drawing lots for all senatorial terms, the senatorial representation shall be allotted so that in the counties having two or more senators, the terms thereof shall be divided, as nearly as may be, between the long and short terms.

SEC. 10. At the general election in A. D. eighteen hundred and sixty-six, and thereafter, the term of senators shall be four years from the day succeeding such general election, and members of assembly for two years from the day succeeding such general election, and the terms of senators shall be allotted by the legislature in long and short terms, as hereinbefore provided, so that one-half the number, as nearly as may be, shall be elected every two years.

SEC. 11. The term of the members of the assembly elected at the first general election under this constitution shall expire on the day succeeding the general election in A. D. eighteen hundred and sixty-five; and the terms of those elected at the general election in A. D. eighteen hundred and sixty-five shall expire on the day succeeding the general election in A. D. eighteen hundred and sixty-six.

SEC. 12.   The first regular session of the legislature shall commence on the second Monday of December, A. D. eighteen hundred and sixty-four, and the second regular session of the same shall commence on the first Monday of January, A. D. eighteen hundred and sixty-six, and the third regular session of the legislature shall be the first of the biennial sessions, and shall commence on the first Monday of January, A. D. eighteen hundred and sixty-seven; and the regular sessions of the legislature shall be held thereafter biennially commencing on the first Monday of January.

SEC. 13.   All county officers under the laws of the Territory of Nevada at the time when the constitution shall take effect, whose offices are not inconsistent with the provisions of this constitution, shall continue in office until the first Monday of January, A. D. eighteen hundred and sixty-seven, and until their successors are elected and qualified; and all township officers shall continue in office until the expiration of their terms of office, and until their successors are elected and qualified; *provided,* that the probate judges of the several counties, respectively, shall continue in office until the election and qualification of the district judges of the several counties or judicial districts; *and provided further,* that the term of office of the present county officers of Lander County shall expire on the first Monday of January, A. D. eighteen hundred and sixty-five, except the probate judge of said county, whose term of office shall expire upon the first Monday of December, A. D. eighteen hundred and sixty-four, and there shall be an election for county officers of Lander County at the general election in November, A. D. eighteen hundred and sixty-four, and the officers then elected shall hold office from the first Monday of January, A. D. eighteen hundred and sixty-five, until the first Monday of January, A. D. eighteen hundred and sixty-seven, and until their successors are elected and qualified.

SEC. 14.   The governor, secretary, treasurer, and superintendent of public instruction of the Territory of Nevada shall each continue to discharge the duties of their respective offices after the admission of this state into the Union, and until the time designated for the qualification of the above-named officers to be elected under the state government; and the territorial auditor shall continue to discharge the duties of his said office until the time appointed for the qualification of the state controller; *provided,* that the said officers shall each receive the salaries, and be subject to the restrictions and conditions provided in this constitution; *and provided further,* that none of them shall receive to his own use any fees or perquisites for the performance of any duty connected with his office.

SEC. 15.   The terms of the supreme court shall, until provision be made by law, be held at such times as the judges of the said court, or a majority of them, may appoint. The first terms of the several district courts (except as hereinafter mentioned) shall commence on the first Monday of December, A. D. eighteen hundred and sixty-four. The first term of the district court in the Fifth judicial district shall commence on the first Monday of December, A. D. eighteen hundred and sixty-four, in the county of Nye, and shall commence on the first Monday of January, A. D. eighteen hundred and sixty-five in the county of Churchill. The terms of the Fourth judicial district court shall, until otherwise provided by law, be held at the county seat of Washoe County, and the first term thereof commence on the first Monday of December, A. D. eighteen hundred and sixty-four.

SEC. 16.   The judges of the several district courts of this state shall be paid, as hereinbefore provided, salaries at the following rates per annum: First judicial district (each judge), six thousand dollars; Second judicial district, four thousand dollars; Third judicial district, five thousand dollars; Fourth judicial district, five thousand dollars; Fifth judicial district, thirty-six hundred dollars; Sixth judicial district, four thousand dollars; Seventh judicial district, six thousand dollars; Eighth judicial district, thirty-six hundred dollars; Ninth judicial district, five thousand dollars.

SEC. 17.   The salary of any judge in said judicial districts may, by law, be altered or changed, subject to the provisions contained in this constitution.

SEC. 18.   The governor, lieutenant-governor, secretary of state, state treasurer, state controller, attorney-general, surveyor-general, clerk of the supreme court, and superintendent of public instruction, to be elected at the first election under this constitution, shall each qualify and enter upon the duties of their respective offices on the first Monday of December succeeding their election, and shall continue in office until the first Tuesday after the first Monday of January, A. D. eighteen hundred and sixty-seven, and until the election and qualification of their successors respectively.

SEC. 19.   The judges of the supreme court and district judges to be elected at the first election under this constitution shall qualify and enter upon the duties of their respective offices on the first Monday of December succeeding their election.

SEC. 20.   All officers of state, and district judges first elected under this constitution, shall be commissioned by the governor of this territory, which commission shall be countersigned by the secretary of the same, and shall qualify, before entering upon the discharge of their duties, before any officer authorized to administer oaths under the laws of this territory; and also the state controller and state treasurer shall each respectively, before they qualify and enter upon the discharge of their duties, execute and deliver to the secretary of the Territory of Nevada an official bond, made payable to the people of the State of Nevada, in the sum of thirty thousand dollars, to be approved by the governor of the Territory of Nevada, and shall also execute and deliver to the secretary of state such other or further official bond or bonds as may be required by law.

SEC. 21.   Each county, town, city, and incorporated village shall make provision for the support of its own officers subject to such regulations as may be prescribed by law.

SEC. 22.   In case the office of any state officer except a judicial officer shall become vacant before the expiration of the regular term for which he was elected, the vacancy may be filled by appointment by the governor, until it shall be supplied at the next general election, when it shall be filled by election for the residue of the unexpired term.

SEC. 23.   All cases, both civil and criminal, which may be pending and undetermined in the probate courts of the several counties at the time when, under the provisions of this constitution, said probate courts are to be abolished, shall be transferred to and determined by the district courts of such counties respectively.

SEC. 24.   For the first three years after the adoption of this constitution, the legislature shall not levy a tax for state purposes exceeding one per cent per annum on the taxable property of the State; *provided,* the legislature may levy a special tax, not exceeding one-fourth of one per cent per annum, which shall be appropriated to the payment of the indebtedness of the Territory of Nevada assumed by the State of Nevada, and for that purpose only, until all of said indebtedness is paid.

SEC. 25.   The county of Roop shall be attached to the county of Washoe for judicial, legislative, revenue and county purpose until otherwise provided by law.

SEC. 26.   At the first regular session of the legislature to convene under the requirements of this constitution, provision shall be made by law for paying for the publication of six hundred copies of the debates and proceedings of this convention in book form, to be disposed of as the legislature may direct; and the Hon. J. Neely Johnson, president of this convention, shall contract for, and A. J. Marsh, official reporter of this convention, under the direction of the president, shall supervise the publication of such debates and proceedings. Provision shall be made by law at such first session of the legislature for the compensation of the official reporter of this convention, and he shall be paid in coin or its equivalent. He shall receive, for his services, in reporting the debates and proceedings fifteen dollars per day during the session of the convention, and seven and one-half dollars additional for each evening session, and thirty cents per folio of one hundred words for preparing the same for publication; and for supervising and indexing such publication the sum of fifteen dollars per day during the time actually engaged in such service.

Although the Schedule is the mechanism by which a transition of government is achieved and its provisions are therefore ordinarily of historical interest only, the Nevada Supreme Court ruled in State ex rel. Herr v. Laxalt *(June 5, 1968) that the Schedule has continuing vitality as a part of the constitution, to the extent that its provisions are still applicable.*

Section 22 was amended in 1976 to eliminate references to judges and added the phrase specifically exempting them from the appointment provisions.

ARTICLE XVIII

RIGHT OF SUFFRAGE

[Right of suffrage not to be withheld]

SECTION 1.   The rights of suffrage and office-holding shall not be withheld from any male citizen of the United States by reason of his color or previous condition of servitude.

The original constitution ended with Article XVII, "Schedule," insofar as the substantive requirements of government are concerned; it included, of course, the Election Ordinance, which provided for the vote on the constitution. Thus both Articles XVIII and XIX are additions to the constitution.

Article XVIII was added in 1880 to conform with the Fifteenth Amendment to the United States Constitution; the Nineteenth Amendment made the word "male" obsolete.

ARTICLE XIX

INITIATIVE AND REFERENDUM

[Law to be submitted to people for approval or disapproval on petition of 10 percent of voters]

SECTION 1.   1. Whenever a number of registered voters of this state equal to 10 percent or more of the number of voters who voted at the last preceding general election shall express their wish by filing a petition in the form provided for in section 3 of this article that any statute or resolution or any part thereof enacted by the legislature be submitted to a vote of the people, the officers charged with the duties of announcing and proclaiming elections and of certifying nominations or questions to be voted upon shall submit the question of approval or disapproval of such statute or resolution or any part thereof to a vote of the voters at the next succeeding election at which such question may be voted upon by the registered voters of the entire state.

2.   If a majority of the voters voting upon the proposal submitted at such election votes approval of such statute or resolution or any part

thereof, such statute or resolution or any part thereof shall stand as the law of the state and shall not be amended, annulled, repealed, set aside, suspended or in any way made inoperative except by the direct vote of the people. If a majority of such voters votes disapproval of such statute or resolution or any part thereof, such statute or resolution or any part thereof shall be void and of no effect.

[Procedure for initiative]

SEC. 2. 1. Notwithstanding the provisions of section 1 of article IV of this constitution, but subject to the limitations of section 6 of this article, the people reserve to themselves the power to propose, by initiative petition, statutes and amendments to statutes and amendments to this constitution, and to enact or reject them at the polls.

2. An initiative petition shall be in the form required by section 3 of this article and shall be proposed by a number of registered voters equal to 10 percent or more of the number of voters who voted at the last preceding general election in not less than 75 percent of the counties in the state, but the total number of registered voters signing the initiative petition shall be equal to 10 percent or more of the voters who voted in the entire state at the last preceding general election.

3. If the initiative petition proposes a statute or an amendment to a statute, it shall be filed with the secretary of state not less than 30 days prior to any regular session of the legislature. The secretary of state shall transmit such petition to the legislature as soon as the legislature convenes and organizes. The petition shall take precedence over all other measures except appropriation bills, and the statute or amendment to a statute proposed thereby shall be enacted or rejected by the legislature without change or amendment within 40 days. If the proposed statute or amendment to a statute is enacted by the legislature and approved by the governor in the same manner as other statutes are enacted, such statute or amendment to a statute shall become law, but shall be subject to referendum petition as provided in section 1 of this article. If the statute or amendment to a statute is rejected by the legislature, or if no action is taken thereon within 40 days, the secretary of state shall submit the question of approval or disapproval of such statute or amendment to a statute to a vote of the voters at the next succeeding general election. If a majority of the voters voting on such question at such election votes approval of such statute or amendment to a statute, it shall become law and take effect upon completion of the canvass of votes by the supreme court. An initiative measure so approved by the voters shall not be amended, annulled, repealed, set aside or suspended by the legislature within 3 years from the date it takes effect. If a majority of such voters votes disapproval of such statute or amendment to a statute, no further action shall be taken on such petition. If the legislature reject such proposed statute or amendment, the governor may recommend to the legislature and the legislature

may propose a different measure on the same subject, in which event, after such different measure has been approved by the governor, the question of approval or disapproval of each measure shall be submitted by the secretary of state to a vote of the voters at the next succeeding general election. If the conflicting provisions submitted to the voters are both approved by a majority of the voters voting on such measures, the measure which receives the largest number of affirmative votes shall thereupon become law.

4.   If the initiative petition proposes an amendment to the constitution, it shall be filed with the secretary of state not less than 90 days before any regular general election at which the question of approval or disapproval of such amendment may be voted upon by the voters of the entire state. The secretary of state shall cause to be published in a newspaper of general circulation, on three separate occasions, in each county in the state, together with any explanatory matter which shall be placed upon the ballot, the entire text of the proposed amendment. If a majority of the voters voting on such question at such election votes disapproval of such amendment, no further action shall be taken on the petition. If a majority of such voters votes approval of such amendment, the secretary of state shall publish and resubmit the question of approval or disapproval to a vote of the voters at the next succeeding general election in the same manner as such question was originally submitted. If a majority of such voters votes disapproval of such amendment, no futher action shall be taken on such petition. If a majority of such voters votes approval of such amendment, it shall become a part of this constitution upon completion of the canvass of votes by the supreme court.

[Text of referendum and initiative petition]

SEC. 3.   Each referendum petition and initiative petition shall include the full text of the measure proposed. Each signer shall affix thereto his or her signature, residence address and the name of the county in which he or she is a registered voter. The petition may consist of more than one document, but each document shall have affixed thereto an affidavit made by one of the signers of such document to the effect that all of the signatures are genuine and that each individual who signed such document was at the time of signing a registered voter in the county of his or her residence. The affidavit shall be executed before a person authorized by law to administer oaths in the State of Nevada. The enacting clause of all statutes or amendments proposed by initiative petition shall be: "The People of the State of Nevada do enact as follows:".

[Initiative and referendum reserved to counties and municipalities]

SEC. 4.   The initiative and referendum powers provided for in this article are further reserved to the registered voters of each county and each municipality as to all local, special and municipal legislation of every kind in or for such county or municipality. In counties and municipalities initiative petitions may be instituted by a number of registered voters equal to 15 percent or more of the voters who voted at the last preceding general county or municipal election. Referendum petitions may be instituted by 10 percent or more of such voters.

SEC. 5.   The provisions of this article are self-executing but the legislature may provide by law for procedures to facilitate the operation thereof.

[Initiative must provide necessary revenue]

SEC. 6.   This article does not permit the proposal of any statute or statutory amendment which makes an appropriation or otherwise requires the expenditure of money, unless such statute or amendment also imposes a sufficient tax, not prohibited by the constitution, or otherwise constitutionally provides for raising the necessary revenue.

As noted above, Article XIX was not part of the original constitution.

Section 1 was added in 1904 and provides for a referendum to the voters of acts of the legislature whenever 10 percent of those voting at the last election submit a petition requesting such referral.

Paragraph 2 of Section 1 was also added in 1904; it strengthens the impact of Section 1 by making laws approved at a referendum election impossible of revocation except by vote of the people. Ordinary acts of the legislature are subject to revocation or modification simply by passage of another act by the legislative body.

Section 2 was added in 1912, amended in 1958, 1962, and 1972. It provides for popular, as distinct from legislative, initiation of measures whenever 10 percent of the voters in thirteen of the seventeen counties sign a petition proposing a law. The petition is presented to the legislature, which must act on it within forty days. If the measure is passed and signed by the governor, or is passed over his veto, it becomes law; if the measure is rejected by the legislature, or if the legislature fails to act on it within forty days, it goes on the ballot and, if passed by the voters, it becomes law. Thus, no measure proposed by 10 percent of the voters can die through legislative opposition or inaction.

In 1962 the voters approved an amendment by which all of Article XIX was rewritten. Two substantive changes were included in this rewriting. One change provided that when an initiative petition proposes a constitutional amendment, such petition shall not be presented to the legislature, but shall be put on the ballot at the next two general elections. If twice approved by the voters, the amendment becomes part of the constitution. The second change reduced the

number needed to propose an initiative from 10 percent of the qualified *voters to 10 percent of those who* voted *in the last general election in thirteen of the seventeen counties.*
Section 6 was added in its entirety in 1972.

ELECTION ORDINANCE

[Obsolete, historical only]

WHEREAS, The enabling act passed by Congress and approved March twenty-first, A. D. eighteen hundred and sixty-four, requires that the convention charged with the duty of framing a constitution for a state government "shall provide by ordinance for submitting said constitution to the people of the Territory of Nevada for their ratification or rejection," on a certain day prescribed therein; therefore this convention, organized in pursuance of said enabling act, do establish the following:

Ordinance

SECTION 1.   The governor of the Territory of Nevada is hereby authorized to issue his proclamation for the submission of this constitution to the people of said territory, for their approval or rejection, on the day provided for such submission by act of Congress; and this constitution shall be submitted to the qualified electors of said territory, in the several counties thereof, for their approval or rejection, at the time provided by such act of Congress; and further, on the first Tuesday after the first Monday of November, A. D. eighteen hundred and sixty-four, there shall be a general election in the several counties of said territory, for the election of state officers, supreme and district judges, members of the legislature, representative in Congress, and three presidential electors.

SEC. 2.   All persons qualified by the laws of said territory to vote for representatives to the general assembly on the said twenty-first day of March, including those in the army of the United States, both within and beyond the boundaries of said territory, and also all persons who may, by the aforesaid laws, be qualified to vote on the first Wednesday of September, A. D. eighteen hundred and sixty-four, including those in the aforesaid army of the United States, within and without the boundaries of said territory, may vote for the adoption or rejection of said constitution, on the day last above named. In voting upon this constitution each elector shall deposit in the ballot box a ticket, whereon shall be clearly written or printed "Constitution—Yes" or "Constitution—No," or other such words that shall clearly indicate the intention of the elector.

SEC. 3.   All persons qualified by the laws of said territory to vote on the Tuesday after the first Monday of November, A. D. eighteen hundred and sixty-four, including those in the army of the United States, within and beyond the boundaries of said territory, may vote on the day last above named for state officers, supreme and district judges, members of the legislature, representative in Congress, and three presidential electors to the electoral college.

SEC. 4. The elections provided in this ordinance shall be holden at such places as shall be designated by the boards of commissioners of the several counties in said territory. The judges and inspectors of said elections shall be appointed by said commissioners, and the said elections shall be conducted in conformity with the existing laws of said territory in relation to holding the general election.

SEC. 5. The judges and inspectors of said elections shall carefully count each ballot immediately after said elections and forthwith make duplicate returns thereof to the clerks of the said county commissioners of their respective counties; and said clerks, within fifteen days after said election, shall transmit an abstract of the votes, including the soldiers' vote as herein provided, given for state officers, supreme and district judges, representative in Congress, and three presidential electors, enclosed in an envelope, by the most safe and expeditious conveyance, to the governor of said territory, marked "Election Returns."

SEC. 6. Upon the receipt of said returns, including those of the soldiers' vote, or within twenty days after the election, if said returns be not sooner received, it shall be the duty of the board of canvassers, to consist of the governor, United States district attorney, and chief justice of said territory, or any two of them, to canvass the returns in the presence of all who may wish to be present, and if a majority of all the votes given upon this constitution shall be in its favor, the said governor shall immediately publish an abstract of the same, and make proclamation of the fact in some newspaper in said territory, and certify the same to the president of the United States, together with a copy of the constitution and ordinance. The said board of canvassers, after canvassing the votes of the said November elections, shall issue certificates of election to such persons as were elected state officers, judges of the supreme and district courts, representative in Congress and three presidential electors. When the president of the United States shall issue his proclamation declaring this state admitted into the Union on an equal footing with the original states, this constitution shall thenceforth be ordained and established as the constitution of the State of Nevada.

SEC. 7. For the purpose of taking the vote of the electors of said territory who may be in the army of the United States, the adjutant general of said territory shall, on or before the fifth day of August next following, make out a list in alphabetical order, and deliver the same to the governor, of the names of all the electors, residents of said territory, who shall be in the army of the United States, stating the number of the regiment, battalion, squadron, or battery to which he belongs, and also the county or township of his residence in said territory.

14

Sec. 8.   The governor shall classify and arrange the aforesaid returned list, and shall make therefrom separate lists of the electors belonging to each regiment, battalion, squadron, and battery from said territory, in the service of the United States, and shall, on or before the fifteenth day of August following, transmit, by mail or otherwise, to the commanding officer of each regiment, battalion, squadron, and battery a list of electors belonging thereto, which said list shall specify the name, residence, and rank of each elector, and the company to which he belongs, if to any, and also the county and township to which he belongs, and in which he is entitled to vote.

Sec. 9.   Between the hours of nine o'clock a. m. and three o'clock p. m., on each of the election days hereinbefore named, a ballot box or suitable receptacle for votes shall be opened, under the immediate charge and direction of three of the highest officers in command, for the reception of votes from the electors whose names are upon said list, at each place where a regiment, battalion, squadron, or battery of soldiers from said territory, in the army of the United States, may be on that day, at which time and place said electors shall be entitled to vote for all officers for which, by reason of their residence in the several counties in said territory, they are authorized to vote, as fully as they would be entitled to vote in the several counties or townships in which they reside, and the votes so given by such electors, at such time and place, shall be considered, taken and held to have been given by them in the respective counties and townships in which they are resident.

Sec. 10.   Each ballot deposited for the adoption or rejection of this constitution, in the army of the United States, shall have distinctly written or printed thereon "Constitution—Yes," or "Constitution—No," or words of a similar import; and further, for the election of state officers, supreme and district judges, members of the legislature, representative in Congress, and three presidential electors, the name and office of the person voted for shall be plainly written or printed on one piece of paper. The name of each elector voting as aforesaid shall be checked upon the said list, at the time of voting, by one of the said officers having charge of the ballot box. The said officers having charge of the election shall count the votes and compare them with the check list, immediately after the closing of the ballot box.

Sec. 11.   All the ballots cast, together with the said voting list, checked as aforesaid, shall be immediately sealed up and sent forthwith to the governor of said territory at Carson City, by mail or otherwise, by the commanding officer, who shall make out and certify duplicate returns of votes given, according to the forms hereinafter prescribed, seal up and immediately transmit the same to the said governor at Carson City, by mail or otherwise, the day following the transmission of the ballots and the voting list herein named. The said commanding officer shall also immediately transmit to the several county clerks in said territory, an abstract of the votes given at the general election in November, for county officers marked "Election Returns."

SEC. 12. The forms of returns of votes to be made by the commanding officer to the governor and county clerks of said territory shall be in substance as follows, viz.:

Returns of soldiers' votes in the (here insert the regiment, detachment, battalion, squadron, or battery).

(For first election—On the constitution.)

I, _____, herby certify that on the first Wednesday, of September, A. D. eighteen hundred and sixty-four, the electors belonging to the (here insert the name of the regiment, detachment, battalion, squadron, or battery) cast the following number of votes for and against the constitution for the State of Nevada, viz.:

For constitution—(number of votes written in full and in figures).

Against constitution—(number of votes written in full and in figures).

(Second election—For state and other officers.)

I, _____, hereby certify that on the first Tuesday after the first Monday in November, A. D. eighteen hundred and sixty-four, the electors belonging to the (here insert as above) cast the following number of votes for the several officers and persons hereinafter named, viz.:

For governor—(names of persons voted for, number of votes for each person voted for, written in full, and also in figures, against the name of each person).

For lieutenant-governor—(names of candidates, number of votes cast for each written out and in figures as above).

Continue as above until the list is completed.

Attest:

I, A.B.

Commanding officer of the (here insert regiment, detachment, battalion, squadron, or battery, as the case may be).

SEC. 13. The governor of this territory is requested to furnish each commanding officer, within and beyond the boundaries of said territory, proper and sufficient blanks for said returns.

SEC. 14. The provisions of this ordinance in regard to the soldiers' vote shall apply to future elections under this constitution, and be in full force until the legislature shall provide by law for taking the votes of citizens of said territory in the army of the United States.

Done in convention, at Carson City, the twenty-eighth day of July, in the year of our Lord one thousand eight hundred and sixty-four and of the independence of the United States the eighty-ninth, and signed by the delegates.

J. NEELY JOHNSON,

President of the Convention and Delegate from Ormsby County.

WM. M. GILLESPIE, *Secretary.*

[List of delegates signing constitution]

Henry B. Brady	Delegate from Washoe County
E. F. Dunne	Delegate from Humboldt County
J. G. McClinton	Delegate from Esmeralda County
G. N. Folsom	Delegate from Washoe County
F. H. Kennedy	Delegate from Lyon County
W. W. Belden	Delegate from Washoe County
F. M. Proctor	Delegate from Nye County
Albert T. Hawley	Delegate from Douglas County
Geo. L. Gibson	Delegate from Ormsby County
F. Tagliabue	Delegate from Nye County
Wm. Wetherill	Delegate from Esmeralda County
John A. Collins	Delegate from Storey County
Jas. A. Banks	Delegate from Humboldt County
J. S. Crosman	Delegate from Lyon County
Saml. A. Chapin	Delegate from Storey County
C. M. Brosnan	Delegate from Storey County
John H. Kinkead	Delegate from Ormsby County
Geo. A. Hudson	Delegate from Lyon County
Israel Crawford	Delegate from Ormsby County
A. J. Lockwood	Delegate from Ormsby County
H. G. Parker	Delegate from Lyon County
J. H. Warwick	Delegate from Lander County
C. E. DeLong	Delegate from Storey County
Lloyd Frizell	Delegate from Storey County
Geo. A. Nourse	Delegate from Washoe County
B. S. Mason	Delegate from Esmeralda County
Almon Hovey	Delegate from Storey County
Thomas Fitch	Delegate from Storey County
J. W. Haines	Delegate from Douglas County

NOTES

Notes to Chapter 1

1. Gloria Griffen Cline, *Exploring the Great Basin* (Norman: University of Oklahoma Press, 1963), p. 187.

2. John Charles Frémont, *Narratives of Exploration and Adventure,* Allan Nevins, ed. (New York: Longmans, Green & Co., 1956), p. 340. Courtesy of David McKay, Inc.

3. Cline, *op. cit.,* p. 188.

4. For a thorough treatment of trapping and exploring expeditions see Cline, *op. cit.,* and Chapters 3, 4, 5, and 6 in Effie Mona Mack, *Nevada* (Glendale: Arthur H. Clark, 1936).

5. This act may be found in Myron Angel, ed., *History of Nevada* (Oakland: Thompson and West, 1881), p. 37. (Reprint ed., Berkeley: Howell-North, 1958); hereafter cited as Thompson & West.

6. Thompson & West, *op. cit.,* p. 41.

7. S. George Ellsworth, "Utah's Struggle for Statehood," *Utah Historical Quarterly,* Winter, 1963, 31:63.

8. Thompson & West, *op. cit.,* p. 42.

9. *Ibid.,* p. 44.

10. *Ibid.,* p. 46.

11. *Congressional Globe,* 35th Congress, 1st sess., pt. III, p. 2090.

12. *Ibid.,* p. 2122.

13. Thompson & West, *op. cit.,* p. 64.

14. Secretary of State (John Koontz), *Political History of Nevada,* 4th ed. (Carson City: State Printing Office, 1960), p. 22.

15. *Territorial Papers of Nevada,* National Archives, vol. 1. Both letters were found in the same folder.

16. Mark Twain, *Roughing It* (New York: The New American Library, 1962), p. 29.

17. A. J. Marsh, *Letters from Nevada Territory,* William C. Miller, ed. (Carson City: Legislative Counsel Bureau, 1972).

18. *Ibid.,* p. 407.

19. *Ibid.,* pp. 577–578.

20. *Ibid.,* p. 457.

21. *Ibid.,* pp. 565–566.

22. *Ibid.*

23. Thompson & West, *op. cit.,* p. 81.

24. William C. Miller and Eleanore Bushnell, eds., *Reports of the 1863 Constitutional Convention of the Territory of Nevada* (Carson City: Legislative Counsel Bureau, 1972), *passim.*

25. David A. Johnson, "A Case of Mistaken Identity: William M. Stewart and the Rejection of Nevada's First Constitution," *Nevada Historical Society Quarterly,* Fall,

1979, 22:196. (This article cites newspaper accounts of Stewart's speeches to refute the contention in earlier editions of this book and numerous other books and articles that Stewart campaigned *against* the 1863 constitution.)

26. *Ibid.,* p. 194.

27. Thompson & West, *op. cit.,* p. 84.

28. *Territorial Papers of Nevada,* vol. 1. (In the same folder as the letters referred to in n. 15.)

29. Thompson & West, *op. cit.,* p. 85.

Notes to Chapter 2

1. *Nevada Constitutional Debates and Proceedings,* Andrew J. Marsh, Official Reporter (San Francisco: Frank Eastman, 1866), p. 325; hereafter cited as *Debates.*

2. *Ibid.,* p. 411.

3. *Ibid.,* p. 367.

4. *Ibid.,* p. 502.

5. *Ibid.,* p. 532.

6. Myron Angel, ed., *History of Nevada* (Oakland: Thompson & West, 1881), pp. 85–86. (Reprint ed., Berkeley: Howell-North, 1958); hereafter cited as Thompson & West.

7. *Humboldt Register,* Unionville, July 23, 1864.

8. *Congressional Globe,* 37th Congress, 3d sess., p. 1549.

9. William C. Miller and Eleanore Bushnell, eds., *Reports of the 1863 Constitutional Convention of the Territory of Nevada* (Carson City: Legislative Counsel Bureau, 1972), p. 412.

10. *Debates,* p. 486.

11. Original letter, July 18, 1864, made available by Keith L. Lee, former controller, State of Nevada.

12. *Debates,* pp. x-xii.

13. *Ibid.,* p. xiii.

14. *Ibid.,* p. 35.

15. *Ibid.,* p. 96.

16. Original letter, October 3, 1864, made available by Keith L. Lee, former controller, State of Nevada.

17. *Debates,* p. 255.

18. *Ibid.*

19. *Ibid.,* p. 256.

20. *Ibid.,* p. 258.

21. *Ibid.,* p. 484.

22. *Ibid.,* p. 493.

23. *Ibid.,* p. 488.

24. *Ibid.,* pp. 121–122.

25. *Ibid.,* p. 588.

26. *Ibid.,* p. 291.

27. *Ibid.,* p. 390.

28. *Ibid.*

29. *Ibid.,* p. 391.

30. *Ibid.,* p. 474.

31. Thompson & West, *op. cit.,* p. 276.

32. *Ibid.,* p. 291.

33. *Debates,* p. 329.
34. *Ibid.,* p. 358.
35. *Ibid.,* p. 224.
36. *Ibid.,* p. 355.
37. *Ibid.,* p. 356.
38. *Ibid.,* p. 361.
39. *Ibid.,* p. 363.
40. *Ibid.,* p. 444.
41. *Ibid.,* p. 521.
42. *Ibid.,* p. 111.
43. *Ibid.,* p. 116.
44. *Ibid.,* pp. 777–778.
45. *Ibid.,* p. 820.
46. *Ibid.,* p. 827.
47. *Ibid.,* p. xiv.
48. Secretary of State (John Koontz), *Political History of Nevada,* 4th ed. (Carson City: State Printing Office, 1960), p. 29.

Notes to Chapter 3

1. *Nevada Constitution,* Art. XVI, Sec. 2.
2. *Ibid.,* Art. XIX, Secs. 1 and 2.
3. *Ibid.,* Art. XIX, Sec. 3.
4. *Nevada Revised Statutes,* 613.230–300; hereafter cited as *NRS.*
5. The original provision had required only 10 percent of the voters of the state to sign an initiative petition, which permitted citizens in either Washoe or Clark County to secure all the necessary signatures entirely within either county. By requiring 10 percent of the voters in thirteen counties, residents of Washoe or Clark could no longer rely just on the relatively urban voters of the two big counties to provide the needed signatures.
6. So stated by Mr. Chief Justice Marshall in *Barron v. Baltimore,* 7 Pet. 243 (1833).
7. *Gitlow v. New York,* 268 U.S. 652 (1925).
8. *Weeks v. United States,* 232 U.S. 383 (1914).
9. *Mapp v. Ohio,* 367 U.S. 643 (1961).
10. *Fahy v. Connecticut,* 375 U.S. 85 (1963).
11 *Escobedo v. Illinois,* 378 U.S. 478 (1964); and *Miranda v. Arizona,* 384 U.S. 436 (1966).
12. *Gideon v. Wainwright,* 372 U.S. 335, at 346 (1963). This "landmark" case ruled that states must provide counsel for indigent defendants.
13. 391 U.S. 510 (1968).
14. 408 U.S. 238 (1972).
15. *Gregg v. Georgia,* 428 U.S. 153 (1976).
16. 431 U.S. 633 (1977).
17. 410 U.S. 113 (1973).
18. *Report of the National Advisory Commission on Civil Disorders* (Washington: Government Printing Office, 1968).
19. *National Commission on the Causes and Prevention of Violence* (New York: Award, 1969), p. xxi.
20. See Joseph N. Crowley, "Race and Residence: The Politics of Open Housing in Nevada," in *Sagebrush and Neon,* Eleanore Bushnell, ed., rev. ed. (Reno: Bureau of Governmental Research, 1976), pp. 59–79.

21. 392 U.S. 409 (1968).

22. *Nevada State Journal,* April 27, 1971, p. 2.

23. *Nevada Constitutional Debates and Proceedings,* Andrew J. Marsh, Official Reporter (San Francisco: Frank Eastman, 1866), p. 59; hereafter cited as *Debates.*

24. *Ibid.*

25. In the 1860 election for president, fourteen of the delegates at the Nevada convention had supported Lincoln; thirteen, Douglas; six, Bell; and two, Breckenridge. *Debates,* p. xvi.

26. *Debates,* p. 63.

27. *Ibid.,* p. 195.

28. *Ibid.,* p. 55.

29. *Ibid.,* p. 56.

30. *Nevada Constitution,* Art. I, Sec. 3.

Notes to Chapter 4

1. Offices used are president, United States senator, United States representative, governor, lieutenant governor, attorney general, secretary of state, treasurer, and controller. Prior to 1914, United States senators were selected by the legislature; these legislative elections are also included in the totals.

2. 405 U.S. 330 (1972).

3. See Leonard Weinberg and Allen Wilcox, "Voting Behavior and Political Attitudes in Washoe County," in *Sagebrush and Neon,* Eleanore Bushnell, ed., rev. ed. (Reno: Bureau of Governmental Research, 1976), pp. 23–40.

4. 424 U.S. 1 (1976).

5. *Arvey v. Sheriff,* 93 Nev. 469, 567 P.2d 470 (1977).

6. *NRS* 294A.010.

7. *Nevada State Journal,* February 28, 1980, p. 21.

8. In two earlier cases the supreme court reviewed ballots in a statewide election as a result of *quo warranto* proceedings brought by the defeated candidates. However, in neither of these contested elections was the appeal to the court preceded by a recount. The first case was *State v. Sadler* (25 Nev. 131, 1899), in which Reinhold Sadler's plurality of twenty-two votes over his closest opponent for the governorship in 1898 was changed by the court to a plurality of sixty-three. The second was *State v. Baker and Josephs* (35 Nev. 301, 1912), in which the final determination of the court, following its review of the ballots, sustained the 1910 election victory of Josephs as clerk of the supreme court, and raised his margin from eleven to forty-one votes.

9. *Laxalt v. Cannon,* 80 Nev. 588 (1964).

10. Don W. Driggs, "Seniority and Power of the States in the United States Senate, 1913–1979," unpublished manuscript.

11. Michael Barone, Grant Ujifusa, and Douglas Matthews, *The Almanac of American Politics 1980* (New York: E. P. Dutton, 1979), pp. 526–528.

12. *Congressional Quarterly Weekly Report,* January 26, 1980, 38:193.

13. *Ibid.,* pp. 195, 198.

Notes to Chapter 5

1. Kenneth Culp Davis, *Administrative Law and Government* (St. Paul: West Publishing Co., 1960), p. 54.

2. *The Book of the States, 1978–79* (Lexington, KY: Council of State Governments, 1978), pp. 14, 15.

3. Secretary of State (William D. Swackhamer), *Political History of Nevada,* 7th ed. (Carson City: State Printing Office, 1979), p. 162.

4. *Nevada Constitution,* Article I, Sec. 13.

5. Don W. Driggs, "Legislative Apportionment," *Governmental Research Newsletter* (Reno: Bureau of Governmental Research), Vol. I, No. 4, January 1961.

6. *Baker v. Carr,* 369 U.S. 186 (1962). Those interested in Supreme Court decisions of immediate bearing on *Baker* should also read *Colegrove v. Green,* 328 U.S. 549 (1946), and *Gomillion v. Lightfoot,* 364 U.S. 319 (1960).

7. *Reynolds v. Sims,* 377 U.S. 533 (1964).

8. *Ibid.,* at 573.

9. *Ibid.,* at 568.

10. 250 F.Supp. 480 (1965).

11. *Dungan v. Sawyer,* 253 F.Supp. 358 (1966).

12. *Nevada State Journal,* September 17, 1971, p. 13.

13. Eleanore Bushnell, "Reapportionment and Responsibility," in *Sagebrush and Neon,* Eleanore Bushnell, ed., rev. ed. (Reno: Bureau of Governmental Research, 1976), pp. 107, 108.

14. *Nevada Constitution,* Article IV, Sec. 5.

15. *Nevada Revised Statutes,* 218.010; hereafter cited as *NRS.*

16. *Nevada constitution,* Article IV, Sec. 33.

17. *Ibid.,* Article IV, Sec. 12.

18. Citizens Conference on State Legislatures, *The Sometime Governments* (New York: Bantam Books, 1971), pp. 253–255.

19. See Leonard Weinberg and Allen Wilcox, "Voting Behavior and Political Attitudes in Washoe County," in *Sagebrush and Neon,* Eleanore Bushnell, ed., rev. ed. (Reno: Bureau of Governmental Research, 1976), pp. 23–40.

20. *Nevada Constitution,* Article IV, Sec. 17.

21. *Ibid.,* Article IV, Sec. 18.

22. Faun Mortara, "Lobbying in Nevada," in *Sagebrush and Neon,* Eleanore Bushnell, ed., rev. ed. (Reno: Bureau of Governmental Research, 1976), p. 55.

23. *Ibid.,* p. 56.

24. *NRS.* 218.926.

25. *Dunphy v. Sheehan,* 92 Nev. 259, 549 P.2d 332 (1976).

26. *NRS.* 281.501.

27. *Ibid.*

28. *Nevada State Journal,* June 9, 1971, p. 22.

29. *NRS.* 281.481.

30. *Nevada Constitutional Debates and Proceedings,* Andrew J. Marsh, Official Reporter (San Francisco: Frank Eastman, 1866), p. 399.

31. *Ibid.,* p. 144.

Notes to Chapter 6

1. *Nevada Revised Statutes,* 223.080.

2. *Nevada Constitution,* Art. V, Sec. 18.

3. *Sawyer v. District Court,* 82 Nev. 53 (1966).

4. *Ibid.,* at 56.

5. *Nevada Constitution,* Art. V, Sec. 7.

6. *Ibid.,* Art. V, Sec. 14.

7. *Ibid.,* Art. V, Sec. 21.

8. *Ibid.,* Art. IV, Sec. 17.

9. Terry Reynolds, "The Executive Veto in Nevada," unpublished paper, p. 4.

10. A. J. Marsh, *Letters from Nevada Territory,* William C. Miller, ed. (Carson City: Legislative Counsel Bureau, 1972), p. 516.

11. See Jerome H. Skolnick, *House of Cards* (Boston: Little, Brown and Co., 1978), p. 117.

12. See Edward A. Olsen, "The Black Book Episode—An Exercise in Muscle," in *Sagebrush and Neon,* Eleanore Bushnell, ed., rev. ed. (Reno: Bureau of Governmental Research, 1976), pp. 1–22.

Notes to Chapter 7

1. 1 Cranch 137 (1803).

2. *United States Constitution,* Article VI.

3. *Nevada Constitution,* Art. VI, Sec. 4.

4. *Nevada Revised Statutes,* 3.030.

5. *The Book of the States, 1978–79* (Lexington, KY: Council of State Governments, 1978), pp. 90–91.

6. *Nevada Constitution,* Art. VI, Sec. 5.

7. Joseph E. Kallenbach, *The American Chief Executive* (New York: Harper & Row, 1966), pp. 205–208.

8. Recall is described in the *Nevada Constitution,* Art. II, Sec. 9.

9. The charges stipulated in the *United States Constitution* are treason, bribery, and other high crimes and misdemeanors; Art. II, Sec. 4.

10. W. H. Young, *Introduction to American Government,* 12th ed. (New York: Appleton-Century-Crofts, 1962), p. 749.

11. Impeachment is described in Art. VII, Secs. 1 and 2 of the *Nevada Constitution.*

12. *Nevada Constitution,* Art. VII, Sec. 3.

13. *Nevada Constitutional Debates and Proceedings,* Andrew J. Marsh, Official Reporter (San Francisco: Frank Eastman, 1866), p. 542; hereafter cited as *Debates.*

14. *Ibid.,* p. 557.

15. *Coyle v. Smith,* 221 U.S. 559 (1911).

16. *Debates,* p. 172.

17. *Ibid.,* p. 173.

18. *Ibid.,* p. 642.

19. *Ibid.,* p. 689.

Notes to Chapter 8

1. Andrew P. Grose, "Taxation in Nevada: A Comparative Perspective," *Nevada Public Affairs Review,* 1979, 2:6.

2. *The Book of the States, 1978–79* (Lexington, KY: Council of State Governments, 1978), pp. 322–323.

3. *Ibid.,* p. 314.

4. See Don W. Driggs, "Taxation and the Financing of Education in Nevada," in *Sagebrush and Neon,* Eleanore Bushnell, ed., rev. ed. (Reno: Bureau of Governmental Research, 1976), pp. 81–98.

5. *Matthews v. State of Nevada, ex rel. Nevada Tax Commission,* 83 Nev. Reports 269 (1967).

6. Grose, *op. cit.,* p. 7.

7. *Nevada Constitution,* Art. IX, Sec. 3.

8. *Brown v. Board of Education,* 347 U.S. 483 (1954).

9. *Nevada Constitution,* Art. I, Sec. 2.

10. *Nevada Revised Statutes,* 328.610; hereafter cited as *NRS.*

11. *Nevada Constitution,* Art. IV, Sec. 36.

12. Nevada Legislative Counsel Bureau, *Bulletin No. 7,* "County Consolidation and Reorganization in Nevada," December, 1948.

13. *NRS.* 268.010.

14. *County of Clark v. City of Las Vegas,* 92 Nev. 323, 550 P.2d 779 (1976).

15. *Journal of the Senate,* 54th Session, Nevada Legislature, 1967, p. 558.

16. *Journal of the Senate,* 55th Session, Nevada Legislature, 1969, p. 417 and *Journal of the Assembly,* 55th Session, p. 207.

17. See Driggs, *op. cit.*

18. *NRS.* 387.195.

19. Peter Steinmann and Richard Ganzel, "The Funding of Public Education in Nevada," *Nevada Public Affairs Review,* 1979, 2:25.

20. *Ibid.,* p. 23.

21. *Ibid.*

22. *Ibid.,* p. 22.

SELECTED BIBLIOGRAPHY

Documents

Annotations to Nevada Revised Statutes. Prepared under the direction of Russell W. McDonald. 6 vols. Carson City: State Printing Office, 1964. Adds to *Nevada Revised Statutes* such information as opinions of attorneys general and decisions of Nevada courts and of federal courts.

The Book of the States. Lexington, KY: Council of State Governments, 1978–79. Published biennially; an important source of data on state governments and for current trends in state practices.

Congressional Globe.

Congressional Record.

Nevada Constitutional Debates and Proceedings. Andrew J. Marsh, Official Reporter. San Francisco: Frank Eastman, 1866.

Nevada Reports. Nevada Supreme Court cases; published annually.

Nevada Revised Statutes. Compiled by Russell W. McDonald. Carson City: State Printing Office. Compliation of Nevada laws of a general, public, and permanent nature; index; revised following each legislative session.

United States Reports.

Periodicals

Congressional Quarterly. Congressional Quarterly, Inc., 1735 K Street, N.W., Washington, D.C. Published weekly; primarily on Congress and national concerns, but includes major issues affecting the states.

Nevada Business Review. Monthly publication of Bureau of Business and Economic Research, College of Business Administration, University of Nevada, Reno.

Nevada Historical Society Quarterly. Published four times a year by the Nevada Historical Society, Reno. Contains valuable articles on early political and social issues in Nevada and the West.

Governmental Research Newsletter. Reno: Bureau of Governmental Research, University of Nevada, 1960–1975.

Nevada Public Affairs Report. Reno: Bureau of Governmental Research, University of Nevada, 1975–1978.

Nevada Public Affairs Review. Reno: Bureau of Governmental Research, University of Nevada, 1979–1980.

The Western Political Quarterly. Salt Lake City: Institute of Government University of Utah. A political science journal of general coverage.

Books

Angel, Myron, ed. *History of Nevada.* Oakland: Thompson and West, 1881. Reprinted in 1958 by Howell-North of Berkeley.

Bancroft, Hubert Howe. *History of Nevada, Colorado, and Wyoming, 1540-1888.* (History of the Pacific States of North America, vol. 20; also in *The Works* of Hubert Howe Bancroft, vol. 25.) San Francisco: The History Co., 1890.

Barone, Michael, Grant Ujifusa, and Douglas Matthews. *The Almanac of American Politics 1980.* New York: E. P. Dutton, 1979. (Earlier editions published in 1972, 1973, 1975, and 1977.)

Burns, James MacGregor, Jack W. Peltason, and Thomas E. Cronin. *Government by the People,* 10th ed. Englewood Cliffs: Prentice-Hall, 1978.

Bushnell, Eleanore, ed. *Impact of Reapportionment on the Thirteen Western States.* Salt Lake City: University of Utah Press, 1970.

............, ed. *Sagebrush and Neon: Studies in Nevada Politics.* Rev. ed. Reno: Bureau of Governmental Research, 1976.

Citizens Conference on State Legislatures. *The Sometime Governments.* New York: Bantam Books, 1971.

Cline, Gloria Griffen. *Exploring the Great Basin.* Norman: University of Oklahoma Press, 1963.

Davis, Kenneth Culp. *Administrative Law and Government.* St. Paul: West Publishing Co., 1960.

Davis, Samuel P., ed. *The History of Nevada.* 2 vols. Reno: Elms Publishing Co., 1913.

Driggs, Don W. *The Constitution of the State of Nevada: A Commentary.* Nevada Studies in History and Political Science, no. 1. Reno: University of Nevada Press, 1961.

Driggs, Don W., comp. "Bibliography on Nevada Politics," in Frank H. Jonas, ed., "Bibliography on Western Politics," *Western Political Quarterly Supplement,* 1958, 11: 73-77.

Elliott, Russell R. *Nevada's Twentieth-Century Mining Boom; Tonopah, Goldfield, Ely.* Reno: University of Nevada Press. 1966.

.... *Radical Labor in the Nevada Mining Booms, 1900-1920.* Nevada Studies in History and Political Science, no. 2. Reno: University of Nevada Press, 1961.

.... *History of Nevada.* Lincoln: University of Nebraska Press, 1973.

Elliott, Russell R., and Helen J. Poulton. *Writings on Nevada: A Selected Bibliography.* Nevada Studies in History and Political Science, no. 5. Reno: University of Nevada Press, 1963. The most comprehensive bibliography of books, monographs, articles, and unpublished theses on Nevada.

Frémont, John Charles. *Narratives of Exploration and Adventure,* Allan Nevins, ed. New York: Longmans, Green and Co., 1956.

Gorvine, Albert. *Administrative Reorganization for Effective Government Management in Nevada.* Supplement to *Nevada State Journal,* 1948. Also Nevada Legislative Counsel Bureau, Bulletin No. 4, 1948.

Hicks, Charles Roger. *The Constitution of the State of Nevada: Its Formation and Interpretation.* 5th ed. University of Nevada Bulletin, vol. 51, no. 1, January, 1957.

Hill, Gladwin. *Dancing Bear: An Inside Look at California Politics.* New York: World Publishing Co., 1968.

Hulse, James W. *The Nevada Adventure: A History. 3d ed.* Reno: University of Nevada Press, 1972.

Jonas, Frank Herman, ed. *Politics in the American West.* Salt Lake City: University of Utah Press, 1969.

............, ed. *Western Politics.* Salt Lake City: University of Utah Press, 1961.

Lewis, Oscar. *The Big Four: the Story of Huntington, Stanford, Hopkins, and Crocker, and the Building of the Central Pacific.* New York: A. A. Knopf. 1938.

Mack, Effie Mona. *Nevada.* Glendale: Arthur H. Clark, 1936.

Marsh, Andrew J. *Letters From Nevada Territory, 1861–1862.* William C. Miller, ed. Carson City: Legislative Counsel Bureau, 1972.

Miller, William C., and Eleanore Bushnell, eds. *Reports of the 1863 Constitutional Convention of the Territory of Nevada.* Carson City: Legislative Counsel Bureau, 1972.

Myles, Myrtle Tate. *Nevada's Governors, from Territorial Days to the Present.* Sparks, Nevada: Western Printing and Publishing Co., 1972.

National Municipal League. *State Constitutional Provisions on Apportionment and Districting.* New York: National Municipal League, 1971.

Rusco, Elmer R. *Minority Groups in Nevada.* Reno: Bureau of Governmental Research, University of Nevada, 1966.

.... *Voting Behavior in Nevada.* Nevada Studies in History and Political Science, no. 9. Reno: University of Nevada Press, 1966.

Scrugham, James Graves, ed. *Nevada: a Narrative of the Conquest of a Frontier Land; Comprising the Story of Her People From the Dawn of History to the Present Time.* 3 vols. Chicago: American Historical Society, 1935.

Secretary of State (William D. Swackhamer). *Political History of Nevada.* 7th ed. Carson City: State Printing Office. 1979.

Sharkansky, Ira. *The Maligned States.* New York: McGraw-Hill, 1972.

Shepperson, Wilbur S. *Retreat to Nevada: A Socialist Colony of World War I.* The Lancehead Series: Nevada and the West. Reno: University of Nevada Press, 1966.

Skolnick, Jerome H. *House of Cards: Legalization and Control of Casino Gambling.* Boston: Little, Brown and Co., 1978.

Sturm, Albert L. *Thirty Years of State Constitution-Making, 1938–1968.* New York: National Municipal League, 1970.

Study of General Fund Revenues of the State of Nevada. Carson City: Legislative Counsel Bureau, 1966. (Lybrand Report.)

The Supreme Court Review. Chicago: University of Chicago. An annual summary of major United States Supreme Court decisions.

Westin, Alan F., ed. *The Uses of Power.* New York: Harcourt, Brace and World, 1962.

Wren, Thomas, ed. *A History of the State of Nevada, Its Resources and People.* New York: Lewis Publishing Co., 1904.

Zubrow, R. A., R. L. Decker, and E. H. Plank. *Financing State and Local Government in Nevada*. Carson City: State Printing Office, 1960.

INDEX

Abortion, 53
Allen, Lem, 89
Amendment: procedure for legislative proposal, 42; by initiative, 42, 45; on legislative pay, 86, 87; on annual sessions, 88; to raise debt limit, 135; in constitution, 187
Amendments: number of, in Nevada, 39; on ballots, 39–40; and voter "fall off," 70–71; votes on, 1970–1978, 70–71
Americans for Constitutional Action, 76
Americans for Democratic Action, 76
Annual sessions. *See* Legislature
Apportionment. *See* Reapportionment
Arizona, and recall of judges, 125
Ashworth, Keith, 89
Assembly, Nevada: size of, 80; apportionment of, 81–83, 85; districting in, 83, 86; organization of, 89–90; party control of, 90–91; minority and female membership in, 93, 95
Attorney general, duties of, 112

Baker, Edna C., 142
Baker v. Carr, and legislative apportionment, 82
Ball, Nathaniel, 55
Ballot: "none of these candidates" option, 68; length of, 68–71
Banks, James A., 33, 125, 126
Bean v. State, and death penalty, 119
Bear Flag War, 4
Belden, W. W., 21
Bell, Frank, 40
Bell, Rex, 95
Bible, Alan, 72, 73
Bidwell-Bartleson party, 2
"Black Book," 109
Blasdel, H. G., 107
Board of Examiners, 104, 166–167
Board of Pardons Commissioners, 103, 165
Board of Regents, University of Nevada, 142

Board of State Prison Commissioners, 104, 166
Bonneville, Benjamin L. E., 2
Boyle, Emmet D., 100
Bradley, Lewis R., 100
Brookman, Eileen, 95
Brosnan, Cornelius M., 21, 36
Bryan, Richard, 67, 102
Bryan, William Jennings, 62
Buchanan, James: dismissed Governor Young, 7; ordered troops to Salt Lake City, 7; signed Nevada Territory bill, 11; attack upon in convention, 26
Buckley v. Valeo, and campaign finance, 67
Budget, procedures for, 105
Bureau of Land Management, 138

California: never a territory, 1; discovery of gold in, 3, 4; petition for annexation to, 5; constitutional convention of, 21; constitution of, basis for Nevada Constitution, 24
California Plan, 125
Campaign finance, 67–68
Cannon, Howard W.: committee position, 72–73; and 1964 recount, 73–74; ratings by ADA and ACA, 76; and "conservative coalition," 76
Capital punishment, 52–53
Carson City: site of first meeting of territorial legislature, 12; replaced Genoa as county seat of Carson County, 12; consolidation with Ormsby County, 140
Carson County: establishment of, 5–7; attachment to Great Salt Lake County, 7
Carter, Jimmy: and 1980 presidential primary, 68; and MX missile, 138
Central Pacific Railroad, 30, 32
Chapin, Samuel A., 21, 57, 58
Child, John S., 9, 11
Cities: government of, 141; amendment of charters of, 141

SPO, Carson City, Nevada, 1980